Evaluating Leadership

A Model for Missiological Assessment of Leadership Theory and Practice

J. Keith McKinley

D1715050

WIPF *&* STOCK · Eugene, Oregon

EVALUATING LEADERSHIP
A Model for Missiological Assessment of Leadership Theory and Practice

Wipf & Stock
An Imprint of Wipf and Stock Publishers
199 W. 8th Ave., Suite 3
Eugene, OR 97401

www.wipfandstock.com

PAPERBACK ISBN: 978-1-6667-7024-7
HARDCOVER ISBN: 978-1-6667-7025-4
EBOOK ISBN: 978-1-6667-7026-1

VERSION NUMBER 02/16/24

For Gail,

Then the LORD God said, "It is not good for the man to be alone; I will make a helper suitable for him."

—Gen 2:18

Contents

Figures and Tables | ix

Preface | xi

Acknowledgments | xvii

Abbreviations | xviii

Introduction | 1

Part 1: Understand and Describe the Leadership Theory

Chapter 1: Development and Description of the Theory | 25

Chapter 2: Exercise of the Theory | 44

Chapter 3: Outcomes of the Theory | 55

Part 2: Appraise the Leadership Theory Theologically

Chapter 4: Analyze the Teleological Aspect | 69

Chapter 5: Analyze the Ontological Aspect | 79

Chapter 6: Analyze the Authority Aspect | 91

Chapter 7: Analyze the Ethic Aspect | 104

Part 3: Assess the Influence of Culture on the Leadership Theory

Chapter 8: Six Dimensions of Culture | 121

Chapter 9: Culture and Transformational Leadership | 136

Part 4: Determine the Appropriateness of the Leadership Theory

Chapter 10: Conclusions about Transformational Leadership Theory | 159

Chapter 11: Conclusions on the Leadership Assessment Matrix | 173

Appendix 1: Outline of a Theology of Leadership | 179

Appendix 2: Thirty Leadership Theory Assessment Questions | 185

Bibliography | 189

Index | 199

Figures

Figure 1. Power in Relation to Intent and Capacity,
Values, and Needs | 27

Figure 2. Wants and Leadership Styles | 30

Figure 3. Values and Practices in Levels of Culture | 142

Figure 4. Need Pairs from MAS and UAI | 146

Figure 5. Organizational Structures by UAI and PDI | 152

Figure 6. A Roadmap for Missiological Assessment
of Leadership Theory | 177

Tables

Table 1. A Philosophical Matrix for Evaluating Leadership Theory | 23

Table 2. Transformational Leadership Behaviors | 50

Table 3. Moral Character of Transformational and
Pseudo-transformational Leaders | 53

Table 4. A Theological Matrix for Evaluating Leadership Theory | 67

Table 5. Hofstede's Dimensions of Culture | 118

Table 6. Comparing Hofstede's Dimensions to the
GLOBE Categories | 119

Table 7. A Leadership Assessment Matrix | 156

Table 8. Transformational Leadership Factors and
the Dimensions of Culture | 170

Preface

MY INTEREST IN THE subject of leadership was piqued when I entered the U.S. Army at the age of nineteen. From the start, I noticed that my squad in basic training needed a leader. We needed someone to keep our task before us, make certain we knew what to do, how and when to do it, represent us and our needs through the command structure, encourage us in our growth, and lead the way in our mission. Later, the Army provided me with opportunities for growth through the Primary Leadership Development Course, job-specific training, and leadership experiences that come with promotions and assignments such as squad leader, platoon sergeant, and so on.

Many years later with the International Mission Board (IMB) in Southeast Asia, I had more opportunities to grow in understanding and experience in leadership. During a debriefing for first-term missionaries in 2000, Keith Williams of the IMB's Member Care department pointed me to a helpful book entitled, *People Skills*, setting me on a path of self-study in leadership.[1] My curiosity on the subject deepened when I attended Situational Leadership II training led by my colleague Charlie Townsend. The Situational Leadership approach from Ken Blanchard introduced me to the science and theory of leadership. Blanchard takes a behaviorist approach to leadership by using a simple diagnostic tool that guides the leader's

---

1. Bolton, *People Skills*.

behavior.[2] At this point in time, I was in a leadership role attempting to guide missionaries who had more field experience than I. Situational Leadership II provided me with a concrete framework.

Don Dent, the IMB Regional Leader in Southeast Asia, began a simple coaching process with me. Don would call or email me about my goals and we discussed relevant issues. The dialogue was purposeful yet informal and I found his mentoring to be a great help. Through his mentoring, I began to see the importance of soft skills, the relational side of leadership, and mostly, the value of encouragement.

Encouragement from my field leaders continued through Todd Lafferty. Todd and I met frequently over coffee and talked about specific problems and my developing philosophy of leadership. I shared with Todd my initial thoughts that organizational structure should follow function and how I envisioned a leadership team approach for the Strategy Group over which Todd had given me responsibility in 2005. My responsibilities grew considerably. I led a group of about seventy people on twelve teams spread over a wide geographic area. Because I was pushed beyond my capacity, I sought the best means to serve my teams and the purposes of our organization. My reading on leadership expanded to include a broad array of theoretical approaches and applications of those theories, such as Robert Greenleaf's Servant Leadership and Lead Like Jesus by Ken Blanchard and Phil Hodges.[3] Instead of solving my problems, my reading only brought more questions. I enjoyed and appreciated studying leadership theory, and the science of leadership intrigued me, but I was left unsatisfied by the lack of theological undergirding of those theories.

In 2008, the IMB began a significant leadership training process in Southeast Asia designed by Larry and Susan Gay. With their co-teachers Darrell and Shirley Seale, the Gay's facilitated LEAD360 seminars that included leadership assessments including SkillScope, Your Leadership Grip, Birkman360, and the Kraybill Conflict Style Inventory; feedback and evaluation from subordinates, peers, and supervisors, and coaching for a development plan.[4] LEAD360 was a significant step forward

2. Blanchard et al., *Leadership and the One Minute Manager*; Blanchard et al., *Situational Leadership II*; Blanchard, *Ken Blanchard's Situational Leadership II: The Article*.

3. Blanchard and Hodges, *Lead Like Jesus*; Greenleaf and Spears, *Servant Leadership*.

4. Larry Gay, "LEAD360 Rollout Plan 2009" (unpublished International Mission Board (IMB) internal document, February 11, 2009); Gay and Gay, *The Servant Leader's Handbook*, an unpublished manual for the Southeast Asia and Oceania Region of the IMB; Ford, *Your Leadership Grip*; Kraybill, *Style Matters*. Birkman360 is the property

in my understanding of leadership because it integrated the notions of strengths, skills, spiritual gifting, preferred work styles, and conflict management. This mix builds a personal leadership profile on traits, personality, behaviors, and values.

IMB field structure underwent a significant reorganization in 2009, giving us a rare opportunity for a fresh start. I assumed the role of Cluster Strategy Leader for part of Southeast Asia and pitched my ideas for a team approach to my Affinity Leader, Steve Smith. He permitted me to move forward with my ideas, and in February 2009, the cluster leadership team met with our Team Strategy Leaders for the first time. There, I shared my understanding of our milieu and a resulting manifesto.

First, I explained how our context had changed. We faced diminishing human and financial resources and had to consider a new way of working. Previously we accomplished our task primarily by managing those who were related to us by the organizational structure of some form or another. Managing involved administration, maintenance, focus on structure and doing things right.[5] The task before us, to reach millions with the gospel of Christ, remained the same, but we could not meet our goals if we limited our influence to those over whom we had managing authority. We had to expand the sphere of our influence far beyond our organization. We needed to innovate, develop people, and push forward toward our goals. We needed to grow from management to leadership.

Second, we acknowledged that God had brought us together as a team of people with a wide variety of personalities, gifting, and skills. With such a diverse team, we could not expect to follow a model that requires everyone to come with a specific set of traits. We had to look toward an interactive, responsive development process.

Third, God had one clear purpose for us: to make disciples of all peoples in fulfillment of the Great Commission toward a vision of a multitude from every language, people, tribe, and nation knowing and worshipping our Lord Jesus Christ. Though we are created with wondrous variety, we have a singular calling. We are many people with one purpose.

Fourth, leadership in missions is a unifying task. God has brought people together to proclaim and teach the gospel and make disciples where Christ has not been named. Because God had brought us together with all

of Birkman International Inc. Houston, TX. SkillScope is the property of the Center for Creative Leadership, www.ccl.org.

5. Bennis, *On Becoming a Leader*, 41–46.

of our variety for one task, the work of both leaders and followers is to determine how we should function together for God's purposes.

What remained unclear was how we should assess general leadership theory and practice for use in Christian missions. What is the relationship between leadership theory and theology, specifically the theology of missions? These questions led me to doctoral studies at The Southern Baptist Theological Seminary, where I would write a missiological assessment of transformational leadership theory, a version of which you now read.

In the introduction, I explain the background to my research and lay out my research purpose. I define essential terms and set the scope of this study. I describe my methodology and begin to explain the critical matrix for evaluating leadership theory—a means by which leadership theory and practice can be assessed. In the remaining chapters, I will demonstrate this critical matrix by applying it to Bernard Bass' transformational leadership theory, interact with critical thinkers in the field of leadership study, consider the theological foundations and implications of transformational leadership, and the effect of culture on the theory and its application.

In part 1, I delve into the background and development of transformational leadership theory, describing Bass and Avolio's Full Range of Leadership model. In addition to a theory's history, understanding a leadership assessment involves examining the application and outcomes of said theory. By the end of this chapter, the reader should have a grasp of the first tier of the evaluative matrix and a good understanding of transformational leadership theory, how to apply it, and its expected results.

In part 2, I examine transformational leadership theory from a theological point of view, including the aspects of teleology, ontology, authority, and ethic, and be able to appraise transformational leadership theory as a practice for Christian missions. By the end of chapter three, the reader should have a theological evaluation of transformational leadership theory and understand the second tier of the matrix.

In part 3, I examine transformational leadership theory through the lens of cultural anthropology. Hofstede's six cultural dimensions form the backbone of this aspect of my missiological assessment of transformational leadership theory. By the end of this chapter, the reader should gain practice with the third tier of the evaluative matrix and a reasoned opinion about the universality of the theory.

I conclude my study and bring together the philosophical, theological, and cultural anthropological aspects of transformational leadership theory and the evaluative matrix. I point out the critical implications of transformational leadership theory in missions, close the study with a final assessment of transformational leadership, and propose a way forward for leadership in missions.

Upon completion of this book, the reader should have a reasonable grasp of my evaluative matrix, a missiological understanding of Bass' transformational leadership theory, and confidence that they can assess other theories and practices with their newly gained knowledge and freshly honed skills.

Acknowledgments

I OWE SPECIAL THANKS to my doctoral committee, George Martin, David Sills, and Timothy Beougher, who helped narrow and intensify my study and honed my research and critical thinking abilities.

I also thank my many friends and colleagues who supported me during my studies. To my readers, Randy Arnette, Jodee Martin, Peter and Jennie Stillman, and Katlyn Thompson, thank you for your arduous work to improve my work. Your time on my behalf is a cherished gift. And to my good friends Trey and Belamy Lyon, thank you for all the laughter and tears that accompanied our journey, for your encouragement and sometimes stern admonishment to push through to the end.

When I began this venture, I asked our children, Wesley, Aaron, Rachel, and Samantha, for their support. They gave me their support and encouragement, each in their own way and not without the occasional joke about Dad's studies. I could not ask for a better household.

No advice or encouragement has been as consistent and valuable to me as that which I gained from Gail. Knowing my penchant for studies and desire to become a better leader, she sacrificed much so that I could complete this work. She challenges me to be clear and remain on target. Gail is my complement and best champion, and though I do not deserve her, I am forever grateful that God has made us one.

Abbreviations

CVS   Chinese Value Survey

CPI   Corruption Perception Index

IDV   Individualism Index

IVR   Indulgence versus Restraint

LTO   Long-term versus Short-term Orientation

MAS   Masculinity Index

MLQ   Multifactor Leadership Questionnaire

PDI   Power Distance Index

UAI   Uncertainty Avoidance Index

VSMs Values Survey Modules

WVS   World Values Survey

Introduction

MISSIONARY VISION AND PURPOSE arise out of deep theological reflection. A leadership theory to undergird missions requires similar theological reflection. But academic work that integrates secular leadership theory and leadership theology seems to be a rare commodity. Christian researchers should make effective use of solid leadership research to further the cause of Christ in organizations and churches. Indeed, Richard Higginson of the Ridley Hall Foundation for the Study of Faith and Works writes that Christian leadership authors should take advantage of the work of notable authors in the secular community.[1]

Leadership theory in an intercultural context is made more complicated because of the widely varied values, assumptions, and worldviews held by people of diverse cultures. Because of this added level of complexity, Edgar Elliston asserts that leaders should be careful, on the one hand, not to apply western leadership theory uncritically to non–western contexts and, on the other hand, not adopt non–western theories of leadership without careful consideration.[2] Leadership theory can serve to inform a contextually appropriate leadership theory through a critical analysis process but what is that process?

In the inaugural issue of the *Journal of Biblical Perspectives in Leadership*, Michale Ayers laments the lack of leadership ability among church

1. Higginson, *Transforming Leadership*, 4–5.
2. Elliston, "Leadership Theory," 567–68.

1

leaders with formal theological training.[3] He argues that little overlap exists between secular leadership research and theological reflection, which may contribute to the general lack of leadership ability among church leaders. He proposes that the gap between leadership theory and theology must be bridged to solve this problem. He argues that the first step to remedy this problem is to establish a common language between leadership philosophy and Christian theology. Ayers recommends leadership theory analysis using shared philosophical and theological terms, specifically: ontology, methodology, and teleology.[4]

Ayers has hit upon something important. Although uncritical adoption of philosophical language alone will not necessarily result in a healthy leadership theology, it is constructive to take up these philosophical notions as a framework for thinking critically and biblically about leadership, and that is what I intend to do.

There is a paucity of research on leadership in missions. To make matters worse, many missionaries try to lead without considering much of anything about leadership. Some uncritically impose a western leadership model on their non–western context, while others simply adopt host culture leadership practices without evaluation. Neither course is healthy.

Gretchen Vogelgesang, Rachel Clapp–Smith, and Noel Palmer argue the case for a view of leadership that balances the leader's value system and those of his host culture.[5] While not writing about missions, in particular, they propose a leadership model whereby leaders can maintain their moral integrity and simultaneously align themselves with the norms and values of their host cultures.[6] They establish the critical need for integrating cultural intelligence with authentic leadership to develop an effective leadership model in intercultural contexts. Studies like that of Volelgesang et al., which deal with intercultural leadership from a non–religious standpoint, are part of a fast–growing field. As globalization becomes a reality, the education and commerce sectors have been quick to establish significant research on intercultural leadership. Research on leadership theory in missions, however, is almost non–existent.

---

3. Ayers, "Toward a Theology of Leadership," 6. He refers to studies by George Barna, Christian A Schwartz, and Robert H. Welch.

4. Ayers, "Toward a Theology of Leadership," 7–8.

5. Vogelgesang et al., "The Role of Authentic Leadership," 102–17. The perspective espoused by Vogelgesang et al. is based in Authentic Leadership theory.

6. Vogelgesang et al., "The Role of Authentic Leadership," 103.

In my preface, I wrote that I came to The Southern Baptist Theological Seminary to write a missiological assessment of transformational leadership theory. I believed the approach to be thoughtful and useful. Still, I had many questions about understanding and applying a general or secular theory in the distinctly sacred work of missions. I soon discovered I needed an organized way to evaluate leadership theory and practice for missions; no such scheme existed. Because of this critical need, I set out to develop a means to evaluate leadership theory and apply the system to Bass' transformational leadership theory.

Transformational leadership is at the forefront of leadership theory. A recent search of the Amazon online bookstore for books under the keywords *transformational leadership* results in over three thousand entries, and a search for *transformational leadership theory* resulted in almost eight hundred results. The theory may be conceived narrowly, in terms of specific behaviors applied to influence followers, or quite broadly, as an approach to help motivate individuals to change themselves and an entire society. Part of the theory's popularity may stem from this characteristic—that it can be a way of thinking about leadership goals and relationships and not only a set of behaviors or traits.

Though transformational leadership has been under the microscope of academic study in the behavioral sciences, as have few other approaches, the theory is worthy of a closer look by Christian researchers. Transformational leadership theory is intriguing because it takes a philosophical approach to leadership and aims for significant change—change so substantial that it is called transformational. Missiologists should find the theory worthy of attention because of the benefit it may offer to those working in intercultural leadership contexts.

Leadership is important. We desperately need biblically grounded, anthropologically informed leadership, true to the purpose of missions. My search for a way to think about leadership theory and practice from a missiological point of view fuels this research.

Purpose

This study aims to design a critical matrix for evaluating leadership theory and assess transformational leadership theory by this matrix as an example. This research answers the following questions:

1. How should I fundamentally understand and analyze a leadership theory or practice?

2. What is essential in evaluating leadership theory and practice theologically?

3. What is a reasonable approach for understanding culture's effect on a leadership theory or practice?

4. What are the implications of a missiological assessment of transformational leadership theory in missions?

Definitions

In this work, I apply Ayers' suggestion for shared language in this study and formulate a critical matrix for evaluating leadership theory that integrates secular leadership theory, theology, and cultural anthropology. I call this schema the Leadership Assessment Matrix. Scholars in leadership theory, theology, and cultural anthropology undoubtedly hold differing worldviews both within and between these fields of study. Researchers and writers have different understandings of leadership, transformational leadership, missions, missiology, teleology, ontology, authority, and ethic; therefore, it is vital to define certain important terms in this research— even the shared terms for which Ayres appeals. I will define those terms in this section. These terms will be developed further in the following chapters, but this starting point will be helpful.

Leadership

In this study, I use the definition of leadership by Peter Northouse, who states that leadership is "a process whereby an individual influences a group of individuals to achieve a common goal."[7] So defined, leadership is made up of three key elements: a process of influence, a group of individuals, and a common goal.

Northouse clarifies that leadership arises from interactions between leaders and followers. Leadership is born out of a relationship between leaders and followers. Northouse's definition is distinct from a trait view

---

7. Northouse, *Leadership*, 6. Now in its 9th edition, this text has gained widespread acclaim and use in over one thousand colleges and universities.

of leadership, which defines leadership based on a leader's attributes, personality, intelligence, and so on.[8] A second distinctive is that the process–oriented definition implies that leadership emerges out of a leader's relationship with his followers, not primarily the leader's position in an organization. Assigned leadership, based on structural authority, is not entirely foreign to Northouse's definition, but his emphasis is on the process of leadership. A process view of leadership is a dynamic and complex understanding of leaders, followers, and leadership.[9]

Leadership is a process of bi–directional influence. Just as the leader influences followers, followers influence their leader. Citing John R. P. French Jr. and Bertram Raven's seminal research on power, Northouse proposes that the leader's influence is personal instead of positional and therefore arises out of French and Raven's referent and expert categories.[10] Referent power pertains to leader–follower identification in the affective domain of the human psyche.[11]

Leadership moves people toward a common goal. Northouse argues that "coercion involves the use of force to effect change . . . to influence someone to do something against his will." But in his definition of leadership, followers are influenced toward mutually held purposes, sidestepping the problem of coercion. By delimiting his definition to goals held in common by the leader and follower, Northouse eliminates from consideration the likes of Hitler and Kim Jong–il.

Transformational Leadership

Bernard M. Bass states that transformational leadership moves followers to extraordinary achievement while growing the leadership ability of the leader.[12] Bass was not the first to define transformational leadership. J. V. Downton used the term in 1973 to define a process for changing people,

---

8. Personality traits are significant in social interaction and play a role in the leader–follower relationship; however, Northouse's definition does not include the understanding that a particular trait, extraversion, for example, is necessary for leadership to occur.

9. Northouse, *Leadership*, 9. Northouse refers to Jago, who argued that because leadership is a process it can be observed and learned. A. G. Jago, "Leadership: Perspectives in Theory and Research," 315–16.

10. French and Raven, "The Bases of Social Power," 263–68.

11. French and Raven, "The Bases of Social Power," 263–68.

12. Bass and Riggio, *Transformational Leadership*, 2.

moving them to do more than normally expected, to act at a higher level for the betterment of others.[13] Political scientist James MacGregor Burns brought transformational leadership to the forefront of popularity and study in his classic work *Leadership*.[14] Burns writes about a kind of leadership process in which the goals and aspirations of the leader and followers are united and undergirded by motives and values of an altruistic nature.[15] At about the same time, Robert J. House developed his theory of charismatic leadership.[16] House's theory emphasizing charismatic personality and behaviors is very similar to Burn's work.

Bass further developed the work of MacGregor and House and brought transformational leadership theory into the mainstream of research. Working with Bruce J. Avolio, Bass produced the Full Range of Leadership model, which consists of seven leadership elements grouped into three categories: transformational, transactional, and laissez–faire.[17] Bass identified four critical factors within transformational leadership. He refers to these factors as the Four I's: idealized influence, inspirational motivation, intellectual stimulation, and individualized consideration.[18] Transformational leadership theory, as defined by the Four I's, is the subject of this research.

Mission and Missions

The terms mission and missions are difficult to define.[19] Craig Ott and Stephen J. Strauss explain that the difficulty with the terms mission and missions stems from the fact that neither are found in most English language Bible translations or in Bible concordances which leads to confusion.[20] Ott and Strauss report that Jesuits first used the term mission to describe their activities to spread the gospel to different geographic locations. The terms

13. Downton, *Rebel Leadership*, 224, 251, 260.

14. Burns, *Leadership*.

15. Burns, *Leadership*, 20.

16. House, *A 1976 Theory of Charismatic Leadership*.

17. Avolio, *Full Leadership Development: Building the Vital Forces in Organizations*; Bass, *Leadership and Performance beyond Expectations*; Bass, "From Transactional to Transformational Leadership: Learning to Share the Vision," 19–32.

18. Bass, "From Transactional to Transformational Leadership," 21–24.

19. The term, missional, is rarely used in the resource materials applied to this study. Therefore a definition of missional is not supplied in this research.

20. Ott, *Encountering Theology of Mission*, xiv.

were used interchangeably to describe the gospel's spread until the 1960s when mission came to refer to "God's sending activity," and missions came to refer to the spread of the gospel by the church.[21]

George Miley writes that God's mission is to "bless all peoples, nations, or cultural groupings" and that this is the church's mission.[22] Kevin DeYoung and Gregory Gilbert contend that mission is not equivalent to the *missio Dei*.[23] The mission of the church is not to do all that Jesus did but to witness to what he has done.[24] De Young and Gilbert explain more precisely that,

> the mission of the church is to go into the world and make disciples by declaring the gospel of Jesus Christ in the power of the Spirit and gathering those disciples into churches, that they might worship the Lord and obey his commands now and in eternity to the glory of God.[25]

DeYoung and Gilbert write that mission used to mean sending cross-cultural missionaries to convert non–Christians and gather them into churches; now, mission means much more. They are correct. Some definitions are very broad. For example, Andrew Walls and Cathy Ross write that the five marks of global mission are (1) proclaim the good news, (2) teach, baptize, and nurture new believers, (3) respond to human need, (4) transform unjust structures of society, and (5) safeguard the integrity of creation and sustain and renew the life of the earth.[26]

Eckhard Schnabel stipulates that mission is an activity of the church, but it is not everything the church does.[27] The church's mission activity includes an intentional geographic movement carried out by those called and sent from the local church, who tell the good news to those who have not heard or believed, teach a new way of life, and establish a new community of faith around the new believers.[28] He argues, further, that the New Testament established no requirement for missions or missionaries to cross cultural boundaries though it is appropriate that they do so.

21. Ott, *Encountering Theology of Mission*, xv.

22. Miley, *Loving the Church*, 30.

23. DeYoung and Gilbert, *What Is the Mission of the Church?*, 62.

24. DeYoung and Gilbert, *What Is the Mission of the Church?*, 56.

25. DeYoung and Gilbert, *What Is the Mission of the Church?*, 62.

26. Walls and Ross, eds., *Mission in the Twenty–First Century*, xiv.

27. Schnabel, *Paul the Missionary*, 21–22.

28. Schnabel, *Paul the Missionary*, 22–29.

Andreas Köstenberger and Desmond Alexander stipulate that any proper definition of mission is a derivative of a biblical–theological approach and conclude that the mission of the church is an extension of Jesus' purpose, which is at the center of God's plan to extend salvation to the ends of the earth. The church's mission is to testify of the saving work of Jesus, to build up believers in Christ, and to form them together as Christian congregations.[29]

George W. Peters writes of mission as "the total biblical assignment of the church of Jesus Christ," and missions to be,

> the sending forth of authorized persons beyond the borders of the New Testament church and her immediate gospel influence to proclaim the gospel of Jesus Christ in gospel–destitute areas, to win converts from other faiths or non–faiths to Jesus Christ, and to establish functioning, multiplying local congregations who will bear the fruit of Christianity in that community and to that country.[30]

Similarly, David Horner defines mission as "God's plan for reaching all nations with the good news of Jesus Christ by sending his people to tell them about and show them the gracious, redeeming love of a gracious God."[31]

Ott and Strauss argue, among other things, for doxology as the purpose of mission, "the broad, comprehensive goal of mission."[32] In common English language use, mission can mean an assignment, a delegation, or purpose. This common use is how mission is primarily used in secular writing on leadership theory. This study interacts with leadership theory literature. Therefore, for the purpose of this study, mission refers to purpose.

Missions is not a term commonly found in secular leadership theory literature. Ott and Strauss use the plural, missions, to refer to the task of the church to fulfill its mission.[33] They assert that the task of missions is the "sending activity of the church to create and expand . . . kingdom communities among every people of the earth."[34]

---

29. Köstenberger, Alexander, and Carson, *Salvation to the Ends of the Earth*, 255–58.

30. Peters, *A Biblical Theology of Missions*, 11.

31. Horner, *When Missions Shapes the Mission*, 4.

32. Ott, *Encountering Theology of Mission*, 79.

33. Ott, *Encountering Theology of Mission*, 106. They posit that doxology is the purpose of mission, redemption is the foundation of mission, the Kingdom of God is the center of mission, eschatology is the hope of mission, the nations are the scope of mission, reconciliation is the fruit of mission, and incarnation is the character of mission.

34. Ott, *Encountering Theology of Mission*, 160.

James E. Plueddemann writes that missions is not limited to those in an intercultural role, and in fact, most Christians are called to serve the Lord in their own cultures.[35] He argues that the Holy Spirit made a distinction between those serving the local church and those called to apostolic functions, adding "Scriptures seem to teach two distinct organizational functions within the church, local and itinerate."[36]

Justice Anderson relies on the work of Olav Myklebust, who "considered missions [to be] the conscious efforts on the part of the church, in its corporate capacity, or through voluntary agencies, to proclaim the gospel (with all this implies) among peoples and in regions where it is still unknown or only inadequately known."[37]

David Horner defines missions as "God's plan for reaching all nations with the good news of Jesus Christ by sending His people to tell them about and show them the gracious, redeeming love of a glorious God."[38]

In the book, *When Everything is Missions*, Deny Spitters defines missions as "the work of the Church in reaching across cultural, religious, ethnic and geographic boundaries to advance the work of making disciples of all nations."[39]

In Romans 15:15–22, the Apostle Paul defines his apostolic purpose as a minister to the Gentiles by a narrowly defined context and a scope that excludes many other good things. Paul declares that he is a minister to the nations so that the offering of the Gentiles may be acceptable. His mission is to see to it that the Gentile contingent of humanity is brought into the worship and praise of God. Paul states that his purpose will be accomplished by the power of the gospel of Christ to bring about obedience of faith. Paul's means of accomplishing his mission, the task of missions, is preaching the gospel and teaching obedience that we call disciple–making.

Paul's ministry and message is geographically religiously defined. He states that his mission is to preach the gospel where Christ has not already been named; where there is no foundation for faith. Finally, his calling is of such a compelling nature that it is to the exclusion of other good things. His mission prevented him from doing other things in other places. Paul

35. Plueddemann, "Theological Implications of Globalizing Missions," 260.

36. He concludes that when this distinction is lost, world mission suffers. Plueddemann, "Theological Implications of Globalizing Missions," 264.

37. Anderson, "An Overview of Missiology," 2.

38. Horner, *When Missions Shapes the Mission*, 6.

39. Spitters and Ellison, *When Everything is Mission*, 37.

describes his apostolic activity in these specific terms as: focused on the lost nations, by the power of the gospel preached and taught, among those who have never heard, to the relative exclusion of other good things.

For the purpose of this study, missions refers to the acts of the Christian church to proclaim and teach the gospel of salvation in Jesus among peoples where the church has not yet been established, in such a way that people turn from sin to faith in Jesus and follow his lordship in the power of the Holy Spirit as part of a local body of believers committed to Jesus and one another to the glory of the Father.[40]

Missiology

Alan Tippett describes missiology as dealing with the intersection of theology, anthropology, and history.[41] The confluence of these three domains results in area studies in ethnography, ethno–history, the expansion of the church, and most centrally, theory and theology of mission.[42]

Anderson introduces missiology as the science of missions including "the formal study of the theology of mission, the history of missions, the concomitant philosophies of mission and their strategic implementation in given cultural settings."[43] Anthropology, in his scheme, is relegated to implementation of that which has been born out of missiology, the rigorous progression through theology, history and philosophy.[44]

Darrell Whiteman makes an argument to include anthropology in mission, and, by implication, missiology. Whiteman's claim is that anthropology is holistic, explanatory, takes an emic view, and is intent on the relational–communicative aspects of life.[45] Whiteman is not

---

40. This does not mean that missions can only exist among Unreached People Groups (UPGs). Preaching the gospel where the church has not yet been established is the starting point for missions, not the finishing point. The notion of UPGs has been helpful to identify blind spots—hidden peoples—in mission strategy. Missions is not complete until the church is established with sufficient maturity.

41. Tippett, *Introduction to Missiology*.

42. Tippett, *Introduction to Missiology*, 21.

43. Anderson, "An Overview of Missiology," 2–8.

44. Anderson, "An Overview of Missiology," 15–17.

45. Whiteman, "Anthropology and Mission: The Incarnational Connection, Part I," 35–44; Whiteman, "Anthropology and Mission: The Incarnational Connection, Part II," 79–88. He explains that anthropology takes a holistic approach to the study of people, paying attention to all the domains of life. Anthropology studies behavior, cognition, and

alone in finding usefulness in adopting an anthropological approach to understanding other cultures. Other scholars join Whiteman's lead. For example, David Hesselgrave, Paul Hiebert, Charles Kraft, and Gailyn Van Rheenen promote the anthropological aspects of missions.[46] In particular, Hiebert applies anthropology's holistic view to the cognitive, affective, and evaluative dimensions of worldviews.[47]

For the purpose of this study, missiology refers to the careful study of missions from viewpoints of Christian philosophy, theology, and cultural anthropology.

Teleology

Teleology is the study of the purposes of things. Michale Ayers draws on Paul Edwards and points out that, in philosophy, teleology includes a distinction between functional and purposive activity.[48] He argues that understanding moves from ontology to methodology and then to teleology. Though his order may work in philosophy, to place teleology and examination of purpose at the end of a logical stream does not bode well for faith in God, who has revealed himself and his purposes. Rather, one must begin with God's revealed purpose and move forward from there. In so doing, purpose helps define being and behavior; knowing God's purpose (in leadership) guides our understanding of who we are (as leaders) and what we should do (leadership behaviors).

---

valuation and these realms of human existence are critical to faith. Whiteman argues that missionaries need to develop their anthropological skills such as identifying intercultural patterns and distinctions to aid understanding. Anthropology can help missionaries gain insights for gospel witness, authentic church planting, and leadership development. Participant observation is a key research tool in anthropology that assists the researcher in gaining an emic understanding of the culture under study. Understanding the emic point of view may go far to help prevent intercultural communication mishaps that result in rejection of the gospel, syncretism, and heresy. Whiteman argues that anthropology focuses on human interaction and communication, critical elements for gospel witness. Importantly, it strives to understand cultural forms and their associated meanings. Finally, anthropology helps us understand cultural change; the transformation of people and culture that the gospel brings.

46. Hesselgrave, *Communicating Christ Cross-Culturally*; Kraft, *Anthropology for Christian Witness*; Rheenen, *Communicating Christ in Animistic Contexts*; Hiebert, *Anthropological Reflections*.

47. Hiebert, *Transforming Worldviews*.

48. Ayers, "Toward a Theology of Leadership," 14.

Teleology in theology points to God's purposes or mission. Ayers does not establish a particular definition of teleology in theology nor for leadership, but he does attempt to draw some boundaries. First, leadership must be about more than "getting results."[49] Second, a follower–centric perspective is inappropriate because it ignores any ontological aspects of the leader and possibly reduces leadership to method. Third, Ayers suggests that teleology in leadership needs to consider moral, ethical, and spiritual aspects of the leader, the leader's motivation, as a guard against overt positivism. In this research, teleology refers to the examination of God's missionary purpose through his church in Christian missions.

Ontology

In philosophy, ontology refers to the examination of being; it is concerned with the nature of existence, the order of first things.[50] Ontology in theology deals with the fact of God's existence, his nature, and character; the non–contingent attributes of God.[51] Ayers defines ontology in leadership as "that sphere concerned with the inner, *a priori* nature of the leader [defined] as a new framework by which to investigate the innate needs, views of reality, internal disposition, and hidden dynamics of leaders, thereby making manifest any evidence of leadership."[52] For this study, ontology refers to the inner domain of a leader which includes but is not limited to the character, values, personality, gifting, and calling of the leader.

Authority

Authority in philosophy refers to the right use of power. French and Raven identify five bases of power: reward, coercive, legitimate, referent, and expert. *Reward power* is the ability to induce or draw forth positive emotions.[53] Reward power increases with the magnitude and probability of reward. *Coercive power* is related to psychological valences, in this case negative or punishment for non–conformity. Once again, the strength

---

49. Ayers, "Toward a Theology of Leadership," 15.

50. Ayers, "Toward a Theology of Leadership," 9.

51. Ayers, "Toward a Theology of Leadership," 10.

52. Ayers, "Toward a Theology of Leadership," 11.

53. French and Raven, "The Bases of Social Power," 263–68.

of coercive power is directly related to its magnitude and likelihood of punishment. *Legitimate power* is related to role or position. This power obtains legitimacy in the internalized norms of the subject (follower) and is often described in terms of ought–ness or right–ness. Cultural norms, social values, and designation by a legitimizing agent are the three bases for legitimate power. Normally legitimate power is very stable because it comes from the subject's value system. The range of legitimate power is usually well specified and defined, for example in a job description. Referent power comes from identification or feeling of unity with or attraction to the leader. *Referent power* is sometimes difficult to distinguish from reward and coercive power. *Expert power* is primarily limited to the cognitive domain but it can cause change in behavior. For expert power to come into play, trust must be established, and this power is limited to the area of expertise. Some halo effect may occur in expert power, extending the leader's power beyond the scope of his expertise. French and Raven conclude that referent power generally has the broadest range of influence. They also note that trying to use power outside the range of that power's base tends to reduce its magnitude. Finally, coercion on the part of the leader will decrease attraction on the part of the follower, thereby reducing referent power in the relationship. Pertinent to this study, legitimate power is related to authority in the sense that some degree of legitimacy comes with position in government, society, or organization. Legitimacy in this view describes right–ness of one's authority. The scope of such authority is commonly defined in law, social norms, or policy.

Robert J. Banks, in *Reviewing Leadership,* writes that many popular authors suggest that we conceive of leadership as influence by means of mutually shared authority.[54] Banks agrees that Christian leaders ought to share authority.[55] In theology, authority refers first to God's revelation and secondarily to human leadership. In this research, I use authority as the right to lead or exert power.

Ethic

The study of application of a theory is called methodology, examining, or explaining behaviors resulting from a theory.[56] In theology one might look

---

54. Banks, *Reviewing Leadership,* 52.

55. Banks, *Reviewing Leadership,* 70.

56. Ayers, "Toward a Theology of Leadership," 11–12.

at what God has done in Christ or how we move from orthodoxy to ortho-praxy. Methodology in leadership, according to Ayers, has to do with the "tactile traits or necessary behaviors of leaders."[57] Most leadership theories come with a set of expected behavioral outcomes or standards of excellence. Transformational leadership theorists posit behavioral sets as well. The term methodology may cause some confusion because it can refer to a process of experimentation and consecutive, related actions. Therefore, in this research I refer to the leader's ethic. Ethic, in this case, refers not to the body of values that one might hold, but to the set of desired behaviors or principles of con-duct that results from a particular leadership theory.

Scope

This research project has three delimitations. First, one of the greatest chal-lenges to research in leadership studies is the vast quantity of literature. Much of the literature is written for a non–academic audience, so the chal-lenge is to delimit the study in such a way that fruitful research can be accomplished. Accordingly, this study will be delimited to Bass and Avolio's work on transformational leadership theory. Furthermore, this theoretical research is delimited to the Four I's of Bass and Avolio.

Second, the point of this research is to develop a tool for missiological assessment of leadership theory and evaluate Bass' transformational lead-ership theory. Therefore, the assessment has the goal of understanding the implications of their theory for the purpose of doing missions effectively in an intercultural setting. The missiological delimitation has implications for the theological assessment of transformational leadership theory. Because of the specific missiological scope of this study, the theological aspect of the assessment is delimited to understanding the theory for the purpose of missions. This study examines the four transformational leadership factors in terms of teleology, ontology, authority, and ethic in missions.

Third, in keeping with the missiological scope of this study, the cultural anthropological aspect is further delimited to the cultural di-mensions proposed by Geert Hofstede. Hofstede argues for six cultural dimensions that help explain intercultural differences. His cultural di-mensions are (1) power distance, (2) individualism and collectivism, (3) masculinity and femininity, (4) uncertainty avoidance, (5) long–term and

57. Ayers, "Toward a Theology of Leadership," 12.

short-term orientation, and (6) indulgence versus restraint.[58] The dimensions are applied as an analytical grid by which to assess the intercultural transferability of transformational leadership theory for the purpose of missions in the context of missions.

Methodology

A study of this type is based on the literature in the fields of leadership philosophy, theology of missions, and cultural anthropology. I read general works on leadership theory, especially textbooks on leadership, and peer-reviewed studies on leadership in academic journals to gain a general sense of the history of the development of transformational leadership theory. Of special note are the journals of Regent University School of Business and Leadership. Regent's journals, such as the *International Journal of Leadership Studies*, *Journal of Biblical Perspectives in Leadership*, and *Journal of Strategic Leadership*, were particularly helpful for this study. Journals and papers published by the International Leadership Association will be of interest for those researching intercultural leadership.

Evaluating a leadership theory or practice requires processing it through three levels: understanding, analysis, then evaluation. As previously argued, the theory or practice needs to be evaluated from three perspectives: philosophically, theologically, and culturally.[59] Combining these levels of evaluation with the three perspectives results in a reasonable, biblically sound, culturally appropriate leadership theory or practice. Explicitly, I mean we must:

1. Understand and describe the theory or practice.

2. Analyze the theory or practice theologically.

3. Analyze the theory or practice for cultural effect.

4. Evaluate the theory or practice to decide if it is a reasonable, biblically faithful, culturally appropriate theory or practice of leadership.

To accomplish this goal, work sequentially through four steps. First, describe the theory or practice and how it works. Second, appraise the theory or practice theologically. Third, assess the influence of culture on the theory or practice. Fourth, determine the appropriateness of the theory or

---

58. Hofstede et al., *Cultures and Organizations*.

59. Philosophically, I mean as a theory in its own right, on its own terms.

practice. Each of these steps is made up of important elements to ensure a reasoned evaluation and form the basis of my Leadership Assessment Matrix. Now, I will describe each step and associated elements in more detail.

Step 1: Understand and describe the leadership theory.

The goal of this first tier is to understand and describe how the theory developed and its core elements, explain the exercise of the theory, and identify the expected outcomes of the theory in practice. First, research to discover and understand how the theory developed. What is the historical context in which the theory developed, were there any theoretical antecedents, or relevant social phenomena surrounding the theory's development? How has the theory developed and morphed over time? Then describe the central tenants of the theory and any norms or values that are part of the theory.

Second, explain how the theory is supposed to work. What is its purpose, and what does the theory purport to accomplish? Where is leadership posited in the theory? For example, does leadership come from the leader, the follower, the context, a collective, dyads, or the group? We often approach a leadership theory with preconceived notions, but we must understand the theory on its own terms so do not presume to know the answer to these questions. How is influence exerted in the theory? Traits, behavior, cognition, affect, and consensual orientation, among others, can be mechanisms of influence. Also, seek to discover who is served by leadership I the theory. What is the relationship between the leaders and individuals, groups, institutions, organizations, or movements in the theory?

Third, identify any expected outcomes of the theory. What performance measures are constituent to the theory? Look for relationships between the theory, behaviors, and results. What lines of causation can you find? Make note of leadership output—what the leader does. Pay attention to the leader's impact, and the result of their actions. This tier includes understanding the contextual elements of the theory. In other words, what factors shape the results of the leadership and how are those factors mediated, moderated, or modified by the local context? What of the theory's universality? How does the theory relate to other theories? Does the theory claim universal or intercultural application? In step three, you will examine these last two elements, contextualization and universality, in greater depth.

Step 2: Appraise the leadership theory theologically.

Whereas the first tier is descriptive, the second tier is analytical. The goal of the second tier is to critique the theory or practice theologically, employing a theology of leadership. As with the previous step, we need an evaluative matrix by which to examine, critique, and assess a theory or practice. My proposed Leadership Assessment Matrix examines a theory or practice at four levels.

First, compare the theory's teleological aspect to a theology of leadership. This comparison requires a solid grasp of the purpose of missions and the role of leadership in working toward that noble cause. A theology of leadership should refer to appropriate leadership motivation as well as aims and concrete objectives or goals in the missionary task.

Second, measure the theory's ontological aspect against a theology of leadership. Delve into the inner domain of leadership from a biblical, theological perspective. This inner domain includes a leader's call, character, competence, and conduct as defined by a biblical theology of leadership. Questions such as: Where do leaders in missions come from, what sort of character should we expect from missions leaders, do they require certain kinds of gifting, abilities, or experience, help flesh out a theory's ontological aspect. These form a basic framework for evaluating a leadership theory or practice and relate to the next section, authority in leadership.

Third, test the theory's views on authority against a theology of leadership. How is a leader's capacity to lead defined or determined? What is a leader's source of authority and to whom are they responsible, whom do they serve?

Fourth, appraise the ethic, the code of conduct, of the theory by a theology of leadership. The code of conduct in question in the theology of leadership answers the question, how does the leader serve God and man?

Step 3: Assess the influence of culture on the leadership theory.

The third aspect of this assessment focuses on culture highlighting potential intercultural blind spots as a result of employing an essentially western view of leadership in non–western cultures.[60] The key activity in

60. Walumbwa and Lawler, "Building Effective Organizations;" Kowske and Anthony,

this step is to measure the assess the theory's potential applicability in a particular culture by holding it up to an established cultural matrix such as Hofstede's six dimensions of national culture. How is transformational leadership affected by power distance, individualism and collectivism, masculinity–femininity, uncertainty avoidance, long–term vs. short–term orientation, and indulgence versus restraint?[61] Assessing how a culture might perceive a leadership theory or practice is an important initial step. Then assess how culture may influence the effect of a leadership behavior.[62] Categorize any instances of mediation, moderation, or modification caused or called for by the cultural milieu.

Step 4: Determine the appropriateness of the leadership theory.

The final step is to summarize the results of the previous three steps and determine the level of appropriateness of a leadership theory or practice for missions or ministry in a specific cultural setting. Only after understanding a leadership theory in its own right, evaluating the theory by God's word, and examining the effect of culture on the theory can we make a sound judgment about the missiological application of a leadership theory for use in missions and ministry.

Organization

In part 1 of this research, I will conduct the first step of a missiological analysis of leadership theory or practice using Bernard Bass' transformational leadership theory as an example. I will examine and describe the historical context, development, elements, exercise, and expectations of his theory. In part 2, I will perform a theological analysis of transformational leadership theory. I will consider teleology, ontology, authority, and ethic in this evaluation. Part 3 will consist of a cultural appraisal of the theory. Geert Hofstede's dimensions of culture will guide this review. Finally, in part 4, I will conclude by giving a summary of my findings and

"Towards Defining Leadership Competence around the World," 21–41.

61. Hofstede et al, *Cultures and Organizations.*

62. Hofstede, "A European in Asia," 16–21; Pekerti and Sendjaya, "Exploring Servant Leadership across Cultures," 754–80; Walumbwa and Lawler, "Building Effective Organizations,"1083–101.

make my recommendations regarding the usefulness of transformational leadership theory for missions and ministry. In addition, I will point out a few implications of this research and draw some conclusions about the Leadership Assessment Matrix.

PART 1

Understand and Describe the Leadership Theory

THE STUDY OF LEADERSHIP theory is relatively new; nevertheless, many well-researched volumes on leadership theory are available.[1] Works that outline a systematic means of leadership theory research are rarer. J. G. Hunt provides one of those rare exceptions.[2] Hunt proposes that the study of leadership should include a discussion of a theory's purpose, historical context, level of analysis, and relational and dynamic aspects. Hunt suggests that researchers consider the ontological issue of the nature of reality (or leadership) and the epistemological question, "How can we know that which we know?" as antecedents to leadership. In his typology, purpose refers to why one focuses on leadership–whether to transform, inform, learn how to do something, or

1. Notable examples are Bass, *Assessment of Managers*; Bass and Bass, *The Bass Handbook of Leadership: Theory, Research, and Managerial Applications*; Burns, *Leadership*; Clark et al., *Measures of Leadership*; DuBrin, *Leadership: Research Findings, Practice, and Skills*; Gardner, *Leading Minds: An Anatomy of Leadership*; Gill, *Theory and Practice of Leadership*; Hackman and Johnson, *Leadership: A Communication Perspective*; Hersey et al., *Management of Organizational Behavior*; Kellerman, *The End of Leadership*; Donna Ladkin, *Rethinking Leadership: A New Look at Old Leadership Questions*; Nohria and Khurana, *Handbook of Leadership Theory and Practice*; Northouse, *Leadership: Theory and Practice*; Rost, *Leadership for the Twenty-First Century*; and Schein, *Organizational Culture and Leadership*.

2. Hunt, "What Is Leadership?" 19–47.

learn about something. Hunt argues that research should specify the level of analysis intended, such as single, multiple, cross-sectional, unidirectional, comparative, or a combination of levels of analysis. He also recommends that the researcher identify the unit of focus in theory. For example, a theory may explain leadership in terms of the leader, follower, dyadic leader-follower interaction, or group relationship as the unit of focus. Finally, Hunt stipulates that researchers consider the dynamic aspect of leadership—how the various aspects of the theory interrelate.

Dmitry Khanin counsels that leadership analysis includes the study of the leading causes of leadership, influence in leadership, and the objectives and aspirations of leadership. Cause, as a domain in Khanin's system, accounts for the study of cultural-organizational aspects, leader and follower characteristics, and their interrelationships. Khanin's influence domain includes leadership's relationship to institutions, norms, and ethics; also, the sources of influence, and whether the method is pure (a single process) or a combination. The domain of objectives and aspirations in his system incorporates the theory's approach, applicability, and contingency or adaptability.[3]

Morela Hernandez calls for an investigation of the locus of leadership. She describes five loci of leadership: the leader, context, followers, collectives, and dyads where *context* includes culture and norms, *collectives* include work groups, teams, and *dyads* refer to the leader-follower relationship. Leadership, she continues, is exercised through mechanisms such as traits, behaviors, cognition, or affect. In her approach, cognition mechanisms are the sense-making approaches that attend related to leadership. Affect, as a mechanism for leadership, refers to the emotions and moods of the relationships of the group's people.[4]

None of the above approaches to understanding leadership theory fully suits the needs of leadership theory in missions. Hunt's insights are helpful in understanding leadership as a notion, but he does not delve into the phenomena or practice of leadership. Khanin's work is a significant step forward, proposing a framework for the study of leadership theory that includes analyzing cause, purpose, and methods, but he ignores historical context and influences. Furthermore, Khanin's system examines the objectives of a theory but not outcomes such as performance.[5] Hernandez's work

3. Khanin, "Contrasting Burns and Bass," 7–25.
4. Hernandez et al., "The Loci and Mechanisms of Leadership," 1165–85.
5. Khanin, "Contrasting Burns and Bass," 15.

on the loci and mechanisms of leadership is excellent but too narrow as a tool for understanding leadership for missions. In this study, I consider the recommendations of these researchers and extend their work in my scheme for evaluating leadership, displayed in Table 1. This new approach forms the first tier of the Leadership Assessment Matrix for a comprehensive assessment of leadership theory for use in Christian missions.

Table 1. A Philosophical Matrix for Evaluating Leadership Theory

Aspect	Element	Description
Development and Description of the Theory	Historical Context	What theoretical or social–cultural antecedents influence the theory?
	Theory Development	How did the theory come to be?
	Theory Description	What are the central elements of the theory?
Exercise of the Theory	Purpose	What does the theory purport to do?
	Locus of Leadership	Where does the theory situate leadership?
	Influence Mechanisms	What are the means of influence in the theory?
	Stewardship Orientation	Whom does the leader serve?
Outcomes of the Theory	Performance Measures	What are the theory outcomes and measures of performance?
	Meta–Relational Aspect	What interrelationships exist between elements of the theory?
	Contextual Influence	What factors shape behavior?
	Universality of the Theory	What are the intercultural applications?

Chapter 1

Development and Description
of the Theory

IN KEEPING WITH THE above matrix, in this section I give attention to the historical context of Bernard M. Bass' transformational leadership theory. I explain Bass and Bruce J. Avolio's development of their theory with particular attention to the seven leadership factors of their Full Range of Leadership theory. This description will serve as part of the framework for understanding transformational leadership theory.

Historical Context: James MacGregor Burns'
Foundational Work

The historical context of Bass' transformational leadership theory begins with James MacGregor Burns, the father of transformational leadership theory.[1] He was a prolific writer about history, politics, U.S. presidential biographies, and leadership and has a tendency to use political leftists and progressives as model transformational leaders. Nevertheless, Burns stands at the fountainhead of transformational leadership theory. He believed that without a solid theoretical foundation, we have no basis for any substantial conversation about leadership, much less any hope of knowing what

---

1. Rost, *Leadership for the Twenty-First Century*, 10–11.

leadership is or how to go about developing leaders.[2] Burns' notions on leadership, especially those concerning power and authority, transactional leadership, and transformational leadership, became the basis for transformational leadership theory and, therefore, essential to understanding.

Power and authority: The basis of leadership.

Burns explains that power has the potential for good and evil, "the glory and burden of most of humanity."[3] In Burns' framework, power does not require dominance over others. Rather, he defines power as a process, "in which power holders . . . have the capacity to secure changes in the behavior of a respondent . . . by utilizing resources in their power base."[4] Therefore, power is the capacity for influencing behavioral change and is derived from what he describes as resources in a relationship process.[5] For Burns, resources are the motivations that arise out of values. Values drive wants and needs, which create motivation for behavioral change.[6] The motives to which Burns refers are those described in Abraham Maslow's hierarchy. Burns offers a caution about the nature of needs and transforming leadership. Motivations can be born out of basic physiological and physical needs, but these motivations tend to grow out of an exchange relationship, or transactional leadership. In transformational leadership, needs of a higher order are called into play, self-esteem being primary among them.[7] The fundamental concept is that power lies in the relationship of motives linked to resources.[8]

Mutually held values motivate followers to follow. Therefore, power is value-laden and emerges out of a leader-follower relationship that grows in proportion to the resources available in those relationships. As leaders and followers grow in their relationships, they discover mutual values. Mutually held values render power to the leader in the form of the follower's willingness to be led by the leader. Followers follow out of the hope and

2. Burns, *Leadership*, 2–3.

3. Burns, *Leadership*, 14–15.

4. Burns, *Leadership*, 13.

5. Burns, *Leadership*, 13.

6. Burns, *Leadership*, 67–72, 425, 461.

7. Burns, *Transforming Leadership*, 142.

8. Burns, *Transforming Leadership*, 198.

conviction that needs arising out of these mutual values will be satisfied. Therefore, the process of relationship develops power.[9]

Power in the leader–follower relationship consists of two variables: intent and capacity. The intent of the members in the relationship defines their direction—what they hope to accomplish. The members' capacity to accomplish their intent defines their potential strength. The magnitude of leadership power is found in the degree to which the mutual needs of leader and follower are met.[10] Figure 1 depicts the relationship of power to a leader's intent and capacity and followers' values and needs.

Intent is essential to power because it is that which draws together the resources and motives of leader and follower powerbases. A leader's power is based on the perception that he can deliver on his followers' needs. In the long run, how much a leader matches up to an iconic perception of the nature of leadership is less important than what he can do for his followers. Followers are motivated to follow and act positively toward a leader when they believe that he has their interests at heart.[11]

Figure 1. Power in Relation to Intent and Capacity, Values, and Needs.

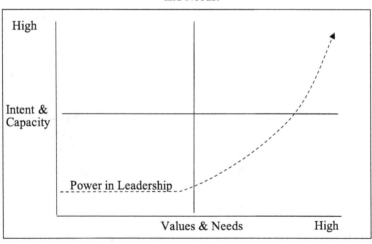

9. Burns, *Leadership*, 17–18.

10. Burns, *Leadership*, 18–22.

11. Burns, *Leadership*, 13, 294.

Authority is formal power located in position. Authority is often exercised by doling out benefits or sanctions according to formal pathways. Such authority is real to the degree that followers associate reliability and credibility to the system. Power, authority, and leadership are intermingled but not synonymous, as Burns explains: "all leaders are actual or potential power holders, but not all power holders are leaders."[12] Legitimate authority in a system is assumed as long as the system provides stability and security, the hallmarks of bureaucracy. Bureaucracies may rob authority from those in formal roles within their system, and Burns sees that as a good thing. Two fears form the basis of common aversion toward bureaucracies: fear of "being swallowed up in the machine," and the fear that the ends have lost to means.[13] Bureaucracies and other formal organizational structures can become so convoluted that the initial purpose for rules, regulations, and procedures gets lost in more rules, regulation, and procedure to the point that the system no longer provides that for which it was intended. As to the second fear, Burns poignantly remarks, "In bureaucracy, as in other social entities, power is arbitrary and feckless unless guided by purpose."[14] Stasis easily sets in and a drive to guard and prolong the system can overtake purpose. When the original purpose of meeting mutual needs is lost for continuation of the entity, ends have abdicated to means. Real authority in systems lies in the power to meet individual needs and wants.[15]

Leader–follower transaction.

Authority and power are intricately linked in organizations and corporations. People are usually predisposed to follow people who are in leadership roles. Burns argues, however, that notions of power and authority are insufficient to explain the basis of leadership in large entities. He asserts

12. Burns, *Leadership*, 18. The idea of wielding power for personal gain makes Burns critical of "how-to manuals" and trainings that promise keys to manage people or to sway them. Such methods are forms of manipulation more like Machiavelli's prince than like leaders. Burns renders a harsh critique of Dale Carnegie's *How to Win Friends and Influence People*. He asserts that Carnegie's system is little more than manipulation, treating people as objects by subtly arousing a desire in the person through flattery, linking that desire to the sales product, then satisfying that modified want. Burns, *Leadership*, 446–48.

13. Burns, *Leadership*, 297–98

14. Burns, *Leadership*, 299

15. Burns, *Leadership*, 296–301.

that punishment and reward used to motivate employees is the most likely explanation for power in large organizations, the mode of leadership. The wants and desires of followers make punishment and reward transactions possible.[16]

Leadership begins with change rooted in want claims Burns.[17] The nature of these wants and how the leader responds to them defines the kind of leader he is. Transactional leadership occurs when a leader acts on the basis of exchanging one thing for another.[18] The exchange may be food, housing, or security for support, armed revolt, or any other matter. Unlike coercion, transactional leadership exchanges are based in the interaction of the followers' motivations and the benefits offered by the leader. Both the leader and followers are conscious of the bargain and relate to one another as persons, not merely objects. Furthermore, this relationship is for a common purpose, or at least not contradictory purposes. Once these purposes are satisfied, the relationship may fade.[19] As lower physiological or security needs are met, the relationship between leader and follower changes and the character of their exchange develops.[20] Higher–level needs are less egocentric and usually last longer.[21] The implication for transactional leadership styles is that the leader is burdened with an ever–changing environment as he strives to understand the followers' needs and how he can apply those needs for the benefit of the organization. Figure 2 illustrates leadership styles as related to leader and follower wants.

Transactional leadership behaviors may emerge suddenly and without much contemplation on the part of the leader. Burns recognizes that in many circumstances a leader may not have the luxury of following a careful, rational decision–making process because the situation has so constrained him that he feels he has no real choice. Burns claims that most leaders at this point will fall into transactional leadership models in response to the pressures. Leaders in such circumstances bargain, take short–term objectives over long–term goals, or acquiesce their purposes.[22]

---

16. Burns, *Leadership*, 372–75.

17. Burns, *Transforming Leadership*, 140.

18. Burns, *Leadership*, 4, 19–20.

19. Burns, *Leadership*, 20.

20. Burns, *Leadership*, 72.

21. Burns, *Leadership*.

22. Burns, *Leadership*, 408–9.

Figure 2. Wants and Leadership Styles

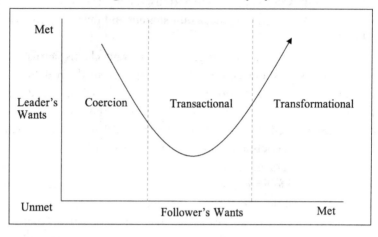

Most of what passes as leadership is not leadership, posits Burns. He claims that typical examples of exemplary leadership are simply the decision-maker acting out the effects of decisions made by circumstances and persons before them. Many leaders follow the path set before them by circumstances out of their control and often without their knowledge. The test of leadership is whether or not the change or decision was real and intended.[23] By *real*, Burns means that a transformation of "attitudes, norms, assumptions, and behaviors of daily life" has occurred.[24] The leader consciously chooses a particular route and moves with the intent to bring about real change.[25] Change must be intentional for genuine leadership to have taken place.

How does one move from simply making decisions to leading? Burns claims that the solution is found in the nature of real change leadership. Leadership that rises and falls on the principle of mutually shared purposes and needs of both the leader and follower.[26] Another name for real change leadership is transformational leadership.

---

23. Burns, *Leadership*, 408–17.

24. Burns, *Leadership*, 414.

25. Burns, *Leadership*, 413–17.

26. Burns, *Leadership*, 417–21.

Transformation: The goal of leadership.

Transformational leadership moves followers to morally higher ground. Leaders who encourage followers to attend primarily to things immediate and possible, fall short of transformational leadership. Burns argues that leaders often rationalize their tendency to act narrowly, striving only to meet basic needs, in terms of responsibility to the leader's needs, or those of his followers.[27] Either way, the result is to choose the mundane over the magnificent. Transformational leadership deals with the magnificent.

Burns defines transformational leadership as that which is reciprocal, value–based, thrives in a competitive environment, and causes change toward mutually–held goals and posits five arguments for his case. First, transformational leadership is reciprocal. It results from a symbiotic relationship between leader and follower that naturally develops structure and even formality.[28] Burns answers that followers need the leader in order to realize the needs that followers cannot satisfy on their own. The critical distinction between leaders and followers is that followers have "unrealized wants, unexpressed attitudes, and underlying predispositions," and leaders have clear motivations and initiative such that they take action to resolve their wants, express their attitudes, working out of their predispositions.[29] He goes further to argue that the leader's personal need–meeting experience, i.e., how his own needs were or were not met, has a direct relationship to the level of leadership to which an individual can rise.[30] Leaders find self–actualization through leading others in their individual and collective process of actualization.[31] Leaders, in Burns' formulation, grow and have their needs met through the growth and need–meeting of those who follow them. Reciprocity of need–meeting is at the heart of transformational leadership and is a kind of servanthood. In Burns' view, bureaucracies are not antithetical to leadership when they remember that they are a "servant of the people."[32] Burns' political leanings make him trust the transformational potential of large, bureaucratic, governing agencies, but his point that systems tend to lose their way and ignore the notion of reciprocity should not

27. Burns, *Leadership*, 42–46.
28. Burns, *Leadership*, 425, 452.
29. Burns, *Transforming Leadership*, 172.
30. Burns, *Leadership*, 66–67.
31. Burns, *Transforming Leadership*, 143.
32. Burns, *Leadership*, 302

be lost. People in organizational systems tend to forget the very reasons for the institution and for the rules and processes of that system. In short, they neglect the principle of reciprocity in relationships.

Second, transformational leadership is value–based. Burns quotes Martin Luther "Here I stand, I can do no other!" as an example of one driven by principles beyond himself and armed with values that power transforming leadership.[33] Parents, teachers, clergy, employers, and eventually society as a whole recognize, validate, and legitimize values and needs.[34] Values form the basis for action in transformational leadership. Values determine needs, at least those apart from physiological needs. Needs or wants form the motivations that Burns refers to as part of what makes up the resources for change.[35] Leadership is transformative when the leader helps followers move from values and needs to aspirations to expectations, and in the end, to demands.[36] Not all values are suitable for transformation. Some values are *modal*, that is, they form the basis for *end* or transformational values.[37] Examples of modal values are integrity, honesty, and fairness. End values are the grand causes that have the potential to raise followers up to higher levels of morality; values such as equality and justice.

Third, transformational leadership thrives in a competitive environment. Burns holds that conflict is necessary for leadership to be legitimate. Conflict proves that the leader–follower relationship is free of coercion. The moral side of conflict is not Burns' only concern. He is adamant that organizational environments be open to conflict. Conflict strengthens and feeds innovation. Leadership is produced in the crucible of conflict where motives are brought to bear, needs are sharpened, and values strengthened.[38] Dissent runs counter to the common expectation that leadership brings unity and uniformity. Yet, without room for contrasting points of view and struggling over core issues, true leadership does not arise. Conflict strengthens leaders and stirs up innovation. Burns believes creativity to be the highest form of efficacy. Creativity is a dynamic force for transformational change that arises out of free interaction, competition, and conflict. Creativity is innovative and, therefore, challenges the *status*

---

33. Burns, *Leadership*, 457.
34. Burns, *Transforming Leadership*, 144.
35. Burns, *Leadership*, 72, 425, 461.
36. Burns, *Transforming Leadership*, 143.
37. Burns, *Leadership*, 426.
38. Burns, *Leadership*, 453.

quo. The challenge to existing structures and power roles might simply be to offer another choice or it might be a call for substantial change, revitalization, reformation, or even revolution.[39]

Fourth, transformational leadership causes change. The drive toward a collective purpose gives birth to the need for leadership. Change toward that purpose, as marked by intent and satisfaction of needs and expectations, is the best measure of leadership.[40] Burns writes that the most important changes are carried on as social or religious movements.[41] Therefore, it should be no surprise that leadership has a moral purpose for its end. Leadership points to higher moral ground. Pointing the way to higher ground is not enough; leaders need to bring about change.[42] Transformation is less about grand schemes and heroic leaders and more about often–unrecognized leaders of opinion acting out of deep–seeded beliefs and values. Parents are the most common transformational leaders. They exhibit the "stronger and clearer motivations and purposes" required for leadership and are teachers who mold the deeply held values of their followers.[43] teaching is a vital role in transformation leadership because leaders can influence and mold the motives, values, and purposes of their followers. Teachers help their students rise to new levels of moral reasoning and critical thinking.[44] Great men of history, argues Burns, are so because they have tapped into a ground–swell of transformation.[45]

Finally, the change brought about by transformation leadership moves the leaders and followers toward mutually–held goals. Near universal moral principles such as equal rights and dignity are examples of the kind of goals to which Burns refers.[46] Change can be nothing more than substitution, but transformation brings about a "metamorphosis in form or structure."[47] Burns' central thesis is that political change of form and structural is brought about by transformational leadership.

---

39. Burns, *Transforming Leadership*, 152, 157, 160–61.

40. Burns, *Leadership*, 3.

41. Burns, *Leadership*, 454.

42. Burns, *Leadership*, 455.

43. Burns, *Leadership*, 429.

44. Burns, *Leadership*, 425, 449

45. Burns, *Leadership*, 443.

46. Burns, *Leadership*, 42.

47. Burns, *Transforming Leadership*, 24.

Transformational leadership is powerful because it calls on leaders to recognize and satisfy higher human needs in a holistic way that results in a relationship whereby both leader and follower are elevated to a greater moral plane. Leadership that elevates all involved parties to higher levels of morality, challenging the leader to re-establish ever-higher mutual goals is transformational leadership. Burns notes that leadership of this kind requires more sacrifice than it offers material benefits. Unfortunately, most leaders fail to provide transformational leadership. The predominance of their leadership activity is "system maintenance."[48] Burns goes so far as to argue that an organization can appear to be transformational and dynamic, all the while be primarily engaged in preserving stasis.

Theory Development: Bernard Bass Extends the Theory

By the time Burns wrote *Leadership*, Bernard M. Bass was already an established authority on leadership and had authored *Leadership, Psychology, and Organizational Behavior* on the subject of leadership and contingent reinforcement. In 1979, after reading Burns' book, *Leadership*, Bass was struck by the notion of transformational leadership and embarked on a life-long study of the subject. His first definition of a transformational leader was "someone who raised their awareness about issues of consequence, shifted them to higher-level needs, influenced them to transcend their own self-interests for the good of the group or organization, and to work harder than they originally had expected they would."[49]

With this new definition of leadership, Bass conducted a pilot study of seventy "high-level" transformational leaders.[50] He concluded that transformational leaders could indeed lead followers to exceed their expectations. Emboldened by the data, he forged ahead and examined leadership from sociological, political, and psychoanalytical perspectives, intertwined with his previous reading in biography and history, and tested by quantitative analysis. This research led to the publication of *Leadership and Performance beyond Expectations*.

48. Burns, *Leadership*, 4, 416, 455.

49. Bass, "Theory of Transformational Leadership Redux," 466–7.

50. Bass, "Theory of Transformational Leadership Redux," 468. Initially, Bass worked under the assumption that transformational leadership was relegated to the realm of high-level leaders, such as CEO's.

At first, Bass' research purposed to demonstrate that transformational leaders worked harder than transactional leaders, but the data did not support the claim. All was not lost though, because he began to see that transformational leaders are not rare. Furthermore, he affirmed that the current research tools and theories did not distinguish transformational leaders from transactional leaders. Bass realized he needed a new instrument to measure leadership and began to develop the instrument that would become the Multifactor Leadership Questionnaire (MLQ), published in 1990.[51]

Early studies demonstrated that 66 percent of the variance in his transformational leadership correlation matrix was attributed to charismatic leadership attributes. The other factors were individualized consideration (6.3%), intellectual stimulation (6.3%), and contingent reward (7.2%). Bass believed that leaders can inspire without necessarily being highly charismatic, and so, pulled out several elements from the charismatic factor items on the instrument and labeled them Inspirational Motivation. Bass' research failed to verify the separation of the charismatic factor from Inspirational Motivation. He was encouraged by others to maintain the separation of the two charismatic–inspirational factors because such a separation seemed to bear out in other research. Conceptually, it makes sense to frame the two factors distinctly. Leaders can learn to be more inspirational, a behavior, even while they are not particularly charismatic, a personal attribute. Because of the broad understandings of charisma as well as its negative political overtones, Bass introduced the term Idealized Influence in its place.[52]

Bass' primary test mechanism is the MLQ, which he developed with Bruce J. Avolio. The MLQ has been used in research for over 3,700 respondents from organizations ranging in size from 45 to over 500 employees.[53] Contingent Reward, Active Management by Exception, Passive–Avoidant Leadership, Charisma/Inspirational, Intellectual Stimulation, and Individual Consideration have a positive inter–correlation. Distinctions between the factors remain useful, however, for assessment, counseling, and training.[54] Bass describes the transformational leader as leading by one of three key means: Charismatic Leadership, Intellectual Stimulation,

51. Bass, "Theory of Transformational Leadership Redux," 468.

52. Bass, "Theory of Transformational Leadership Redux," 469–72. Charisma was too highly associated with Benito Mussolini, Adolph Hitler, and Emperor Tojo.

53. Avolio and Bass, "Re–Examining the Components," 444.

54. Avolio and Bass, "Re–Examining the Components," 444–45, 457.

and Individualized Consideration.[55] The best leaders display both transactional and transformational leadership behaviors that Bass named the Full Range of Leadership.[56]

Theory Description: Components of the Full Range of Leadership

Transformational leadership theory is a descriptive, inductive theory that began from observations that led to hypotheses that were tested, modified and re-tested. Full Range of Leadership theory is made up of seven factors: Contingent Reward, Management by Exception, Laissez-Faire, Idealized Influence, Inspirational Motivation, Intellectual Stimulation, and Individual Consideration.

Contingent Reward.

Leaders strong in the Contingent Reward factor clarify rewards, give assistance based on effort, and recognize and reward achievement.[57] They make contracts and they provide reward for effort.[58]

Management-by-Exception.

The Management-by-Exception factor identifies leaders who notice aberrations to standards. Leaders strong in this factor track and focus on mistakes and failures. Followers view them as those who put out fires.[59] These managers may be seen as standard-bearers, upholding policy and procedure.[60] Management-by-Exception is a corrective behavior on the part of the leader. The corrective actions taken by the leader may be active or passive, but neither action is as effective as Contingent Reward or transformational leadership behaviors. The active aspect of

55. Bass, "From Transactional to Transformational Leadership," 21–22.

56. Hatter and Bass, "Supervisor's Evaluations and Subordinates Perceptions" 695–702.

57. Avolio and Bass, "Re-Examining the Components," 450.

58. Bass, "From Transactional to Transformational Leadership," 22.

59. Avolio and Bass, "Re-Examining the Components," 450.

60. Bass, "From Transactional to Transformational Leadership," 22.

Management–by–Exception occurs when a leader monitors for non-standard behavior and reacts accordingly.[61]

Laissez–Faire.

Laissez–Faire leadership is the absence of leadership either by avoidance or abdication.[62] Also referred to as Management–by–Exception/Passive, the Laissez–Faire leader is one who believes the adage––if something's not broke, don't fix it. Passive leaders avoid involvement and decision–making and are viewed by subordinates as absent when needed. They respond to problems of a serious or chronic nature, but delay in doing so.[63]

Idealized Influence.

Bass distinguishes charismatic qualities and behaviors of leaders from other transformational characteristics. He describes the Idealized Influence leader as envisioning, confident, with high moral standards, model behavior, morally uplifting, trustworthy, and responsible, who promotes ethical standards and procedures.[64] A transformational leader holds high expectations and yet communicates these purposes in down–to–earth terms.[65] Idealized Influence refers to those characteristics and behaviors that cause followers to imitate their leaders.[66] Serving as a role model is an important factor of transformational leadership that comes about when followers respect, admire, and trust their leader. Bass' research indicates that such leaders are perceived to have unusual capabilities and persistence. Some of these characteristics are related to leader behavior and others are attributed to the leader by their followers. Together, these behaviors and attributes result in the feeling that the leader can be counted on to do the right thing. Such leaders are willing to take risks and are consistent.[67]

61. Bass and Riggio, *Transformational Leadership*, 8.

62. Bass and Riggio, *Transformational Leadership*, 8; Bass, "From Transactional to Transformational Leadership," 22.

63. Avolio and Bass, "Re–Examining the Components," 450.

64. Bernard M. Bass and P. Steidlmeier, "Ethics, Character, and Authentic Transformational Leadership," *Leadership Quarterly* 10 (1999): 187.

65. Bass, "From Transactional to Transformational Leadership," 22.

66. Bass and Riggio, *Transformational Leadership*, 6.

67. Bass and Riggio, *Transformational Leadership*, 6.

Followers who are proud of their leader and who believe that their leader goes beyond self–interest, indicate the presence of Idealized Influence in leadership.[68] These leaders hold their followers' respect. Transformational leaders with a high Idealized Influence factor display power and confidence. They speak about values and model ethical standards. Their decision–making reflects consideration of moral and ethical standards. Influential leadership gives meaning and challenge to followers. Transformational leaders paint an optimistic future, molding follower expectations.[69]

An egotistic outlook and manipulative behavior are ethical boundaries for Idealized Influence. According to Bass and Steidlmeier, pseudo–transformational leaders, those who pose as transformational for their own benefit, create false dichotomies of values leading to an "us versus them" mentality.[70] Such leaders tend to cast grandiose visions with little apparent understanding of how to reach their lofty goals. They profess strong follower attachment but are ready to sacrifice followers for their own sakes. Inconsistency and lack of responsibility are hallmarks of pseudo–transformational leaders.

Inspirational Motivation.

Inspirational Motivation paired with Idealized Influence forms the charismatic leadership factor.[71] The Inspirational Motivation leadership factor describes leaders who provide followers the opportunity to share goals and join in activities to reach those goals.[72] Leaders who empower focus on the best in people.[73] They do not simply paint a rosy picture, but speak truthfully to followers and demonstrate genuine concern for good and achievement.

Transformational leaders inspire and motivate. Leaders with the Inspirational Motivation factor provide meaning and challenge to the work.

---

68. Avolio and Bass, "Re–Examining the Components," 450.

69. Bass and Riggio, *Transformational Leadership*, 6.

70. Bass and Steidlmeier, "Ethics, Character, and Authentic Transformational Leadership," 187.

71. Bass and Riggio, *Transformational Leadership*, 6.

72. Bass and Steidlmeier, "Ethics, Character, and Authentic Transformational Leadership," 188.

73. Bass and Steidlmeier, "Ethics, Character, and Authentic Transformational Leadership," 188.

These leaders develop *esprit de corps*. They are optimistic and excited about the future. Not prone to wild, unattainable vision, these leaders lay–out expectations and demonstrate commitment to the shared goals as they empower followers toward self–actualization.[74] They are persuasive and help followers gain understanding and the meaning of goals set forth by the leader.[75]

Inspirational leaders are consistent and willing to take risks for the common purpose.[76] They reassure followers that, though obstacles may stand in the way, success is possible, even likely. Their speech is optimistic and enthusiastic, but such leaders do not shy away from reality.[77] They draw awareness to important issues and communicate expectations.[78]

Pseudo–transformational leaders focus on the worst in people. Their speech is misleading and may be filled with subtlety, not clarity. Although they sound empowering, these leaders retain control and create dependency. Theirs is an egotistic view of leadership.[79]

Intellectual Stimulation.

Intellectual Stimulation promotes cognitive growth, rational processing, and careful problem–solving.[80] Intellectual Stimulation refers to the behaviors of a leader that drive followers' cognitive and imaginative growth. Open to questioning and new approaches to problems, transformational leaders encourage creativity and new solutions. Criticism of mistakes is private, while praise is public.[81]

Intellectual stimulation is present when superiors question assumptions, encourage subordinates to employ intuition, entertain ideas that seem unusual, create imaginative visions, ask subordinates to rework problems, and see unusual patterns. Intellectually stimulating leaders are observed by

---

74. Bass and Steidlmeier, "Ethics, Character, and Authentic Transformational Leadership," 188

75. Bass and Riggio, *Transformational Leadership*, 6.

76. Bass and Riggio, *Transformational Leadership*, 6.

77. Avolio and Bass, "Re–Examining the Components."

78. Bass and Riggio, *Transformational Leadership*, 6.

79. Bass and Steidlmeier, "Ethics, Character, and Authentic Transformational Leadership," 188–89.

80. Bass, "From Transactional to Transformational Leadership," 22.

81. Bass and Riggio, *Transformational Leadership*, 6.

followers as those who question assumptions, are never satisfied with the *status quo*, and are always seeking out new and different views as a means for accomplishing the group purpose. An open and dynamic environment for solving problems and planning is part of the Intellectual Stimulating factor of transformational leadership. Bass and Paul Steidlemeier write of this factor as addressing a "transcendent spiritual dimension."[82] They assert this dimension is an altruistic stance of open–mindedness for searching for the "ground of meaning for truth."[83]

Bass and Steidlemeier describe Intellectual Stimulation as the factor whereby leaders persuade followers with logical arguments with clear warrant. The rational discourse of such leaders can bring about change in values through cognitive processes that are both satisfying and beneficial for the follower. The pseudo–transformational form of Intellectual Stimulation is narrow–minded, ridged, and egotistic. These leaders base behaviors on false assumptions, are manipulative, fed by follower ignorance, and work through emotional appeal for the narcissistic interests of the leader.[84]

Individualized Consideration.

Individualized Consideration is marked by the act of rendering personal attention to followers.[85] The leader strong in this factor believes in equity, not necessarily equality. Individually, considerate leaders coach and advise.[86] Transformational leaders who work through this factor give attention to followers' individual needs and contributions. As a coach or mentor, the transformational leader discovers and spurs the followers' growth. Often, growth comes through new opportunities and challenges well–suited for the follower along with appropriate autonomy in a supportive environment. Leader behaviors are dependent on the follower's needs, similar to those leader responses described by Ken Blanchard in his situational leadership

82. Bass and Steidlmeier, "Ethics, Character, and Authentic Transformational Leadership," 188.

83. Bass and Steidlmeier, "Ethics, Character, and Authentic Transformational Leadership," 188

84. Bass and Steidlmeier, "Ethics, Character, and Authentic Transformational Leadership," 188–89.

85. The leader emphasizes tailor–made activities towards followers as opposed to behaving the same way toward all follower. Bass, "From Transactional to Transformational Leadership," 22.

86. Bass, "From Transactional to Transformational Leadership," 22.

theory.[87] A clear understanding of followers and transparent communication is necessary for Individualized Consideration.[88]

Individualized Consideration is demonstrated as individual care for others. Attention to a follower's needs for growth and acting on an individual's behalf to provide opportunities for advancement are individualized consideration behaviors that spring from specific knowledge and understanding of the follower as an individual.[89] Bass writes,

> Individualized consideration was apparent to interviewees when their bosses answered them with minimum delay, showed they were concerned for their subordinates' well–being, assigned tasks based on subordinate needs and abilities, encouraged two–way exchanges of ideas, were available when needed, encouraged self–development, practiced walk–around management, and effectively mentored, counseled, and coached.[90]

Individualized Consideration focuses on motivation of the follower as a moral category, not only on the desired behavior. The desired result of Individualized Consideration in transformational leadership is positive behavior out of a new, higher moral motivation to serve others.[91] A leader strong in Individual Consideration is altruistic.[92] Leader Individualized Consideration behaviors include: general support for a follower's work, encouragement of autonomy, empowering for more responsibility, and creating opportunity for growth at work.[93] As the follower's needs are addressed, he also undergoes transformation such that his perspectives begin to include the good of the group. Leaders with high Individualized Consideration can affect followers' behavior by setting expected behaviors and by exhibiting normative behaviors.[94]

---

87. Ken Blanchard, Patricia Zigarmi, and Drea Zigarmi, *Situational Leadership II* (San Diego: The Ken Blanchard Companies, 2007).

88. Bass and Riggio, *Transformational Leadership*, 6–7.

89. Bass, "Theory of Transformational Leadership Redux," 473.

90. Bass and Riggio, *Transformational Leadership*, 12.

91. Bruce J. Avolio and Bernard M. Bass, "Individual Consideration Viewed at Multiple Levels of Analysis: A Multi–Level Framework for Examining the Diffusion of Transformational Leadership," *Leadership Quarterly* 6 (1995): 202.

92. Bass and Steidlmeier, "Ethics, Character, and Authentic Transformational Leadership," 189.

93. Avolio and Bass, "Individual Consideration Viewed at Multiple Levels of Analysis," 202.

94. Avolio and Bass, "Individual Consideration Viewed at Multiple Levels of

The pseudo transformational leader is self-centered, maintaining tight control over his followers. Although he may seem to provide opportunities for growth, but they are half-hearted and often simply means by which to manipulate the worker. Manipulation by the pseudo-transformational leader is used to gain power. Often these leaders try to enhance their status by maintaining social distance from their subordinates as they project a grandiose vision of the future of the organization, which is out of touch with reality and the organization's capacity.[95]

Summary

Burns' scholarship in leadership theory laid the groundwork for Bass. Burns brought clarity to the notion that purpose, values, needs, and wants are part of power and authority. Power is not restricted to force, neither is authority limited to coercion. Power and authority result from the relationship process between leaders and their followers such that people follow leaders who have followers' best interest at heart. As Burns continued to think about these notions, he began to conceive of leadership in terms of transactions between leaders and followers. These transactions are need–meeting and want–meeting exchanges. Meeting only one party's needs is coercion. Meeting mutually held needs and want in common purpose with the bounds of common values is the realm of transformational leadership.

Burns offers four groups of questions for reflection to aid the would–be transformational leader. First, why does the individual seek to lead? Is the leader's motivation and purpose vocational? Is gaining a better status in life the driving force? The leader's purposes may be so interwoven with a high moral cause that they are difficult to draw apart. Nevertheless, the question is worth asking. It may reveal that one is really trying to lead no one other than himself; that his purposes serve only himself. Second, who should follow? Burns argues that leadership is a collective action and so it makes sense to try to envision who would be natural followers. Third, to what end will the leader lead? He is asking for something different than specific, measurable, achievable, and time–bound objectives. He is asking for the ultimate nature, the transformative direction, the life–changing and enduring end of the leader's vision. Finally, how will the leader overcome obstacles in his

---

Analysis," 202–5.

95. Bass and Steidlmeier, "Ethics, Character, and Authentic Transformational Leadership," 189.

path? Transforming leadership seeks to understand the mutually held purpose in terms of the followers' mindset. Burns end his volume by stating, "In real life the most practical advice for leaders is not to treat pawns like pawns, nor princes like princes, but all persons like persons."[96]

Moving from Burns' leadership theory to practice is difficult. Bass worked from Burns' theoretical foundation and moved from theory into practice. The MLQ provides a means by which scholars, leaders, and organizations can identify and encourage transformational leadership characteristics and teach and implement transformational behaviors.

---

96. Burns, *Leadership*, 460–61.

Chapter 2

Exercise of the Theory

WHAT IS THE PURPOSE of this approach to leadership? Where does authority lie? How are followers influenced? Who is served by such leadership? These questions serve to further define and describe transformational leadership theory.

Purpose: What Does the Theory
Proport to Accomplish?

Transformational leaders motivate followers to perform beyond their expectations. Bass explains that the purpose of transformational leadership is "to challenge followers to perform beyond normal expectations, to stimulate them to be creative and innovative, and to develop their collective leadership capacity."[1] The desire of a transformational leader is to change the follower, to help him grow as a leader in his own right. In Avolio and Gardner's authentic leadership development theory, the leader may not actively develop followers into leaders, but may inadvertently do so through role modeling. Conversely, in transformational leadership, active effort to change followers is central.[2]

---

1. Bass and Riggio, *Transformational Leadership*, 2.
2. Avolio and Gardner, "Authentic Leadership Development," 327.

Transformational leaders have a strong sense of purpose If the leader is sufficiently charismatic, his purposes may be adopted by followers. If sufficiently strong in Intellectual Stimulation, leaders may persuade followers to adopt their purposes.

In keeping with Burns' theory, purpose is a central element around which both leaders and followers gather. Bass argues that a deep level of transformation can be achieved when the purposes of the organization coalesce with that of the members of the organization.[3] Strong alignment of purpose, values, and interests are the core elements that drive a group to perform beyond its expectations.

The phrase, leading from the front, reflects this notion of leading through a strong, mutually held, guiding purpose. Leading from the front conjures up the image of a leader who calls people forward to a higher purpose, rather than one who pushes from behind by policy and procedure. Bass and Ronald E. Riggio find that elements of command and control may be absent in strongly transformational leadership organizations—even to the extent that some loss of predictability occurs. Groups without either highly structured rules and regulations or clear and commonly-held purposes are "formless, confused, [and] shapeless."[4] Groups formed around mutual purpose are highly responsive and adaptable to changes in their environment.[5]

Some organizations excel in both transactional and transformational leadership approaches to a distinct advantage. These "high-contrast" groups maintain both strongly transformational leadership and highly structured procedures. Elite military forces are an example of high-contrast groups. High-contrast organizations have firm procedures for operations and communications together with a high degree of individual and team decision-making practices aligned through common purpose and values. A strong mutual purpose is essential to high-contrast groups. This unique blend makes for an organization that works within predictable internal procedures to perform highly flexible and context-oriented missions.[6]

Mutual purpose does not simply appear out of thin air-it is taught. At first glance, the idea of persuasively conveying purpose to a group may seem in contradiction to Burns' ideal of mutually-held values and

---

3. Bass and Riggio, *Transformational Leadership*, 50.
4. Bass and Riggio, *Transformational Leadership*, 109.
5. Bass and Riggio, *Transformational Leadership*, 106.
6. Bass and Riggio, *Transformational Leadership*, 106.

purposes. Burns argues that teachers, parents, and religious leaders are often the most prominent value–teachers and transformational leaders. For Burns, the main concern is that the follower, be they a child or a co-worker, have the freedom of conscience to choose whether or not to align themselves with the values and purposes being taught.[7]

Locus of Leadership: Who Leads?

Hernandez's typology, as explained in the introduction to part 1, places authority in one of five categories: the leader, context, followers, collectives, or dyads. In transactional leadership, the source of leadership is primarily the leader. In contrast, the locus of leadership in transformational leadership is in dyadic leader–follower relationships. Hernandez warrants this claim based on her assessment that transformational leadership is a follower–focused system attending to leader–follower relationships.[8] Bass' form of transformational leadership theory contends that elected or appointed leaders lead from the authority of their position, legitimized by those who follow them.

Bass and Riggio postulate that those elected to position are more likely to be transformational than those appointed because of the consistent pressure on elected officials to be responsive to their constituents. Conversely, appointed leaders are more likely to display legitimate, reward, or coercive power. Pure coercion notwithstanding, followers must ratify a leaders' position no matter how the leader came to it. The degree to which a leader is trusted to meet follower expectations is related to that ratification. Bass and Riggio claim that transformational leaders can use legitimate or reward power.[9] Legitimate power is perceived by followers to be right or good based on their values and cultural norms. Reward power is the ability to elicit positive emotions based upon the likelihood of reward.[10] Both sources of power can be used by the transformation leader as he applies the Full Range of Leadership model. The key to transformational use of otherwise transactional factors is for the leader's purpose or mutually–held goals to motivate and guide the application of power.

---

7. Burns, *Leadership*, 428.

8. Hernandez et al., "The Loci and Mechanisms of Leadership," 1170–77.

9. Bass and Riggio, *Transformational Leadership*, 182.

10. French and Raven, "The Bases of Social Power," 263.

Bass and Steidlmeier argue for a locus of authority as somewhere between the libertarian notion of free choice and the common good. Common good must be understood as more virtuous than individual good and more than the aggregate sum of individual good. Stakeholders must come together for the good of the whole for truly common good to be done and may have to set aside their individual desires for the good of the whole.[11] This civic virtue is the key moral ground of transformational leadership. Authority grounded in Bass and Steidlmeier's view of civic good supports Hernandez' argument that the locus of leadership in transformational leadership is in dyadic leader–follower relationships.

Transformational leadership rejects the notion of purely participative decision–making. Leaders emerge and initiate a way forward that others are willing to follow. Transformational leadership can be participative or directive depending on the circumstance.[12] Leaders are transformational when followers believe that the values and interests upheld by the leader are good and right. In the final analysis, the locus of leadership in transformational leadership is with the leader who processes, decides, and acts for the purpose of the organization with the needs and values of the group and individual in mind. Leadership is a relational process, dyadic or otherwise, but the place of leadership is with the one who initiates behaviors toward the common goal.[13]

Influence Mechanisms: How do Leaders Lead?

Following Hernandez's typology, mechanisms of influence can be categorized as trait, behavior, cognition, or affect. Trait mechanisms are some of the longest studied means of influence. Hernandez refers to research by R. R. McCrae and P. P. Costa that demonstrated significant association between conscientiousness, extraversion, openness, emotional stability and leadership.[14] Cognition as an influence mechanism refers to the means by

11. Bass and Steidlmeier, "Ethics, Character, and Authentic Transformational Leadership," 200–201

12. Bass and Steidlmeier, "Ethics, Character, and Authentic Transformational Leadership," 202. Situational leadership theory by Paul Hersey and Ken Blanchard addresses the notion that differing circumstances require different types of leader behavior. Hersey et al., *Management of Organizational Behavior*.

13. Dave Logan et al. make a compelling argument for triadic over dyadic relationships in leadership. See Dave Logan et al., *Tribal Leadership*.

14. Hernandez et al., "The Loci and Mechanisms of Leadership," 1178. McCrae and

which leadership is understood, "how the scripts and schemas influence the ways leadership is conducted and ultimately perceived and interpreted."[15] Essentially, a leader teaching or tapping into a referential cognitive framework or model in the follower is using a cognitive mechanism. Affect refers to any means that appeals to follower's emotions.[16]

Trait as influence.

Traits matter in leadership. Followers are concerned that their leaders are moral, concerned over ethical issues, consistent, tenacious, self–less.[17] In general, leaders are more likely to be extroverts, those who are outgoing and enjoy group settings. Extroversion is correlated to transformational leadership at weak levels (r=0.19 to 0.25). Ascendancy, the tendency to assume leadership roles, is only mildly associated with transformational leadership. Self–confidence is much more strongly associated with transformational leadership (r=0.53). Transformational leaders tend to have an internal locus of self–control. Such leaders are confident that they have control over their lives. This confidence is substantially correlated with Individual Consideration (r=0.33 to 0.44) as well as significantly with Inspirational Motivation (r=0.33).[18]

In addition to the association of certain traits with transformational leadership, some measures of multiple intelligences have similar correlations. Social intelligence seems to be strongly related to transformational leadership (r=0.3 to 0.6) with regard to openness, frankness, and careful

---

Costa, "Validation of the Five–Factor Model of Personality across Instruments and Observers," 81–90.

15. Hernandez et al., "The Loci and Mechanisms of Leadership," 1168.

16. Hernandez et al., "The Loci and Mechanisms of Leadership," 1168, 1179.

17. Avolio and Bass, "Re–Examining the Components."

18. Bass and Riggio, *Transformational Leadership*, 168–69. Bass explains that r values of 0.3 to 0.4 indicate moderate correlation, values of 0.5 to 0.6 indicate substantial correlation, and those above 0.7 indicate strong correlation. Valuation of the regression coefficient, *weak, moderate, strong*, varies somewhat from researcher to researcher. Richard Taylor explains that correlation analysis measures the strength of linear relationships. Correlation (r) values of <0.36 are weak, 0.36 to 0.67 are moderate, 0.68 to 0.89 are strong, and > 0.89 are very strong correlations. The coefficient of determination ($r2$) relates to how much the variance measured is explained by the dependent variable. For example, an $r2$ value of 0.04 (r=0.20) means that 4% of the total variation can be accounted to the variable. Correlation measures association, not cause. Taylor, "Interpretation of the Correlation Coefficient: A Basic Review," 35–39.

listening. As might be expected, emotional intelligence tends is moderately associated to strongly associated with transformational leadership.[19]

Some of the differences in correlations between studies of traits and intelligences in transformational leadership can be explained by contextual variance. But Bass maintains, "No matter where you put some people, they will emerge and succeed as leaders."[20]

Behavioral influence.

Hernandez asserts that transformational leaders primarily exercise influence through behavior and the cognitive domain, while some exercise influence through trait, and a few, through affect. Leadership behavior is moderated by the context, culture, and norms of the group.[21]

Organizational change is necessary and difficult and requires more than management of the *status quo* can offer. Early on in Bass' work, he writes about influence in transformational leadership stemming from drawing forth motivation from followers by satisfying needs.[22] In particular, the leader seeks to meet followers' higher needs.[23] The result is "mutual stimulation and elevation that converts followers into leaders and may convert leaders into moral agents."[24] Bass' transformational leadership process is to bring follower awareness of the importance and value of organizational goals to the forefront, help followers see beyond themselves for the sake of the group and organization, and motivate followers on the basis of high value needs as associated with the organization's purpose.[25] Certain behaviors influence this process such as setting goals and articulating a clear path. When the leader gives guidance, shows concern for, and is attentive to his followers, he exhibits behaviors that influence others.[26] Other transformational leadership behaviors are displayed in Table 2.

---

19. Bass and Riggio, *Transformational Leadership*, 172–74.

20. Bass and Riggio, *Transformational Leadership*, 177.

21. Hernandez et al., "The Loci and Mechanisms of Leadership," 1170.

22. Bass, *Bass and Stogdill's Handbook of Leadership*, 20.

23. In terms of Abraham Maslow's hierarchy of needs.

24. Bass, *Bass and Stogdill's Handbook of Leadership*, 20.

25. Jay A. Conger, "Charismatic and Transformational Leadership in Organizations: An Insider's Perspective on These Developing Streams of Research," *Leadership Quarterly* 10 (1999): 151.

26. Hernandez et al., "The Loci and Mechanisms of Leadership," 1170.

Table 2. Transformational leadership behaviors

Concerned beyond self	Shows power and confidence	Communicates expectations
Talks about values	Models ethical standards	Communicates rewards
Emphasizes mutual purpose	Speaks optimistically	Seeks different views
Expresses confidence	Gives individual attention	Questions assumptions
Articulates compelling vision	Raises awareness	Suggests new methods
Works within follower's strengths	Teaches and coaches	

Compiled from Bass, *Transformational Leadership*, 11–12 and Avolio, "Re-Examining the Components," 441–62.

Gretchen Vogelgesang, Hannes Leroy, and Bruce J. Avolio find association between behavioral integrity and follower perception that the leader communicates in a transparent manner. Belief is further associated with improved follower engagement at work and performance. Communication transparency means that the follower perceives that the leader listens, follows–up, recommends, and exhibits open communication. She claims that transparent communication is a necessary antecedent to behavioral integrity, alignment between word and deed. Communication transparency is a group–level behavior positively correlated to behavioral integrity that mediates follower engagement and performance.[27]

Influence through reason.

Bass makes little reference to reasoning or the cognitive realm in the sense defined by Hernandez. Generally, Bass articulates cognitive strategies as a means of reward such as a sense of competency, self–control, and purpose on the part of the followers as a result of Intellectual Stimulation.[28]

Other aspects of Bass's work may reflect that which Hernandez identifies. In casting vision for an organization, the leader establishes the beginnings of a cognitive framework that followers, in turn, may use to interpret

27. Vogelgesang et al., "The Mediating Effects of Leader Integrity," 405–13.
28. Bass and Riggio, *Transformational Leadership*, 174.

and understand future ideas put forth by the leader. Strong vision statements reflect optimism and confidence, values and intrinsic rewards, challenges and opportunities, specificity, and direction. For example, Yair Berson, Boas Shamir, and Bruce J. Avolio assert that transformational leaders articulate more than grandiose goals in their statements, a critique of Jim Collins' "Big Harry Audacious Goals."[29] Followers are more strongly motivated by reasonable goals, those they perceive are achievable albeit very hard to reach.[30]

Affect and influence.

Jay A. Conger concludes that charismatic leaders are prone to exaggerate claims to support their visions, even to the point of misleading followers. Charismatic leaders may inadvertently create in-groups and out-groups, promoting rivalries. Charismatic leaders often have difficulty cultivating successors because they enjoy being in the limelight and are reluctant to share it with others.[31]

Organizational culture has a powerful effect on how followers feel about an organization. Weichun Zhu and colleagues argue that moral action stems from moral decisions that stem from a moral climate and identity. The entire moral context—behavior, decisions, climate, and identity—is under the influence of authentic transformational leaders. Authentic transformational leaders can be positive role models, moral coaches, set moral standards and processes, provide constructive feedback, integrate moral standards within their vision, apply moral decision-making

---

29. Yair Berson and Bruce J. Avolio, "Transformational Leadership and the Dissemination of Organizational Goals: A Case Study of a Telecommunication Firm," *The Leadership Quarterly* 15 (2004): 625–46; Jim Collins, *Good to Great: Why Some Companies Make the Leap... and Others Don't* (New York: HarperCollins Publishers, 2001).

30. Bass and Steidlmeier, "Ethics, Character, and Authentic Transformational Leadership," 189.

31. Conger, "Charismatic and Transformational Leadership in Organizations," 171. William H. Bommer, Robert S. Rubin, and Timothy T. Baldwin studied the effect of cynicism about organizational change (CAOC) and peer leadership behavior on transformational leadership behavior. One of the few studies using transformational leadership behavior as a dependent variable, the researchers found that higher levels of peer leadership behavior attenuated the negative effect of CAOC to the point that CAOC was insignificant. They also found that management members with high CAOC were less likely to engage in transformational leadership behavior and that transformational leadership behavior exhibited by managers had a positive correlation to transformational leadership behavior among peers. In other words, transformational leadership behavior is infectious. Bommer et al., "Setting the Stage for Effective Leadership," 195–210.

processes, and give moral rewards and discipline to influence the moral context within their sphere of influence.[32]

In another study, Zhu and colleagues determined that affective trust, the emotional trustor–trustee bond, is related to harder work and commitment from employees. Cognitive trust, related to an employee's belief that the leader is competent, reliable, and a person of integrity, was found to be negatively associated with job performance.[33] This startling research highlights the vital importance of the affective aspect of leader–follower relationships over against character or competency alone.

Influence through affect may be measured in terms of psychological capital. James B. Avey, Bruce J. Avolio, and Fred Luthans studied positive leadership defined by psychological capital and its effect on follower productivity.[34] Psychological capital refers to efficacy, hope, optimism, and resiliency.[35] The researchers found that a correlation was present, but weak, indicating that positive leadership only partially explained positive follower performance.

A. C. McClough, S. G. Rogelberg, and G. G. Fisher offer a warning about affect and influence. They maintain that cynical employees are often highly engaged and concerned about the organization. Therefore, it is prudent to understand the heart of their feelings of frustration and resolve or redirect those negative emotions. Once a hopeful outlook is obtained, these former cynics are often the best cheerleaders for the organization.[36]

Stewardship Orientation: Who is Served?

Transformational leaders are dominated by altruism and transparency instead of manipulation. Bass posits that they work for the benefit of followers, not treating them as ends to means. They respect individual dignity and interests. The transformational leader draws upon virtuous behavior as a

---

32. Weichun Zhu et al., "The Effect of Authentic Transformational Leadership," 801–17. Zhu proposes four interventions: (1) establish and strengthen follower moral identity through modeling, (2) make decisions by means of an authentic and transparent process, (3) choose authentic transformational leaders in order to develop authentic moral followers, and (4) senior leaders establish an ethical climate that socializes moral values and principles. Weichun Zhu et al., "The Effect of Authentic Transformational Leadership," 815.

33. Weichun Zhu et al., "Revisiting the Mediating Role of Trust," 96, 102–3.

34. Avey et al., "Experimentally Analyzing the Impact of Leader," 282–94.

35. Luthans et al., *Psychological Capital Developing the Human Competitive Edge.*

36. McClough et al., "Cynicism and the Quality of an Individual's Contribution to an Organizational Diagnostic Survey," 31–41.

moral base for leadership. Similar to Plato's philosopher king and Confucius' moral sage, Bass describes the transformational leader as "humble . . . virtuous, obeying the dictates of one's conscience, maintaining old friendships and forming new ones, being loyal, generous and forgiving, helping others, conforming to custom, and maintaining good faith."[37]

Avolio and Bass contend that transactional leaders work within the culture and structure of the organization whereas the transformational leader works to change the organization for the better.[38] Outward orientation, such as seeking to better an organization, is a form of stewardship. Table 3 displays the moral elements of transformational leadership identified by James B. Avey, Bruce J. Avolio, and Fred Luthans versus false expressions of those elements. Transformational leadership characteristics, such as confidence in a noble cause and responsibility toward others and the organization, indicate a sense of stewardship or responsibility on behalf of another—an outward orientation of purpose.

Table 3. Moral Character of Transformational
and Pseudo–transformational Leaders

Transformational Idealized Influence	Pseudo–Transformational Idealized Influence
Envisions a better future	Creates false *us vs. them* differences in values
Self–confident in noble cause	Grandiose vision
High standards	Standards ostensibly for the good of the organization
Model behavior worthy of imitation	Profess strong attachment to followers, but ready to sacrifice them
Morally uplifting	Argues that *our* values are good, *theirs* are not
Trustworthy	Untrustworthy
Responsible for followers and organization	Lack responsibility to followers and organization
Promotes ethical policies and procedures	Inconsistent and unreliable

Data from Bass and Steidlmeier, "Ethics, Character, and Authentic Transformational Leadership Behavior," 187.

37. Bass and Steidlmeier, "Ethics, Character, and Authentic Transformational Leadership, 185, 193."

38. Avolio and Bass, "Individual Consideration Viewed at Multiple Levels of Analysis," 203.

Summary

Transformational leadership's purpose is to motivate followers to perform beyond expectations. A leader's charisma or persuasive argument may be sufficient motivation to woo followers to follow. Strong mutual alignment of purpose, values, and goals is essential to transformational leadership. Such alignment does not simply appear, therefore purpose and values must be taught. Leadership is found in the relationship between the leader and the follower. Leaders who have sufficient character and competency and take initiative have their leadership ratified by their followers. Their relationship is one of trust built upon the belief that the leader holds in stewardship the organization's and followers' best interest. Trust in the leader is built upon the leader's character, behavior, rational argument, and the affective nature of the corporate culture he builds.

Chapter 3

Outcomes of the Theory

UNDERSTANDING TRANSFORMATIONAL LEADERSHIP THEORY, its historical context, development, purpose, authority, mechanisms, and service are essential aspects of a missiological assessment. Just as essential are the more pragmatic aspects of a theory. Does it work? Does the theory accomplish that which it predicts? How do the different aspects of the theory interrelate and modify one another in practice? Is the theory applicable in other contexts? In this section, I analyze transformational leadership's performance, interrelationships, contextualization, and universality aspects

Performance Measures: How do we Know Leadership is Working?

Transformational leadership is inherently outcome–based leadership. In keeping with the goal of transformational leadership to help followers perform beyond their expectations, Bass stipulates, "leadership is effective if followers achieve their goals or meet their needs as a consequence of the successful leadership."[1] The core of Bass' argument is that transactional leadership explains a great deal of effective leadership, but transformational leadership significantly augments follower effort, effectiveness, and

---

1. Bass, "Theory of Transformational Leadership Redux," 464.

satisfaction.[2] The questions remain, how should evaluators assess transformational leadership outcomes and what is the result of those assessments?

Transformational leaders are more effective communicators than non–transformational leaders, regardless of the style of communication they use, report Yair Berson and Bruce J. Avolio. The communications styles measured were open communication, careful transmitter, and careful listener. Leaders who rated lower in transformational leadership tended to show more *defender* orientation, emphasizing stability. Those who rated higher in transformational leadership took attended to take a *prospector,* more risk–oriented, approach.[3]

Berson and Avolio demonstrated support for the hypothesis that transformational leaders are able to generate followers' support for organizational goals. This finding is especially true where transformational leadership occurs at the top levels of the organization. In situations in which leaders were rated as less–transformational, confusion over strategic goals occurred.[4] Janka I. Stoker, Hanneke Grutterink, and Nanja J. Kolk offer an important caveat to the above findings. Their research reveals no particular differentiation between transformational and non–transformational CEOs among teams who exhibit high levels of feedback–seeking behavior.[5] Therefore, unit culture and behaviors can make up for a lack in transformational leadership at the executive level. Mid–level managers can make significant contributions within their areas of influence which impact the organization.

YoungHee Hur, Peter T. van den Berg, and Celeste P.M. Wilderom give evidence that transformational leadership positively mediates emotional intelligence and leadership performance, but not team effectiveness. Emotional intelligence related positively to transformational leadership ($r=0.46$), specifically at the leader effectiveness level ($r=0.66$). Because they are more transformational than their peers, emotionally intelligent leaders are rated as more effective by followers and better at developing service–oriented work climates. Transformational leadership explains why emotionally intelligent leaders are more effective managers.[6]

2. Bass and Riggio, *Transformational Leadership*, 55.

3. Berson and Avolio, "Transformational Leadership."

4. Bass and Riggio, *Transformational Leadership*, 4.

5. Stoker et al., "Do Transformational CEOs Always Make the Difference?" 582–92.

6. Hur et al., "Transformational Leadership as a Mediator," 591–603.

In a unique study of thirty-nine leaders who lead both on-site and virtual teams, Radostina K. Purvanova and Joyce E. Bono found that the most effective leaders were those who increased their transformational leadership behaviors with virtual teams.[7] The effect of transformational leaders was stronger with virtual teams than those face-to-face. Measuring the moderating effect of physical distance on transformational leadership, Jane M. Howell, Derrick J. Neufeld, and Bruce J. Avolio establish that performance was higher with lower physical distance under transformational leadership conditions.[8] The seemingly contradictory results from the two studies above can be explained by the fact that virtual teams are structured to work over greater physical distance than regular teams whose members are simply distant from one another.

John J. Sosik, Veronica M. Godshalk, and Francis J. Yammarino find that transformational leaders who form mentor-mentee relationships have a positive effect on the followers' learning goal orientation and expectations of career success independent of the organization's environment when both parties take the same view of the learning goals.[9] In other words, mutual goal agreement in the leader-follower relationship is necessary in order to obtain positive outcomes and in learning-goal contexts. Mentor-mentee matches are vitally important. If the two parties do not see eye-to-eye on goals and processes, the effort is simply a frustration for both.

What about employee turnover? Affective Commitment, "an individual's perception of his/her emotional attachment and affective identification with his organization," positively mediates transformational leadership and employee turnover intention, report Herman H. M. Tse, Xu Huang, and Wing Lam.[10] The findings bore out in employee turnover intent, and subsequent behavior over a year-and-a-half period. The researchers argue that the cause of this higher retention rate is not high-quality leader-follower relationships; rather, the higher retention rate is attained because the leader is able to stir up follower commitment to the

7. Purvanova and Bono, "Transformational Leadership in Context," 343–57.

8. Howell et al., "Examining the Relationship of Leadership and Physical Distance with Business Unit Performance," 273–85.

9. Career success means career achievement, development, and balance. Sosik et al., "Transformational Leadership, Learning Goal Orientation, and Expectations for Career Success," 241–61.

10. This study employed a sample of 490 full-time employees in a telecommunication company in the People's Republic of China. Tse, et al., "Why Does Transformational Leadership Matter for Employee Turnover," 764.

organization's purpose and goals. The more a leader is seen to represent the organization's goals, the stronger the follower affective commitment to the leader and the organization.

An experimental study of 214 participants investigated the effect of transformational and transactional leadership behaviors on perceived social support, self–efficacy beliefs, and emotions during a stressful task.[11] Transformational leadership was associated with better task performance and generally more positive affective responses. Furthermore, the researchers found a direct, causal relationship between transformational leadership and these positive outcomes.

A leader's perceived behavioral integrity is positively correlated to followers' perception that the leader is transparent in his communication, as evidenced in a study of 451 military cadets.[12] Gretchen Vogelgesang, Hannes Leroy, and Bruce J. Avolio conclude that transparent communication, in turn, is associated with a higher level of engagement and performance as rated by a third party. Transparent leadership communication, therefore, directly mediates leadership behavioral integrity which mediates follower engagement that mediates follower performance. Their findings extend those by Suzanne J. Peterson et al. who demonstrated that followers' performance was partially mediated and fully mediated by their leader's influence on social capital.[13] Maria Tims, Arnold B. Bakker, and Despoina Xanthopoulou have also found a positive affective response to transformational leadership behaviors.[14]

In their 1996 review of literature evaluating the link between the MLQ and effectiveness, Kevin B. Lowe, K. Galen Kroeck, and Nagaraj Sivasubramaniam ascertain that Charisma was most strongly related to leader effectiveness by all measures.[15] Individualized Consideration was more strongly related to follower's estimation of leader's effectiveness than unit performance.

---

11. Lyons and Schneider, "The Effects of Leadership Style on Stress Outcomes," 737–48.

12. Vogelgesang et al., "The Mediating Effects of Leader Integrity."

13. Suzanne J. Peterson et al., "The Relationship between Authentic Leadership and Follower Job Performance," 502–16.

14. Maria Tims et al., "Do Transformational Leaders Enhance Their Followers' Daily Work Engagement?" 121–31.

15. Lowe et al., "Effectiveness Correlates of Transformational and Transactional Leadership," 385–425.

Weichun Zhu et al. verified that transformational leadership leads to higher levels of cognitive and affective trust.[16] Affective trust is correlated to follower organizational commitment and performance; not so with cognitive trust. Cognitive trust was even found to negatively mediate transformational leadership and performance. The authors suggest that this polarized mix of mediating effects of trust on transformational leadership and performance is because affective trust is a result of mutual concern and care, whereas cognitive trust comes by the follower's perception of the leader's character.

Another leadership outcome is employee satisfaction. Transformational factors correlate higher with employee effectiveness and satisfaction than does the contingent reward factor which, in turn, is more highly correlated to effectiveness and success than management–by–exception factors.[17] Bass and Riggio report that transformational leadership showed strong correlation with effectiveness, satisfaction, and extra effort perceived by the followers (r=0.76, 0.71, and 0.88, respectively).[18]

One of the few longitudinal studies on transformational leadership is by Jane M. Howell, Derrick J. Neufeld, and Bruce J. Avolio. They found that transformational leaders have a positive correlation to group performance after one year whereas transactional leadership had no correlation to group performance over the same time–frame.[19] Howell and her colleagues render further warrant to the claim that the assumptions of transformational leadership theory bear out in performance research.

Some measures of transformational leadership are more subjective. Successful leadership is indicated by group coalescence and conformity.[20] Success simply means that the group has formed and is able to function as a group instead of vaguely associated individuals. Furthermore, effective leadership is defined by group effectiveness or approaching the group's full potential to accomplish what it is they seek to do.

16. Zhu et al., "Revisiting the Mediating Role of Trust."

17. Bass, "Theory of Transformational Leadership Redux," 475.

18. Bass and Riggio, *Transformational Leadership*, 26, reporting from a study by Gasper, "Transformational Leadership: An Integrative Review of the Literature."

19. Howell et al., "Examining the Relationship of Leadership and Physical Distance."

20. Bass, "Theory of Transformational Leadership Redux," 465.

Meta–Relational Aspect: How do the Elements of the Theory Relate to One Another?

Both expected and normative behaviors can be analyzed at the individual, group, and organizational level. With these varied levels and categories of behavior, we should expect contextual variance. Because of this variance, multi–level consideration must be made for transformational leadership factors. As far back as 1995, Avolio and Bass proposed analyzing Individualized Consideration at individual, group/team, and organizational levels to understand if and how a leadership behavior becomes embedded in an organizational culture. Contingency or situational models attend to leadership as a consideration of the leader's behavior, the effect on the follower, and the structure of the work situation as a natural outworking of that theory.[21]

Meta–analysis of Full Range of Leadership factors demonstrate that leadership effectiveness is most strongly associated with Idealized Influence and Inspirational Motivation, grouped together as Charisma–Inspiration. Intellectual Stimulation, Individualized Consideration, Contingent Reward, and Management–by–Exception follow Charisma–Inspiration with decreasing correlational strength, respectively. Effective transformational leaders bring together follower commitments to the organization and individual values and aspirations in such a way that the follower can see how these varied commitments interrelate in pursuit of their common goal.[22]

The four factors of transformational leadership are interactive.[23] Inspirational leaders create meaning for the followers out of Individualized Consideration, an awareness of what is essential to the follower. Transformational change is found first and foremost in the leader. The leader's motivation and behavior moves from satisfying needs and tasks to recognizing the individual character of needs within the group.[24] An example of interdependency between transformational leadership factors is that although initiation and consideration scales support performance

21. Avolio and Bass, "Individual Consideration Viewed at Multiple Levels of Analysis," 200.

22. Bass and Riggio, *Transformational Leadership*, 25–26.

23. Avolio and Bass, "Individual Consideration Viewed at Multiple Levels of Analysis," 204.

24. Avolio and Bass, "Individual Consideration Viewed at Multiple Levels of Analysis," 202.

and satisfaction, levels are even higher when other transformational leadership behaviors are added to the mix.[25]

Bass writes that although every social science approach to leadership prior to his work was based on a task–people dichotomy, transformational leadership demonstrated that orientation to both task and people could be important perspectives that attend to leadership.[26] D. A. Waldman, Bernard M. Bass, and E. Y. Yammarino found that rather than replacing transactional leadership, transformational leadership behaviors augment transactional leadership.[27] Their findings substantiate Bass' claim by accommodating and serving the needs of both the task and the individuals who make up the team.

Contextual Influence: How Does the local Situation Influence the Theory?

Context may be understood as opportunities and constraints that affect behavior in the organization.[28] Context in transformational leadership should also consider the interrelationships of the people in the organization. Research on the powerful positive influence of peers, in a study by William Bommer, Robert Rubin, and Timothy Baldwin, indicates that leadership is indeed a collective notion, or at least intensely relational.[29] Their study suggests that broad leadership development, i.e., widening the pool of peer transformational leaders, will have a strong positive effect for the organization because of the augmenting effect that peers have on one another.

Transformational leadership is grounded in a deep–level association where the values and ideals of leaders and followers are intertwined and shared. This deep–level association forms the context of transformational leadership. The obvious but sticky problem in this context is the notion of universal core values. What core values, or civic virtues, should guide

25. Seltzer and Bass, "Transformational Leadership: Beyond Initiation and Consideration," 693–703. Initiation has to do with clarifying requirements, giving necessary information, and structuring the task—arguably a Contingent Reward behavior. Consideration refers to creating a sociable, participative, egalitarian environment with concern for individual welfare.

26. Bass and Riggio, *Transformational Leadership*, 4.

27. Waldman et al., "The Augmenting Effect of Transformational Leadership," 151–69.

28. Johns, "The Essential Impact of Context or Organizational Behavior," 386.

29. Bommer et al., "Setting the Stage for Effective Leadership."

transformational leadership? Bass answers that benevolence and altruism are universal virtues, transcending cultural boundaries. He adds that the expression of these core values will differ from culture to culture, as will their relative importance. Bass claims that this cultural diversity of norms substantiates the need for transformational leaders at "all levels of human society."[30] Bass leaves any question of a fixed moral code unanswered and simply calls for an authentic commitment to "the process of searching out moral excellence."[31]

Universality of the Theory: Is the Theory Applicable in Other Cultures?

How universal is transformational leadership? Is it reasonable to assume that the theory will function well in non–western cultures? Transformational leadership is positively linked to performance in the North American and international contexts. Hur's study revealed that transformational leadership is also effective in non–western cultures. The study produced a high correlation between transformational leadership and leader effectiveness in South Korean companies at a level of $r=0.66$, even though South Korean culture is generally considered bureaucratic and highly oriented toward maintaining the *status quo*.[32] The universality of transformational leadership is an idea strengthened by the work of Tse, Huang, and Lam.[33]

Geert Hofstede contends that western management theories hold to certain precepts that may not be globally accepted. Three such assumptions are: "a stress on market processes, a stress on the individual, and a focus on managers rather than workers."[34] Bass and Steidlmeier admit that the concern over freedom of ideals, behaviors, and the search for truth so prominent in transformational leadership theory is a Western concern. In other cultures, welfare of others may be more important than the leader's welfare.[35] How a leader, or any individual for that matter, views

30. Bass and Steidlmeier, "Ethics, Character, and Authentic Transformational Leadership," 192, 209–10.

31. Bass and Steidlmeier, "Ethics, Character, and Authentic Transformational Leadership," 192, 209–11.

32. Hur et al., "Transformational Leadership as a Mediator."

33. Tse et al., "Why Does Transformational Leadership Matter."

34. Hofstede, "Cultural Constraints in Management Theories," 81.

35. Bass and Steidlmeier, "Ethics, Character, and Authentic Transformational

himself in relation to others, specifically other groups, is related to the In-clusivism–Collectivism scale that will be discussed later.

Bass claims, however, that research from the GLOBE project demon-strates the efficacy of transformational leadership in sixty–two countries. The precise characterization of charisma may differ from one country to another, but the concept is almost universally present and important to leadership. D. I. Jung, B. M. Bass, and J. J. Sosik argue that transforma-tional leadership is actually more likely to be found in collectivistic than individualistic cultures like the United States.[36] Their claim is that the group orientation of collectivistic cultures sensitizes those cultures to the mutual nature of transformational leadership and their tendency toward high obedience to authority makes for a strong environment for transfor-mational leadership. Cultures high in uncertainty avoidance might place unusually high demands on leaders to avoid risk, and masculine cultures are likely to prefer strong, dominant leaders.

Jane M. Howell, Derrick J. Neufeld, and Bruce J. Avolio found only one study on physical distance as a moderator of follower–leader perfor-mance.[37] Physical distance was negatively associated with the positive ef-fect of transformational leadership. Their findings suggest that although transformational leadership may be present and effective in non–western cultures, those cultures have a moderating effect on theory application.

Summary

Transformational leadership is outcome–based by design. Proponents of the theory place a great emphasis upon moving people to achievement, even achievement beyond expectations. Transformational leaders tend to com-municate effectively. Regardless of their place in organizational hierarchy, transformational leaders tend to generate considerable follower support for organizational goals. Virtual teams that tend to be more independent than on–site teams respond very well to transformational leaders. Their response might be because of the encouraging and supportive climate created by transformational leaders while maintaining focus on the organization's pur-poses. The corporate climate nurtured by transformational leaders also has a positive effect on personnel retention rates and satisfaction. An important

---

Leadership," 186.

36. Jung et al., "Bridging Leadership and Culture," 3–18.

37. Howell et al., "Examining the Relationship of Leadership and Physical Distance."

part of the climate created by these leaders rests in the leaders' integrity. Integrity and transparent communication lead to trust that results in followers working harder and an improvement in performance and satisfaction. One of the strengths of transformational leadership theory is that it is transferable across cultures. Not limited to western cultures, transformational leadership can be effective in non–western societies. This transferability involves adaptation in each new culture—a contextualization of the factors in terms of how the transformational factors are identified and expressed in different cultures. The transferability and universality of transformational leadership and any leadership theory and practice will be assessed in part 3 of this study. Before that assessment, we must set all theory and practice under the light of Scripture, the subject of part 2.

PART 2

Appraise the Leadership Theory Theologically

A LEADERSHIP THEORY OR practice may pass philosophical muster, but is it for missions? Missions leadership occurs when someone, through their character, competence, and conduct, influences individuals to band together and work to achieve a mutual objective in missions. Because the leading in question occurs in the field of missions, it is a missiological enterprise of which theology is crucial.

Mark Green articulates four reasons behind the difficulty of extracting a leadership theory from the Apostle Paul's ministry as reported in the Bible. First, leadership is a new field of study and was certainly conceived of differently two millennia ago. Second, Paul's leadership style changed over time as he grew as a leader. This change is no doubt true for all leaders in the Bible. Third, a limited volume of source material is available for study, especially when trying to study the leadership of any single individual in the Bible. Finally, researchers cannot fully appreciate the culture of the specific contexts to which Paul wrote.[1]

Similar difficulties hinder the study of leadership from any biblical character. Because of these difficulties, missions leaders do well to start from contemporary leadership theories and submit them to theological

---

1. Mark Green et al., "Assessing the Leadership Style of Paul," 4–5.

scrutiny. Leadership theory must be subject to theology and undergo a theological critique prior to use in missions.[2] In this section, I develop the second tier of my Leadership Assessment Matrix pertaining to theological aspects of leadership.

Theology is generally not considered in leadership studies according to Michale Ayers, Associate Professor and Director of the Christian Leadership program at the College of Biblical Studies in Houston, Texas. He claims that the two domains of study, one of the things of God, the other of the things of man and society, rarely intersect.[3] He argues that leadership theory critiques must consider the ontological, methodological (ethic), and teleological aspects of leadership.[4]

The preceding chapter examined transformational leadership theory from a philosophical–theoretical standpoint. An evaluative matrix that included the history, development, exercise, and outcomes of transformational leadership theory guided that examination. Theological assessment of leadership theory requires a similar scheme—a matrix that addresses the issues particular to theology and missions. Therefore, what should a matrix of missions leadership include?

James E. Plueddemann is Professor of Missions and Chair of the Department of Missions and Evangelism at Trinity Evangelical Divinity School. He poses five questions about leadership: (1) What is the purpose of leadership? (2) What assumptions lie behind the theory in question? (3) What are the leadership goals—outcomes sought under the primary purpose? (4) How do leaders accomplish their tasks? (5) What is the nature of intercultural leadership practice? Plueddemann argues that good leadership practice grows from good leadership theory, influenced by good theology. These five questions will inform the theology for missions leadership presented in this research.[5]

---

2. For example, James Plueddemann asserts that Christian theology places the authority of the Bible above culture. Leadership theory is subject to biblical scrutiny just as culture is. Plueddemann, *Leading across Cultures*, 64–67.

3. Ayers, "Toward a Theology of Leadership," 3–4. Aubrey Malphurs argues that Christians can understand leadership by means of both general and special revelation. Those researchers investigating leadership from secular sources must take care to maintain a Christian worldview. Malphurs, *Being Leaders*, 16–17.

4. Ayers, "Toward a Theology of Leadership," 6–8.

5. Plueddemann, *Leading across Cultures*, 157, 170–71, 185.

In keeping with Ayers' recommendation, I ask four questions of a theological nature using language common to both philosophy and theology.[6] These questions form a theological matrix by which a theory can be examined. First, what are the teleological aspects of the theory? Second, what are the ontological aspects of the theory? Third, what view of authority does the theory espouse? Fourth, what leadership ethic is expected as a result of this theory?[7] The Theological tier of the Leadership Assessment Matrix in Table 4 extends Ayers' work and includes three of Plueddemann's five questions, namely, his questions about purpose, outcomes, and means.[8]

Table 4. A Theological Matrix for Evaluating Leadership Theory

Aspect	Element	Description
Teleology	A Leader's Purpose	What should leaders do?
	A Leader's Motivation	What drives leaders?
	A Leader's Objectives	What are biblical goals for leaders?
Ontology	A Leader's Calling	Where do leaders arise from?
	A Leader's Character	What character traits are essential in leaders?
	A Leader's Competency	How do gifting, strengths, and experience come to bear?
Authority	A Leader's Capacity	What kind of power do leaders have?
	A Leader's Authority	What is a leader's source of authority?
	A Leader's Responsibility	To whom is a leader responsible?
Ethic	The Leader as Servant of God	How do leaders serve the Lord?
	The Leaders as Servant to Others	How do leaders serve others?

The matrix includes three aspects from Ayers' work: teleology, ontology, and ethic with the additional aspect, authority. Authority is a central

6. Ayers, "Toward a Theology of Leadership," 4.

7. Ethic as expected behavior(s) resulting from the theory.

8. Plueddemann's second question relating to a theory's background assumptions was dealt with in Part 1 and his fifth question on the nature of intercultural leadership practice is considered in Part 3 of this research.

aspect of leadership, though not part of Ayers' original scheme.[9] Each aspect in the typology is further divided into elements derived from Plueddemann's questions outlined above. In this research, the issues raised in answering the aforementioned questions will be compared to theological viewpoints in evangelical missions literature.

9. Authority is so important to leadership that is was the 2007 theme for the annual meeting of the Academy of Religious Leadership. Gelder, "Defining the Issues Related to Power and Authority in Religious Leadership," 1.

Chapter 4

Analyze the Teleological Aspect

TELEOLOGY IN THIS RESEARCH refers to the examination of God's missionary purpose through his church. Teleological concepts of Christian leadership vary greatly. Darrin Patrick and George Miley conceive of leadership in terms of personality and gifting.[1] J. Oswald Sanders and Henry Blackaby define leadership as the ability to influence.[2] Robert Clinton, and Thomas Steffen define leadership by the leader's performance.[3] Robert Banks argues that Christian leadership is showing the way, influencing, and empowering people to bring about change in line with God's character and ways.[4] Andreas Köstenberger articulates leadership as faithfully serving God's mission by bringing glory and honor to God, knowing and abiding in him, doing his will, speaking his words and bearing witness to him, being accountable to him, and acting in his authority.[5]

How one starts determines how one will finish. Definitions of leadership are conceptual frameworks that shape the authors' theories. Therefore, the teleological aspect is the first aspect to consider. The teleological aspect

---

1. Patrick, Church Planter, 72–74; Miley, Loving the Church . . . Blessing the Nations, 98, 106.

2. Sanders, Spiritual Leadership, 27; Blackaby and Blackaby, Spiritual Leadership, 20.

3. Clinton, The Making of a Leader, 66, 213; Steffen, Passing the Baton, 50–51.

4. Banks, Reviewing Leadership, 16–17.

5. Köstenberger, "The Challenge of a Systematized Biblical Theology of Mission, 448–49.

of leadership includes cognitive, volitional, and behavioral features or, as Ott explains, the purpose, motivation, and task of missions.[6] What should missions leadership accomplish? What drives missions leadership? What are the proper goals for missions leadership? These three questions outline the assessment of teleology in leadership theory.

A Leader's Purpose: What Should Leaders Do?

An uncritical application of leadership theory results in a distorted missiology. Much of Christian leadership is based on popular theories emphasizing individual success and ability.[7] George W. Peters highlights this problem when he argues that leadership has failed the church in her mission. He reasons that many church leaders lead as if the church is just another corporation and thus "misdirected [the church] in purpose and mission."[8] Harsh as it may be, Peters' critique is a wake-up call for the church to think carefully about leadership—carefully and theologically. Leaders must think through purpose and leadership. Purpose in missions determines the direction, motivations, and objectives of missions. Therefore, what should leaders do?

Missionary, missions leader, and theologian Don N. Howell asserts that the Apostle Paul's attention to purpose, values, and message kept him from mission ambiguity, drift, and confusion. He contends,

> Servant leaders take the initiative to bring others to a passionate commitment to what is on the heart of God, the extension of his saving rule over individuals and communities both qualitatively (holiness of character) and quantitatively (expansion to the un-reached frontiers).[9]

The commitment referred to by Howell is not passive, but active and results in holy and Kingdom-expanding behavior or, as Albert Mohler puts it, "putting the right beliefs into action, and knowing, on the basis of convictions, what those right beliefs and actions are."[10]

---

6. Ott, *Encountering Theology of Mission*, 79–80, 106, 165–66.

7. Strawbridge, "The Word of the Cross," 78.

8. Peters, *A Biblical Theology of Missions*, 206.

9. Howell, *Servants of the Servant*, 301.

10. Mohler, *Conviction to Lead*, 26.

Awareness of purpose is vital. Plueddemann relates that he once heard a missions executive mock his organization's ultimate purpose to glorify God. In his anecdote, the organization's purpose was taken for granted, reduced to a meaningless phrase with little or no relationship to the goals of the organization, and even became a point of ridicule. When such disconnect occurs, goals such as programs, numbers of missionaries, or even fund–raising, may creep to the forefront of organizational life and replace its original purpose. Leadership has lost its way when goals, which once supported the purpose, become the purpose.[11] Thus, awareness of and connectedness to purpose is vital. Christian leadership in missions exists to promote God's ultimate purpose.

Leadership rooted in God's will and purpose is a biblical theme.[12] Leaders are called to uphold God's will before the people so they may know God's will and purpose.[13] Submission to the will of God is the highest of callings. Isaiah's servant songs depict this submission to God's will by extolling the servant of the Lord who brings delight to the Lord, has the Spirit upon him, and brings forth the Lord's justice.[14] The servant is God's messenger in whom God is glorified and calls back the tribes of Jacob, and the nations, that they may know the Lord's salvation.[15] Ultimately, the Lord prospers his will in the servant's hands.[16] Leadership in the Old Testament is exemplified in the Lord's servant, who perfectly serves God's purposes.

The servant motif continues in the New Testament, where the *servant of Christ* or *servant of God* is common nomenclature for leaders.[17] God's will revealed in Scripture is the standard for leaders.[18] The author of Hebrews instructs followers to heed the words and imitate their leaders' faith, doing good for others and submitting to leaders because this is pleasing to God

11. Plueddemann, *Leading across Cultures*, 161.

12. For example, Hezekiah and Josiah exemplify God–ward purpose in leadership and Scripture commends both of these kings because they led in accordance to God's law (1 Kgs 18:5; 23:25).

13. Deut 6:1–9; Josh 1:1–9.

14. Isa 42:1–7.

15. Isa 49:1–7.

16. Isa 53:10.

17. Rom 1:1; 13:4; Gal 1:10; Col 4:12; 1 Tim 4:6; Titus 1:1; Jas 1:1; Jude 1:1; Rev 15:3. Two exceptions to this pattern are Rom 16:1, where Phoebe is referred to as *servant of the church* and Mark 9:35, where Jesus is quoted saying, "If anyone would be first, he must be last of all and servant of all."

18. Howell, *Servants of the Servant*, 11–19.

through Jesus to whom eternal glory.[19] As in the Old Testament, the New Testament portrays leadership as serving God's purposes.

Christian leadership in missions exists to promote God's ultimate purpose. Concerning missions, that purpose is to preach the gospel of salvation in Jesus among peoples where the church has not yet been established. Leaders in Christian missions should work to influence groups of individuals, whether those groups be churches, organizations, institutions, corporations, or missionary entities, to achieve the mutual purpose of God. Paul wrote of this missionary purpose in Romans as proclaiming the gospel where Christ has not been named to bring about the obedience of faith for God's name and his glory.[20]

The Bible depicts leaders as those who follow, teach, and model God's Word so that others may know God's purpose and will.[21] God's people are emissaries of Christ to all peoples, proclaiming the good news and making disciples in the name of the Father, Son, and Holy Spirit for the glory of God.[22] The purpose of missions is to preach the gospel of salvation in Jesus among peoples where the church has not yet been established to bring about the obedience of faith for his name's sake.[23] God has gifted his church with leaders to lead for his purposes, namely to bring glory and praise to himself.[24]

Analysis of Transformational Leadership.

Revealed or objective purpose is not an explicit concern in Bass' formulation of transformational leadership. Transformational leaders influence followers to work toward mutual purposes, a higher purpose, or the common good. A strong sense of altruism undergirds Bass's theory as opposed to a divinely revealed purpose. If altruism is the end goal, then indeed the theory must be rejected outright because missions' ultimate purpose is the glory of God, his worship and praise, not altruism. Bass' bent toward altruism does not necessarily disallow a Christ–centered worldview, but such a biblical purpose for Christian missions must be explicit in any

19. Heb 13:7–21.

20. Rom 1:5; 15:18–21.

21. Deut 6:1–9; Josh 1:1–9.

22. Matt 24:14; 28:18–20; Mark 16:15–16; Luke 24:46–48; Acts 1:8.

23. Rom 1:5; 15:18–21.

24. Eph 4:11–14; Rom 12:6–8; John 16:13–15.

missions leadership theory. A transformational leader in Christian missions must call his people to their Christ-exalting purpose and constantly keep that sacred purpose before them.

A Leader's Motivation: What Drives Leaders?

The second element of the teleological aspect is motivation. What drives missions leadership? The Bible presents at least three basic motivations for missions: the plight of the lost, the greatness of God's glory, and the power of the cross.[25] Following is a brief discussion of these three motivations.

Motivated by the plight of the lost.

The Bible is clear, the state of un-regenerate people is that they are dead in their sins and objects of wrath.[26] Without the gospel, people are already dead, and the Apostle Paul writes of his strong desire to reach the lost that they might be saved.[27] Part of the motivation for missions is love:

> By this the love of God was revealed in us, that God has sent His only Son into the world so that we may live through Him. In this is love, not that we loved God, but that He loved us and sent His Son to be the propitiation for our sins. Beloved, if God so loved us, we also ought to love one another.[28]

Ott expresses this motivation as compassion.[29] Though compassion can be due to temporal suffering and the eternal consequences of sin, Ott contends that the eternal destiny of unbelievers is paramount. Furthermore, compassion is penultimate and, on its own, can be anthropocentric. Christians are motivated to missions out of love for the lost in the same manner that God demonstrated his love in Christ, but God's self-giving love through his Son must qualify our compassion. In so doing, our love glorifies the Lord.

---

25. Carson, "Conclusion: Ongoing Imperative for World Mission," 185–195.

26. 2 Kgs 22:13; Ps 90:1–11; John 3:36; Rom 1:18.

27. Rom 9:1–3; 11:13–15; 1 Cor 9:19, 22.

28. 1 John 4:9–11.

29. Ott et al., *Encountering Theology of Mission*, 177–79.

Motivated by the glory of God.

Leaders in missions are motivated by the desire to know Christ and glorify him. David Horner argues that missions built on duty is misplaced and weak. Motivation for missions should be the desire to know more of Christ. Horner continues, "If our hearts are not held in the grip of a profound love for Jesus Christ and a deep appreciation for the treasure He is, we will not be motivated to continue in our commitment to speak of His glory among the nations for very long."[30] Only a consuming love for Christ and passion for his glory will sustain missions.[31]

But certainly, many are motivated for missions out of obedience to the Lord. After all, the Bible explicitly commands the church to missions.[32] God's glory, his nature is the basis for such obedience. Eckhard Schnabel points out that Paul's motivation to labor for Christ was a necessity set on him by God.[33] Charles Van Engen's position is that proper motivation for missions comes from a call to something greater, rather than gain for self.[34] In his influential work, *Let the Nations be Glad*, John Piper makes the argument that the point of missions is that God should be worshipped because he is worthy of our complete adoration.[35] The apostles were motivated by their view of Jesus as Savior and Lord to obey and follow his commands. These authors bring together what the gospel brings together, that these two basic Christian concepts, faith and obedience, belong together. One is never present without the other.[36]

Motivated by the power of the gospel.

Perry W. H. Shaw, professor at the Arab Baptist Theological Seminary in Beirut, Lebanon, concludes that the primary motivation for leadership in the early church was a compelling desire to promote the spread of the

---

30. Horner, *When Missions Shapes the Mission*, 52. Also, Ott et al., *Encountering Theology of Mission*, 179–80, 184–85.

31. Horner, *When Missions Shapes the Mission*, 98.

32. Matt 28:18–20; Mark 16:15; Luke 24:46–48; Acts 1:8.

33. Schnabel, *Paul the Missionary*, 32.

34. Van Engen, *God's Missionary People*, 165.

35. Piper, *Let the Nations Be Glad!*

36. 1 John 2:3–4, 29; 3:7, 24; 5:2–4. Peters, *A Biblical Theology of Missions*, 142.

gospel.[37] Missions is motivated by the power of the gospel—that which compelled the apostles to forsake all others and become men who "upset the world."[38] Peters argues that the apostles were motivated because they knew God had moved in history.[39] They were witness to the power of the gospel to propitiate God's wrath, redeem sinners, justify the elect, and reconcile us to God.[40]

None of the above motivations, the plight of the lost, the awesomeness of God's glory, and the power of the gospel to propitiate God's wrath, redeem sinners, and reconcile us to God—are mutually exclusive. Missions leaders will express their motivation to lead in missions in various ways, but the biblical root motivation in missions leadership is that God is worthy. God is supremely worthy of worship and praise because of his love powerfully expressed in Christ's substitutionary atonement. God's worthiness is the essential motivation for missions. Missions exists because worship of God is not universal.[41]

Analysis of Transformational Leadership.

The motivation for missions leadership is that God is worthy of worship. How does motivation in transformational leadership theory measure up to this biblical standard? Transformational leadership theory proponents appeal to followers' needs for motivation in leadership, but Bass and his colleagues stress that self-interest should be replaced with more transcendent interests that are understood best in terms of Maslow's higher-level needs. Transcendent interests—followers need for esteem—can be powerful motivators in the hands of leaders with high capability in Idealized Influence and Inspirational Motivation. Transformational leadership theory relies on a leader who is able to provide followers with opportunities and encouragement. These leaders focus on the best in people and speak truth to correct them out of genuine concern for their development—aspects of Idealized Influence and Inspirational Motivation.

37. Shaw, "The Missional-Ecclesial Leadership Vision of the Early Church," 138.

38. Acts 17:6.

39. Peters, A Biblical Theology of Missions, 136.

40. Propitiate, Rom 3:24–25; 1 John 2:1–2; 4:10. Redeem, Mark 10:45; Gal 3:13; 4:4–5; 1 Tim 2:5–6; 1 Pet 1:18–19. Justify, Rom 5:1–9; Gal 2:16; Phil 3:9, Jas 3:23–26. Reconcile, Eph 1:3–6; 2:13–16; Heb 10:19–22. See also Stott, The Cross of Christ, 167–203.

41. Piper, Let the Nations Be Glad! 228.

Motivation in Bass' transformational leadership theory is expressed in psychological terms and sounds incompatible to Christian missions. This discord can be overcome. The leader must specify and consistently remind followers of the shared biblical motivation for missions. The Christian transformational leader should point to God's worthiness as the primary motivator of missions.

A Leader's Objectives: What Are Biblical Goals for Leaders?

What are appropriate biblical goals for missions leadership? Shaw contends that the goal of Christian leadership is two-fold: to make disciples and promote the spread of the gospel. i.e., to go into all the world and make disciples. Christian leadership has a two-fold goal: to make disciples and to promote disciple–making to all peoples. This inseparable pair of goals, according to Shaw, was so significant that the twelve quickly adjusted their leadership structure to accommodate teaching and care of the church as the gospel spread.[42] For example, the twelve apostles added the seven deacons to take up administrative responsibilities.[43] Shaw explains that Agabus was one prophet among others in addition to the use of the plural, *teachers*, indicating the presence of multiple leaders in the growing church.[44] The first mention of elders occurs about fifteen years after Pentecost.[45] Subsequently, Paul begins to ensure that elders are appointed in new churches and reports to elders.[46] Shaw's point is that the church adjusted its leadership structure to meet the changing demands brought on by numerical and geographic growth to maintain the task of making disciples and taking the gospel to the ends of the earth.

Preach the gospel throughout the world.

Jesus assured his followers of the certainty and scope of his mission and missions teaching that the gospel will be preached throughout the world,

---

42. Shaw, "The Missional–Ecclesial Leadership Vision of the Early Church," 133, 139.

43. Acts 4:37; 5:2.

44. Acts 11:27–28; Acts 13:1.

45. Acts 11:30.

46. Shaw, "The Missional–Ecclesial Leadership Vision of the Early Church," 134–35.

to all nations before the end comes.[47] The spread of the gospel is the foundational missions leadership task. The whole world must hear so that by hearing, they might believe.[48] Paul sees his primary duty as preaching the gospel.[49] As "an apostle set apart for the gospel of God," his first task can be no other.[50] Jesus explained his work for the Father in much the same way—as the "herald of good tidings."[51] The first goal of missions and missions leadership defines the breadth of that purpose so that the whole world hears the gospel.

Make disciples of all peoples.

Paul aimed to be persuasive in his preaching and sought the conversion of the lost. He sought the "transformation of traditional patterns of religious, ethical, and social behavior," argues Schnabel.[52] Schnabel is getting at the second part of missions leadership goals—to make disciples. This emphasis points to the corporate task of Christian leadership.[53] Other researchers agree. For example, Russell L. Huizing, pastor and student of leadership with experience in a Global Fortune 500 corporation, concludes that leaders "cannot think of discipleship simply as a means among other means . . . to lead others. Discipleship, to the extent that it is an imitation of Christ, is the means of leading others."[54] The second goal of missions, and therefore, missions leadership, defines the depth of missions purpose—that we make disciples.

The New Testament has a two-fold focus to be held in balance: preach the gospel and make disciples. Leadership in missions has two primary goals, each inextricably bound to the other. The first is to lead the church and organizations to proclaim the gospel throughout the world. The second is to lead the church and organizations to make disciples of all nations.

47. Matt 24:14.

48. Rom 10:11–15.

49. Schnabel, *Paul the Missionary*, 210.

50. Rom 1:1.

51. Schnabel, *Paul the Missionary*, 213.

52. Schnabel, *Paul the Missionary*, 225. Subsequent tasks for Paul are establishing local churches, teaching new converts, and training new missionaries. Schnabel, *Paul the Missionary*, 231–32, 236–37, 248–49.

53. Shaw, "The Missional–Ecclesial Leadership Vision of the Early Church," 137, 139.

54. Huizing, "Leaders from Disciples," 344.

Analysis of Transformational Leadership.

Leadership in missions has two primary goals that define the breadth and depth of missions. Transformational leadership theory focuses on achieving more than expected by maintaining a compelling vision, modeling the way forward, creating a corporate environment of healthy competition and support, and facilitating personalized development. The supporting goals of Christian missions and transformational leadership theory are compatible.

As with all the teleological elements in question, explicit attention to the primary purpose, motivation, and goals of Christian missions can provide a reasonable path to apply transformational leadership theory to missions. The burden rests upon the leader to keep the goals to take the gospel to those who have never heard and to teach converts how to become disciples of Jesus.

Summary.

The purpose of transformational leadership is follower–oriented, designed to lead followers to higher plans of work performance and goal attainment. The theory accomplishes this goal, in part, by appealing to the higher–level transcendent interests of the followers and expressing mutually held goals in a compelling vision. At first glance, these aspects of transformational leadership may not seem contrary or incompatible with leadership in Christian missions. The problem is that missions has a definite, revealed, Christ–exalting goal. For the transformational theory to be applied in missions, leaders must maintain this revealed purpose in mind and in front of the people. In like manner, transformational leadership addresses motivation from a psychological perspective, but missions must draw upon biblical motivations such as God's holiness, justice, love, and self–giving compassion as the primary motivators. Finally, leaders can make full use of transformational leadership in working toward the dual goals of gospel proclamation and disciple–making.

Chapter 5

Analyze the Ontological Aspect

WHAT MAKES A LEADER? The Lord appeared to Solomon after he finished building the temple and challenged him to be a leader like his father, saying, ". . . if you walk before Me as your father David walked, in integrity of heart and honesty, acting in accordance with everything that I have commanded you . . . then I will establish the throne of your kingdom over Israel forever."[1] God called David and Solomon to lead Israel and challenged them to lead with integrity of heart and honesty. Calling and character are two vital parts of a biblical ontology of leadership. Skill, or competency, is the third vital part of a biblical ontology of leadership. Psalm 78 describes how all three components—calling, character, and competency—made up the core of David's leadership:

> He also chose David His servant. And took him from the sheepfolds; from the care of the ewes with suckling lambs He brought him to shepherd Jacob His people, and Israel His inheritance. So he shepherded them according to the integrity of his heart, and guided them with his skillful hands.[2]

David's leadership was established in God's call. God called David into service for the sake of his divine purposes. David was called out of his circumstances to lead. Leadership does not require an exfiltration from our

---

1. 1 Kgs 9:4–5.
2. Ps 78:70–72.

personal history and experience. David's leadership was qualified by his character as a man after God's own heart. Finally, he led. Through God-given skill and ability, David lead the people under his care.

Calling, character, and Spirit–empowered competency are essential elements of a leadership ontology that makes a mission leader. How do these three theologically based aspects integrate with leadership theory and practice? This section describes the core ontological elements of a leader's calling, character, and competency from a biblical point of view and evaluates transformational leadership by this standard.

A Leader's Calling: Where do Leaders Arise From?

Writing about missions pastors, Horner stipulates that to claim that everyone is a missionary is an overestimation of most people or an underestimation of missions.[3] Schnabel suggests that it would be a strange church if all were sent out on missionary travels and left behind no local community of faith.[4] If all are called but only few go, then most are unfaithful. Such is the logical result of the notion that all believers are missionaries.[5] God blesses his people with a variety of gifts and various ministries, activities, and roles associated with those gifts.[6] God gifts all believers with some gifts, but none are gifted with all gifts. This fact implies a particular nature to a believer's gifting and calling. For example, Peter was called to reach the Jews with the gospel, and Paul was called to reach the Gentiles.[7] Indeed, both Peter and Paul preached the gospel and taught Gentiles and Jews respectively, but their calling was to serve a particular people. The point is that not all Christians are gifted for the particular service of taking the gospel to where it has not been heard. Not all are called to missions.

Peters asserts that the Bible describes a three–fold call: to salvation, to discipleship, and to ministry of the Word. The call to salvation is the basis for all other calls. The call to discipleship is to all believers, but the call to ministry of the Word is narrower.[8] Peters draws out the four following biblical themes regarding the ministry of the Word. First, God calls people

3. Horner, *When Missions Shapes the Mission*, 142.

4. Schnabel, *Paul the Missionary*, 384.

5. Schnabel, *Paul the Missionary*, 384.

6. 1 Cor 12:4–6, 27–30.

7. Acts 13:2; Rom 1:1; Gal 2:8–9.

8. Peters, *A Biblical Theology of Missions*, 270–71.

to this ministry by the sovereign work of the Holy Spirit. The Gospel of John reminds us that we have not chosen God, rather, he has chosen us.[9] God's call of his ministers is evident in Acts when the Lord calls Barnabas and Saul and instructs the Antioch church to set them apart for that mission.[10] Peters reminds us that this principle of God's sovereign hand over the leaders of the church is clearly depicted in Eph 4:11–12 "And he gave the apostles, the prophets, the evangelists, the shepherds and teachers, to equip the saints for the work of ministry, for building up the body of Christ."[11] The call to missionary service is from God and does not begin out of human volition. Second, God's call to the ministry of the Word is individual.[12] Peters posits that many leaders of Israel and in the New Testament church were individually called to serve the Lord and lead his people. Specifically, he highlights the missionary calling expressed by Paul as an apostle, preacher, and teacher to the Gentiles. Third, the call to missions is unique and life–long. Fourth, the call to mission is a call to work. Peters posits that the call to work in ministry is contemporarily expressed in three areas: shepherding the church, evangelism, and teaching.[13]

A deeper look at the issue of a call service reveals more areas of difficulty. M. David Sills points out that not only does the Bible not define the missionary call, the Bible does not outline vital elements of such a call either. Within the scope of God's purpose to glorify himself by redeeming a people for himself, clearly his Kingdom—the rule of God—will expand. The expansion of the Kingdom of God is accomplished by the power of the Holy Spirit through human agency—that which we call missions. Individual members of God's kingdom participate in God's missionary work by sending or as those sent.[14] Although the specific nature of a missionary call is difficult to articulate, the Bible is clear that God calls some to the missionary task.

---

9. John 15:16.

10. Acts 13:2.

11. Peters, *A Biblical Theology of Missions*, 274.

12. Zane Pratt, David Sills, and Jeffrey Walters argue from Romans 10 that church members are either sent as missionaries or senders of missionaries. Pratt et al., *Introduction to Global Missions*, 4.

13. Peters, *A Biblical Theology of Missions*, 273–76.

14. Sills, *The Missionary Call*, 54–59.

The Apostle Paul recognized the need for other leaders to be called. He instructs the church to seek the man who aspires to lead.[15] Leadership aspiration, that which secular researchers may refer to as *drive*, is what the church usually considers *calling* and is the first characteristic.[16] Christ's calling is not simply a personal decision.[17] Paul served at God's pleasure and so too should missions leaders. Bill Allen, a British Baptist minister and leadership researcher, writes that the primary distinctive of Christian leadership is vocation in its most basic sense—a calling from God.[18] The call, tested by the local church, is the center that holds everything else together in the leader's life of service.[19] Derek J. Prime and Alistair Begg argue from the Apostle Paul's call that the pastoral call is a call to lead and includes an inward awareness of God's desire for the potential leader, associated gifting, and awareness on the part of the body of Christ, by observation and prayer, that the individual shows signs of leadership potential.[20] From where do missions leaders come? They are called. The mission leader's call is the center that holds everything else together. A leader's call is that which binds him to God's purpose and keeps him moving forward during the ordinary and extraordinary challenges of missions service. Leaders in missions are called to missions and to lead.

Analysis of Transformational Leadership.

Transformational leadership theory does not directly address the notion of a call. Motivation to serve through leadership in missions begins with a calling from God, but motivation in transformational leadership is based in meeting needs. Bass argues that truly transformational leaders are motivated to serve the higher needs of humanity, but such a call is substantially different from the call of God.

---

15. 1 Tim 3:1.

16. Patrick, *Church Planter*, 34; Blackaby and Blackaby, *Spiritual Leadership*, 99.

17. Schnabel, "Paul the Missionary," 30–32.

18. Allen, "Pathways to Leadership," 46.

19. Allen argues that a leader's call is that spirituality which invigorates him during the drudge of life-long demands as well as during extraordinary challenges and is related to a leader's deep spiritual conviction and notion of purpose. Allen, "Pathways to Leadership," 46.

20. Prime and Begg, *On Being a Pastor*, 18, 30–33.

The Inspirational Motivation factor is indirectly related to calling. Transformational leaders inspire and empower followers to reach their dreams. In similar fashion, a missions leader's calling may undergird his desire and ability to motivate others to achieve God's purposes in missions. Although transformational leadership theory does not articulate a biblical understanding of calling, neither is calling contradicted by any aspect of the theory. Moreover, a missions leader's sense of calling strongly supports the charismatic factors, Idealized Influence and Inspirational Motivation, of a transformational leader with compelling vision and confidence.

A Leader's Character: What Character Traits are Essential in Leaders?

What character traits are essential for missions leaders? Leadership researchers Shelly A. Kirkpatrick and Edwin A. Locke claim that while traits alone do not make the leader, some character traits seem to be necessary precursors for success.[21] They articulate five critical traits for success. Chief among them is a drive defined as personal ambition expressed as high energy, tenacity, persistence, and initiative. Other important traits include a desire to lead, truthfulness and integrity, self-confidence, and cognitive ability. Traits are not necessarily innate and can be taught. An oversimplification of leadership trait theory associates certain personality types with certain jobs. An entire industry of life coaching and vocation advising has grown out of such thinking. For example, some make the association that quiet people make good librarians, extroverts make good executives and entrepreneurs, introverted thinkers make good ministers and artists, and sensitive people who are well-organized make good nurses.[22] Most behaviorists and psychologists studying leadership traits argue that the character necessary to lead is teachable.

British and United States Army researchers posit several generic character requirements for leaders. The United States Army lists loyalty, duty, respect, selfless service, honor, integrity and personal courage as essential values for all military leaders.[23] John Adair lists the character

21. Kirkpatrick and Locke, "Leadership: Do Traits Matter?" 49–55. Some research demonstrates a genetic or hereditary link to leadership traits. Johnson et al., "Nature vs Nurture," 216–23.

22. Bredfeldt, *Great Leader, Great Teacher*, 117.

23. Army Center for Leadership, *The U.S. Army Leadership Field Manual*, 22.

traits sought at Sandhurst Academy, the British military training center, as enthusiasm, integrity, toughness, humanity, confidence, humility, and courage.[24] Golden Gate Baptist Theological Seminary president Jeff Iorg argues for nine character qualities in Christian leaders in his book *The Character of Leadership*.[25] His list consists of integrity, security, purity, humility, servanthood, wisdom, discipline, and courage.[26] Iorg's study of leadership character is less formal than that by the United States Army and Adair. Still, it comes from his considerable personal experience as a leader, observing other leaders, and teaching leadership. All three of these authorities on leadership include three foundational characteristics: integrity, humility, and courage. If these three traits are vital to leadership in general, how should they be defined for leadership in missions?

Integrity.

The common understanding of integrity is the matter of keeping one's word or the correlation between one's words and deeds. The Bible teaches a similar correlation but bases integrity in righteousness—adherence to God's standards. For example, in Psalm 101 David writes that he will "walk with integrity of heart," and he contrasts such integrity with unrighteousness. First Kings 9:4, Job 2:3, Psalm 7:8; 25:21, Proverbs 10:9; 11:3; 28:6 and Titus 2:7 all reflect this same understanding that personal integrity means uprightness and walking in God's ways—righteousness. Iorg defines integrity as "consistently applying biblical principles in character and action."[27]

Aubrey Malphurs, Senior Professor of Educational Ministries and Leadership and Pastoral Ministry at Dallas Theological Seminary, contends that people willingly follow those they trust; therefore, credibility is a core characteristic for leadership. Malphurs argues that trust begins with God and is extended through human relationships. God has proven to be faithful and insomuch as his servants are faithful to God, they have credibility.[28] Credibility is rooted in a leader's integrity—consistent righteousness. Integrity is measured against God's standards, not simply one's word.

24. Adair, *How to Grow Leaders*, 32.

25. Iorg, *The Character of Leadership*.

26. Iorg, *The Character of Leadership*, 19.

27. Iorg, *The Character of Leadership*, 25.

28. Malphurs, *Being Leaders*, 49.

Humility.

Iorg acknowledges the leader's need for humility. God opposes the proud, but he exalts, leads, empowers, and surrounds the humble. Humility is not self–deprecation. Such debasing behavior may actually draw more attention to a leader instead of putting the spotlight on God.[29] Iorg writes "Humility is the attitude that emerges from . . . thinking about yourself like God thinks of you." Leaders are humble toward God and others. True humility is born out of dependence on God.[30] Humility is not ascetic self–abasement, for such is false wisdom.[31] Humility is putting others first in service to Christ for the glory of God.[32] Humility means that the leader recognizes that his abilities, gifts, talents, strengths, and accomplishments are God's work.

Courage.

Fear is a significant theme in the Bible. Iorg points out that there are over six hundred references to fear in the Bible, beginning in Genesis 3. Apart from appropriate fear of the Lord, fear is a destructive force that causes God's people to miss out on God's blessing, keeps them from using God's gifts, and induces poor decision–making.[33] Courage is the opposite of fear. Courage is necessary for leadership.[34] Courage is the strength to hold steady onto God's will in opposition or to challenge the *status quo* and align with God's will.

Leaders in Christian missions must be models of godly character—men of integrity, humility, and courage. The Apostle Peter urges these leadership traits in his first letter. He charges leaders to demonstrate integrity as they lead by example and exercise self-control.[35] He teaches that leaders are humble toward God and others and that humility ultimately consists of dependence on God.[36] Leaders are courageous—faithful to the

---

29. Iorg, *The Character of Leadership*, 93, 101–4.

30. Deut 8:1–3, 11–20; 17:19–20; 2 Kgs 22:11–13, 18–19; 1 Pet 5:5–7.

31. Col 2:23.

32. Col 2:23; Phil 2:1–16; Eph 4:2.

33. Iorg, *The Character of Leadership*, 182–87.

34. Malphurs, *Being Leaders*, 63–64.

35. 1 Pet 5:3, 8.

36. 1 Pet 5:5–7.

Lord amidst danger and temptation, asserts the Apostle Peter.[37] Courage is trusting in God and his care.[38] Courage in God remains steadfast despite circumstances.[39] In short, leaders must be models of godly character—men of integrity, humility, and courage.

Analysis of Transformational Leadership.

Leaders in Christian missions should be models of godly character—people of integrity, humility, and courage. Lists of desirable leadership character traits, both secular and biblical, have many of the same traits. Followers desire leaders who are trustworthy and responsible, not arrogant, and ready to take risks for the sake of that which is good and right.

Transformational leadership theory promotes moral behavior and concern for ethical behavior. The theory recognizes that people want leaders who are willing to stick with the job when times are tough and who are consistent in their treatment of others. Transformational leadership theory identifies that good leaders are optimistic. The Bible teaches persistence, consistency, and optimism. In biblical theology, God's character, will, and acts form the basis and rationale for these leadership characteristics.

As with other aspects of transformational leadership theory, the key difference between the personal qualities in Bass' theory and those in the Bible is the source and standard of the qualities. While Bass' theory promotes a humanistic worldview of self–development and altruism, the Bible charges leaders and followers alike to turn to the power of the Holy Spirit and the new birth for change in character and look to God's revealed Word for the standard.

A Leader's Competency: How do Gifting, Strengths, and Experience Come to Bear?

God calls leaders to serve his church. He instructs the church to look for leaders on the basis of character, first, then competency. How do gifting, strengths, and experience come to bear on leadership in Christian missions? God displays his care for the church by gifting her with the leaders

---

37. 1 Pet 5:8–9.

38. Ps 56; 1 Sam 14:6–15; 16:1–13; Dan 3:17–18.

39. Ps 119:46; Matt 14:26–31; Mark 8:38; 2 Tim 1:8–12.

she needs.[40] Ken Hemphill provides three basic principles from 1 Thessalonians 5 to explain spiritual gifts and leadership: First, God's people are a community for mutual encouragement. This encouragement is born out of individual competency and responsibility for the good of others. Second, God gifts some in the community with leadership ability. Third, the church performs best when the gifted members of the church work in harmony. God provides leaders for the body of Christ to exercise stewardship for the well–being of the body and the purposes of his kingdom.[41]

Leadership is a spiritual gift.

God gifts the church with leaders to care for the body, not to rule over them. Spiritual gifts do not establish a spiritually elite class.[42] The Apostle Paul, in 1 Corinthians 12:18, teaches that the variety of gifts does not indicate a class system, but it provides warrant for the doctrine that God has gifted the church with a broad variety of gifts for his singular purpose.[43]

Hemphill argues that one of the issues that occasioned Paul's letters to the church at Corinth was their confusion over the gifts. The gifts of certain influential people in the church became a source of pride. Paul corrected this sin by teaching that the gifts are for the building up of the body, not for creating a multi–tiered system of Christian classes.[44] Gordon Fee agrees. He asserts that a clergy–laity dichotomy is inconsistent with leadership in the New Testament. He argues for an identifiable leadership who are part of the whole people of God, not a separate class of believers with different rules and expectations. The whole church is called to recognize they are members of one another, to build up and care for one another, to bear one another's burdens, to be kind, compassionate, and forgiving to one another, to submit to one another, and devoted to one another. Leadership in the New Testament is not about governance, but service, Fee contends. The key to leadership is not individuals in their inherited stations or individuals in newly created offices, but rather the gifting of the Spirit for the good of the body.[45] Leaders "did not consider themselves 'or-

40. 2 Cor 4:5–7; 1 Cor 12:28; Eph 4:11.

41. Hemphill, *You Are Gifted*, 4, 7–9.

42. Fee, "*Laos* and Leadership under the New Covenant," 3–13.

43. Hemphill, *You Are Gifted*, 52–53.

44. Hemphill, *You Are Gifted*, 23–36.

45. 1 Cor 12:11, 7.

dained' to lead the people, but 'gifted' to do so as one gift among others.[46] All members of the body are gifted to varying degrees.

The universality and variety of gifts points to the principle of interdependence for the common good. Interdependence is founded, in part, on the truth that the Lord gives varied gifts to the body and the associated truth that not all are gifted with the same gifts and the same capacity. Therefore, we are interdependent—we need one another. One of the gifts God lavishes upon the church is leadership.[47] The biblical theme here is that God provides some members of the body with leadership competency.[48] Whatever the level of competency, the gift of leadership or gifts for leadership are not intended for personal gain but for the benefit of the body of Christ and God's purposes.

Leadership ability must be nurtured.

Supernatural gifting does not imply that a gift does not need to be nurtured or "fanned into flame."[49] Chuck Lawless posits that Paul sought to develop leaders as part of his ministry. The Apostle mentored future leaders, taking the initiative by selecting whom he would mentor. Lawless describes Paul's method as relationship oriented. In the case of Paul and Timothy, their mentoring relationship was strengthened by their mutual commitment to the cause of Christ.[50] Mentoring appears to be the primary means of Timothy's growth as a leader. Not only was this Paul's pattern with Timothy, argues Lawless, but Paul also encouraged the elders at Crete to teach the younger brothers, repeating Paul's leadership development pattern.[51]

---

46. Fee, Laos and Leadership under the New Covenant," 3–13.

47. Hemphill, *You Are Gifted*, 158–59; Plueddemann, *Leading across Cultures*, 173.

48. Christian leadership gifts may come by supernatural event, part of one's natural personality and character, or developed through training and experience concludes Eugene B. Habecker, president of Taylor University. Habecker affirms that the core reason for the leadership gifts is to maintain unity of the faith and to prepare the saints for ministry. Habecker, *Rediscovering the Soul of Leadership*, 205.

49. Habecker, *Rediscovering the Soul of Leadership*, 184; Plueddemann, *Leading across Cultures*, 174.

50. Lawless, "Paul and Leadership Development," 227–29. In the context of their close relationship, Paul saw Timothy's areas of need, weaknesses that needed to be addressed, drew Timothy's attention to those areas of required growth and, finally, commended Timothy to his own work.

51. Titus 2:1–8.

The ability to teach is a vital leadership competency.

Bill Allen calls for seven particular competencies for Christian leaders. Leaders must be able to (1) think theologically and to make application of that reflection, (2) develop a spiritual foundation to support their ministry, (3) conduct their ministry with integrity, (4) communicate in public and in private, 5) lead others, (6) provide effective care and support, and (7) manage himself and his work.[52] These skills make sense and are at least implied by the biblical text. In the New Testament, the explicit and most common skill required of leaders is the ability to teach.[53] The Apostle Peter argues that unscrupulous teachers can lead believers astray from the faith.[54] The preventative measure to defend the church from false teachers is to remember good teaching, even hard teaching.[55] Many ought to be teachers, declares the author of Hebrews, but apparently, some continue in immaturity and discount themselves as teachers and leaders.[56] To paraphrase Paul's letter to the Ephesian church, Christ gave leaders to the church to prepare her for service to build up the body of Christ. Leaders who teach are necessary so that the church is not thrown off-point by false teaching and clever deceit.[57]

Missions leaders, unlike entrepreneurs, are not necessarily people with innovative strategies, but those who are dedicated to lead others toward God's purposes for his glory through the qualitative measure of our holiness and the quantitative measure of his ever-expanding kingdom.[58] To accomplish this goal, the missions leader requires skilled hands—leadership competency, especially the competency to teach God's Word.

Analysis of Transformational Leadership.

Leaders in Christian missions are dedicated to leading others toward God's purposes for his glory. The accomplishment of this goal requires leadership competency. The ability to teach is the primary leadership skill

52. Allen, "Pathways to Leadership," 40–42.

53. 1 Tim 3:2–3; 2 Tim 2:2, 24; Titus 1:9; Jude 1:3.

54. 2 Pet 2:1–3.

55. 2 Pet 3:1–3, 14–16.

56. Heb 5:12.

57. Eph 4:11–14.

58. Howell, *Servants of the Servant*, 301.

mentioned in the New Testament. Transformational leadership theory recognizes that the best leaders apply both transactional and transformational behaviors. In particular, transformational leaders provide opportunities for their followers, demonstrate genuine concern for the good and for achievement, are self–confident, able to articulate a clear path forward, able to teach and coach, and communicate effectively. A biblical view of leadership can accept these same skills and abilities—after all, David led his people with skillful hands.

Summary

Calling is not a category in transformational leadership theory. Nevertheless, certain aspects of transformational leadership can be helpful in missions leadership. Transformational leaders are inspirational and often use their life story as a motivational concept. Character or ethical behavior plays a significant role in the theory and sets transformational leadership apart from despotic leaders who are out for their own good and to the detriment of others. Communication and the soft skills of human interaction are highly valued in transformational leadership, and leaders are expected to display competence in these areas. In like manner, missions leaders can refer to their calling in an exemplary fashion, illustrating the power of their calling upon their life and work. Character, like the other aspects of transformational leadership theory, must be understood biblically. The leader's character is a moral category and is brought about by the Spirit's transformative work in the believer. Failure to recognize both the fixed biblical standard and our dependence on God for personal righteousness will undoubtedly lead to disaster because of the force of the ever–malleable public value system. The competencies required by Scripture are similar to those delineated in transformational theory. The missions leader would do well, however, to point to the Bible as the basis for these leadership competencies rather than to Bass' transformational leadership theory.

Chapter 6

Analyze the Authority Aspect

POWER AND AUTHORITY ARE interrelated concepts. Power concerns the capacity to act, whereas authority refers to the right to act. On the night of his betrayal, Jesus confirmed the astonishing truth that his followers have the power to do his works and even greater works than he had done.[1] Jesus asserted his authority when he said "All authority in heaven and on earth has been given to me," and he gave his disciples the authority to do his will (Matt 28:18). Jesus developed the theme of power and authority further in the parable of the talents. The parable depicts three vital aspects of authority. The servant was given (1) *capacity*—the power to do the master's will, (2) *right*—the authority to do the master's will, and (3) *responsibility*—he was held accountable for the results of doing the master's will.[2]

A theological assessment of leadership includes an examination of power, authority, and responsibility from a biblical point of view. What kind of power do mission leaders have? What is the source of authority in missions leadership? To whom is a leader in missions accountable?

---

1. John 14:12–14.
2. Matt 25:13–30.

A Leader's Capacity: What Kind of Power do Leaders Have?

Power is the capacity to act or influence others to act. Most believers tend to avoid discussing power in the context of their faith.[3] Perhaps this aversion is because the term, power, conjures up images of coercion and despotism and, therefore, seems off–limits for Christian leadership. Although many feel reluctant to think about power in missions leadership, the New Testament describes at least two general categories of power: the infinite power of the Holy Spirit and finite power in human relationships.

The infinite power of the Holy Spirit is the ultimate power for missions leadership. The deeper discussion of God's infinite power, especially as it relates to the work of the Holy Spirit and the Word of God, is beyond the scope of this research, but it would be an error to consider the finite power of human relationships without recognizing God's limitless power in missions through his Spirit.[4]

French and Raven identify five bases of power: reward, coercive, legitimate, referent, and expert. *Reward power* is the ability to elicit or draw forth positive emotions. Reward power increases with the magnitude and probability of reward. *Coercive power* is related to psychological valences, in this case negative or punishment for non–conformity. Once again, the strength of coercive power is directly related to its magnitude and likelihood of punishment. *Legitimate power* is related to role or position. This power obtains legitimacy in the internalized norms of the subject (follower) and is often described in terms of ought–ness or right–ness. Cultural norms, social values, and designation by a legitimizing agent are the three bases for legitimate power. Normally legitimate power is very stable because it comes from the subject's value system. The range of legitimate power is usually well specified and defined, for example in a job description. *Referent power* comes from identification or feelings of unity with or attraction to the leader. Referent power is sometimes difficult to distinguish from reward and coercive power. *Expert power* is primarily limited to the cognitive domain but it can cause change in behavior. For expert power to come into play, trust must be established, and this power is limited to the area of expertise. Some halo effect may occur in expert

3. Malphurs, *Being Leaders*, 103.

4. Peters articulates three major facets of the Spirit's power: to write and preserve Scripture, to grow and support believers, and the Spirit's general activities in the world. Peters, *A Biblical Theology of Missions*, 301.

power, extending the leader's power beyond the scope of his expertise. French and Raven conclude that referent power generally has the broadest range of influence. They also note that trying to use power outside the field of that power's base tends to reduce its magnitude. Finally, coercion on the part of the leader will decrease attraction on the part of the follower, thereby reducing referent power in the relationship.[5]

Power bases in the New Testament.

All five power bases are evident in the New Testament. A clear example of the *reward power* base is found in Luke 16:1–13, where Jesus teaches his followers to use everything at their disposal for righteousness' sake so that one may gain eternal reward. The Apostle Paul taught Titus that *coercive power* is a part of leading when he urged Titus to "declare, exhort and rebuke with all authority."[6] *Legitimate power* plays a significant role in the New Testament. Malphurs argues that Paul exercised legitimate power in Philemon when Paul writes, "Though I am bold enough in Christ to command you to do what is required, yet for love's sake I prefer to appeal to you."[7] Matthew writes about a centurion who recognized the power of position. The centurion knew that he had power as a leader in the Roman army and recognized much greater power in Jesus.[8] Jesus knew that he was from God and would return to God and that he had all power.[9] God puts people in roles, such as the apostles, the prophets, the evangelists, the shepherds and teachers for the sake of the church.[10] The *referent power* base is displayed in Hebrews: "Remember your leaders, those who spoke to you the Word of God. Consider the outcome of their way of life, and imitate their faith."[11] Finally, the *expert power* base expressed in teaching is probably the single most common power base extolled in the New Testament. There we see that leaders are commanded and inspired to teach;

5. French and Raven, "The Bases of Social Power," 263–68.

6. Titus 2:15.

7. Phil 1:8–9. Malphurs, *Being Leaders*, 106.

8. Matt 8:5–13.

9. John 13:3–5.

10. Eph 4:11.

11. Heb 13:7. Also in 1 Cor 4:16; 11:1; Phil 3:17; 4:9; 1 Thess 1:6–7; 2 Thess 3:7, 9; 1 Tim 4:12; Titus 2:7; 1 Pet 5:3.

teaching is sought in prayer, directed by earthly leaders, exemplified by Jesus, and modeled and commanded by the apostles.[12]

God has given some with the expertise of leadership and expects leaders to take that gift seriously.[13] Teaching the Word of God—expert power—and modeling the Christian life—referent power—are the most commonly promoted types of power in the New Testament. Jesus gave his church the authority to conduct his mission and make disciples of all nations. Jesus' disciples assemble and teach in the name of the Lord.[14] Jesus has all authority and gave the right for disciples to teach and live out his will. Leaders teach, exhort, and rebuke with all authority.[15] Leaders instruct and correct the church as part of being a good servant of God.[16] Legitimate, referent, and expert power are given by God and can be used properly or abused. Malphurs reasons that leadership should stem from referent and expert power, not legitimate power or personal power—a theory corroborated by French and Raven.[17]

Leighton Ford articulates four lessons about leadership from Jesus' life that refine the exercise of leadership power in missions.[18] First, Jesus' leadership was marked by great power but selective exhibition of that might. Second, Jesus' leadership is marked by service for the glory of God. Third, Jesus led and served without contradiction. Jesus centers his leadership on his authority, but his behaviors are selfless. Fourth, Ford adds that Jesus was not calling for the end of leadership. Jesus said the leader must become as the one who serves.[19] Therefore, biblical leadership does not mean abdication of authority. Jesus did not teach that leadership should be given up.

12. Commanded to teach, Lev 10:11; Deut 4:10, 14; 5:31; 6:1, 7; 11:19; 31:19; 33:10; Ezra 7:25; Ps 78:5. Inspired to teach, Exod 35:34; Ps 51:13; Ps 94:12; Ps 119:171; Mic 4:2; John 14:26. Sought in prayer, Judg 13:8; 1 Kgs 8:36; 2 Chr 6:2; Pss 25:4, 5; 27:11; 32:8; 45:4; 51:6; 86:11; 90:12; 119:12, 26, 29, 33, 64, 66, 68, 108, 124, 135; 143:10. Directed by earthly leaders, 2 Chr 17:7; Ezra 7:10; Ps 34:11; Pro 9:9; Isa 2:3; 28:9; Jer 9:20. Exemplified by Jesus, Matt 11:1; 22:16; Mark 4:1; 6:2, 34; 8:31; 12:14; Luke 11:1; 20:21; Acts 1:1. Modeled and commanded by the apostles, Acts 5:21; 1 Cor; 1 Tim 3:2; 4:11; 6:2; 2 Tim 2:2; 24; Titus 2:3; Heb 5:12; Jas 3:1.

13. Rom 12:6–8.

14. Matt 28:18–20; 1 Cor 5:4; Acts 4:18; 5:40; 9:27–28; Acts 19:5; Col 3:17.

15. Titus 2:15.

16. 1 Tim 1:3; 4:6; 4:16; 6:17–18; 2 Tim 4:2.

17. Malphurs, *Being Leaders*, 107; French and Raven, "The Bases of Social Power," 268.

18. Ford, *Transforming Leadership*, 153.

19. Luke 22:26.

What kind of power do missions leaders have? Missions organizations have trustees, executives, managerial, and supervisory positions. These positions all come with legitimate power supported by policy and procedure. Additionally, missions leaders may have considerable referent power that they earn and have attributed to them over time.[20] All missions leaders must have expert power—power that comes from the ability to understand and teach the Word of God.

Analysis of Transformational Leadership.

Capacity to lead in Bass' transformational leadership theory. Bass' formulation of transformational leadership emphasizes positive character traits and not power derived from position. Character builds up a leader's referent power. Transformational leaders demonstrate referent power when they articulate a compelling vision, are confident role models, and are trustworthy of being followed. Transformational leaders should be respected, optimistic, and enthusiastic and thereby inspire others to follow them. Referent power is important in the Bible. Leaders are expected to be people worthy of following. They may not be charismatic, larger–than–life visionaries, but they must be model servants of God. Transformational leadership also places a premium on the leader's cognitive ability. This expert power supports a leader's ability to persuade followers—a key element of the Intellectual Stimulation factor. Expert power as a teacher of God's Word is vital to missions leadership. Whereas Bass' transformational leadership relies most heavily on the charismatic factors, Idealized Influence and Inspirational Motivation, the New Testament emphasizes the leader's ability to teach, persuade, correct, and defend the faith on the basis of his knowledge of God's Word.

A Leader's Authority: What is a Leader's Source of Authority?

A leader can have the capacity to lead, but does he have the right? Leadership with low power and low authority is not leadership. Leadership with high power and low authority is despotism. Leadership with low power and

---

20. Malphurs, *Being Leaders*, 105.

high authority is weak and ineffectual. Leadership with power and authority has a solid moral base and the potential to accomplish its mission.

Derek Tidball writes that Jesus introduced a new way of leading—by sacrificial service.[21] Tidball draws four conclusions from his brief survey of leadership in the New Testament: (1) proper leadership is a concern, (2) the church is not egalitarian—governance is apparent, (3) the New Testament writers did not shy away from using secular leadership terminology, and (4) leadership is re-shaped in terms of caring servanthood. Yet Jesus led with authority. What is the source of authority in missions leadership?

Authority comes from God.

Paul, in Romans 13, teaches that God has established governments and civic authorities. Jesus asserted that his authority came from God.[22] In the Old Testament, God's servants minister in the name of the Lord; they stand, walk, and live in the name of the Lord.[23] God's servants bless others in the name of the Lord and speak in the name of the Lord.[24] Their authority comes from God insomuch as they live and speak his will and word. In the New Testament, Jesus gives his church the authority to carry out his mission, expressly to make disciples of all the nations.[25] Jesus' disciples assemble and teach in the name of the Lord.[26] Jesus has all authority and gave the right for disciples to teach and live out his will.

Paul charged Titus to teach, exhort, and rebuke with all authority and not to be put-off by others in this duty.[27] Paul writes letters or sent his teammates, Timothy and Titus, exerting his authority in the churches.[28] In at least six letters, Paul refers to his authority as given by the will of God, according to the commandment of God, by the gospel, preaching

---

21. Tidball, "Leaders as Servants," 31.

22. John 5:7; 7:17; 8:28; 10:18; 12:49; 14:10; 17:2.

23. Deut 18:5–7; 21:5; 1 Sam 17:45; Mic 4:5; Ps 118:26; Zep 3:12.

24. Bless others in the name of the Lord, 2 Sam 6:18; 1 Chr 16:2. Speak in the name of the Lord, 1 Chr 21:19; 2 Chr 33:18; Ezra 5:1; Jer 26:16, 20; 44:16.

25. Matt 28:18–20.

26. 1 Cor 5:4; Acts 4:18; 5:40; 9:27–28; Acts 19:5; Col 3:17.

27. Titus 2:15.

28. 1 Tim 6:13–16; 2 Tim.1:16; 2:22–24; 3:10; Titus 2:1–15. Banks, *Reviewing Leadership*, 41.

Christ.[29] Paul charges Timothy to instruct and correct the church as part of being a good servant of God.[30] Paul has the authority and teaches his fellow servants that they have the right to teach, correct, and encourage others in the way of the Lord.

Authority lies in leadership positions.

Organizations create structures and roles for leadership and those positions come with a degree of authority to lead. Christian organizations, be they churches or para–church missions organizations, often associate spiritual authority with certain positions.[31] Pastors are a clear example of such authority.

Not only does the New Testament teach that leaders have authority by God's will and in God's Word, but also that God gifts leaders of the church to fulfill this role.[32] Churches affirm the calling, gifting, and authority of leaders in the church, but it is the Holy Spirit who makes them leaders.[33]

Authority lies in God's Word.

As noted previously, the requirements for church leaders in 1 Timothy and Titus include the need for both biblical knowledge and character that is worth following. Followers may attribute authority to organizational leaders because of the leader's presumed or demonstrated character, teaching skill, or wisdom that comes from God and his Word.[34] Attributed authority is not limited to those in leadership positions. Leaders who

---

29. 1 Cor 1:1; Col 1:1; 2 Tim 1:1; 1 Tim 1:1; 2 Tim 1:11; Gal 2:11–14; 2 Cor 4:5.

30. 1 Tim 1:3; 4:6; 4:16; 6:17–18; 2 Tim 4:2.

31. Lawrenz, *Spiritual Influence*, 152.

32. 1 Cor 12:28; Rom 12:6–8; 1 Tim 4:14; 2 Tim 1:16.

33. Acts 20:28. Ben Merkle cautions, though, that church leadership authority is not absolute. Jesus and his work have ultimate authority over the church. Merkle, "Paul's Ecclesiology," 67. Schnabel writes that an essential missions leadership characteristic is that he understands and expresses an apostolic calling and, subsequently, behaves in such a manner that demonstrates accountability to God who called them. Schnabel, *Early Christian Mission*, 982.

34. Lawrenz, *Spiritual Influence*, 152.

demonstrate authority from God's Word can lead without position or formal recognition of their authority.[35]

Gary Bredfeldt argues that all church leaders are teachers at heart. Furthermore, he asserts that church leaders who behave as CEOs instead of teachers lose authority. Bredfeldt is not writing for the missionary context. He argues for authority church leadership, but the basis for authority for Christian leaders should be the same whether in local church or in missions contexts. He argues that Church CEO–leaders are those dependent upon their social status and demonstrable success as the basis for authority, a bias that is not biblical. Bredfeldt explains that success, status, and standing are the world's standards for leadership. He posits that Jesus had little or no success, did not seek status, and lacked social or political standing because he did not seek office. His argument is misleading. One can substantiate that Jesus had great success and that he taught in parables that his servants should be faithful and strive to work successfully for their master. Second, Jesus had status. Many called him teacher and revered him, for he taught as one with authority. Third, Jesus had standing. Though he never became a CEO, he led a movement that is still changing the world. Jesus' apostles enjoyed similar qualifications. The question is what is the basis and measure of a leader's success, status, and standing, the source of power and authority.[36]

George Miley takes a different approach and distinguishes church leaders from apostolic leaders. He describes church leaders in the same way many describe managers. Miley stipulates that church leaders are nurturers who strive for stability. They seek consensus and stress risk avoidance. Church leaders, he argues, are over–extended and seek gradual change. Apostolic leaders, on the other hand are innovators who seek change. They are visionary and anxious to move forward, taking on necessary risks for breakthroughs. When looking for potential apostolic leader types, Miley claims the church should look for those with "notable areas of character immaturity," who are "overextended in their commitments," and of whom the church leaders are "unsure how far we can trust them."[37]

---

35. Lawrenz, *Spiritual Influence*, 152. John Carter argues that a leader's spiritual authority is a derivative of their integrity and includes "wisdom, courage, and humility." Carter, "Power and Authority in Pentecostal Leadership," 203–04.

36. Bredfeldt, *Great Leader, Great Teacher*, 18, 20, 50–51, 60.

37. Miley, *Loving the Church . . . Blessing the Nations*, 88.

A leader's persuasive power gains its authority from God's Word, which is why the role of teaching is so important. Teachers of God's Word rest in the authority of the Bible as the revealed Word of God.[38] Viewing authority this way establishes power in God's will and not an individual's or organization's might. The leader is responsible to God in this view of authority. A biblical example of this view can be found in 2 Timothy, where Paul charges Timothy in the presence of God to teach sound doctrine even in the face of opposition from his hearers.[39] James teaches the same responsibility and warns that teachers will be judged according to a high standard.[40] God is the source of power and authority for the leader who will work and accomplish his purposes. In the New Testament, a leader's primary role is to teach God's Word. The ability to teach, knowledge of God's Word, Spirit-imbued wisdom, and righteous character are, therefore, essential to authority in missions leadership.[41]

What is the source of authority in missions leadership? The New Testament reveals three principles about the right to lead. First, leadership authority comes from God. God places rulers and leaders in their positions to serve his will. That placement does not render *carte blanche* authority to leaders. Second, formal positions and roles come with a degree of authority. Third, the right to lead comes from knowledge and the ability to teach God's Word.

Analysis of Transformational Leadership.

A leader's right to exercise power comes from God and is strongly associated with a leader's obedience to God's will, demonstrated over time. Leaders in the church are called by God and the church affirms their calling. A leader's calling, church affirmation, and his role in the church are indicators of a right to lead. A leader's knowledge of and/or reliance on the Word of God is the final and most substantial source of authority.

---

38. Bredfeldt, *Great Leader, Great Teacher*, 63.

39. 2 Tim 4:1–4.

40. Jas 3:1.

41. Henry Blackaby and Richard Blackaby establish that God's affirmation of the leader, their reputation over time, evidence of a changed life, and Christ-likeness are all-important factors in selecting a leader or attributing authority to him. Blackaby and Blackaby, *Spiritual Leadership*, 93–100.

How does transformational leadership theory compare to a biblical view of the right to lead?

Burns regards power and authority as dependent upon the relationship between the leader's intent and capacity to act in coherence with, or on behalf of, follower values and needs. Therefore, power is primarily a psychological aspect—the interrelationship of motivations and needs. Whether this relationship is coercive, transactional, or transformational depends on the met and unmet needs of the leader and followers.

A Leader's Responsibility: To Whom is a Leader Responsible?

Jesus' parable of the talents in Matthew explains power and authority in terms of capacity, right, and responsibility. Responsibility refers to one's accountability for his behavior. With power and authority comes responsibility. To whom is a missions leader responsible? The New testament teaches that leaders are responsible to God and responsible to those in their care.

Leaders are responsible to God. Leaders are stewards of their gifts, including the gift of leadership. The Apostle Peter reminds his readers that the purpose of the gifts is to serve to serve others in order that God may be glorified.[42] With the power and authority in leadership comes responsibility.[43] Because of this responsibility, teachers and leaders are subject to stricter judgment—accountable to God for their behavior and that which they teach others, by word and deed.[44] Leaders are responsible to followers. Jesus taught his disciples that the path to spiritual leadership was paved with suffering and sacrifice and demonstrated through servanthood. Seeking position for the sake of honor is not the way of spiritual leadership, but sacrificial service is.[45]

---

42. 1 Pet 4:10–11.

43. 1 Cor 8:9–13.

44. Jas 3:1–4.

45. Matt 16:24–25, Mark 8:34–35, Luke 9:23–25.

Leaders are responsible to God.

Leaders are stewards of their gifts, including the gift of leadership. The Apostle Peter reminds his readers that the purpose of the gifts is to serve others in order that God may be glorified:

> As each has received a gift, use it to serve one another, as good stewards of God's varied grace: whoever speaks, as one who speaks oracles of God; whoever serves, as one who serves by the strength that God supplies—in order that in everything God may be glorified through Jesus Christ. To him belong glory and dominion forever and ever. Amen.[46]

With the power and authority in leadership comes responsibility. Paul teaches this concept in 1 Corinthians:

> But take care that this right of yours does not somehow become a stumbling block to the weak. For if anyone sees you who have knowledge eating in an idol's temple, will he not be encouraged, if his conscience is weak, to eat food offered to idols? And so by your knowledge this weak person is destroyed, the brother for whom Christ died. Thus, sinning against your brothers and wounding their conscience when it is weak, you sin against Christ. Therefore, if food makes my brother stumble, I will never eat meat, lest I make my brother stumble.[47]

Because of this responsibility, teachers and leaders are subject to stricter judgment—accountable to God for their behavior and that which they teach others, by word and deed.[48]

Leaders are responsible to followers.

Some scholars claim that servanthood is the most definitive aspect of missionary leadership. Van Engen argues that Jesus is both Lord and suffering servant, manifesting absolute sovereignty and sacrifice simultaneously; therefore, leaders should follow Jesus' example and serve rather than rule.[49] Jesus taught his disciples that the path to spiritual leadership was paved

46. 1 Pet 4:10–11.

47. 1 Cor 8:9–13.

48. Jas 3:1–4.

49. Van Engen, *God's Missionary People*, 168–70.

with suffering and sacrifice and demonstrated through servanthood.[50] Jesus' point to James and John in Mark 8:34–35 is that seeking position for the sake of honor is not the way of spiritual leadership, but sacrificial service is.[51] Van Engen presses the argument further and asserts that "When leaders rule rather than serve, they lose their right to lead."[52]

The servant role that Jesus uses to define spiritual leadership is no more palatable today than it was in Jesus' time. No matter how appropriate the titles "minister," "missionary," or "pastor" may be, the titles are not the point.[53] Jesus calls leaders to a role that goes against the grain of society, then and now.[54] In this view of leadership, the leader is responsible to his followers—those served by his leadership.

To whom is a leader in missions responsible? The two perspectives discussed above need to be held in tension. A missions leader's primary responsibility is to his Lord. A leader's secondary responsibility is to his followers and organization. Leaders are accountable to God for the gifts and leadership that God sovereignly bestows upon them and leaders are accountable to their followers and to their organization to faithfully fulfill their God-given purpose. These vectors of accountability do not need to be set one against the other, but neither are they co-equal. Responsibility to God is ultimate, responsibility to others is penultimate.

Analysis of Transformational Leadership.

In missions leadership, accountability is first to God, second to followers, and, if relevant, to one's organization. Paul Hiebert summarizes this aspect well.[55] Hiebert posits that the leader's role is based in the conviction that God calls him and he is not his own. The leader knows, follows, and teaches the Scriptures. He is aware of the importance of others and seeks to influence them for God's sake. A leader must be ready to persist in the work, for

50. Hutchison, "Servanthood: Jesus' Countercultural Call to Christian Leaders," 62–64.

51. Hutchison, "Servanthood," 65. Also Matt 16:24–25 and Luke 9:23–25.

52. Van Engen, God's Missionary People, 170. Hutchison agrees and reasons that Jesus' call to radical, deep personal humility in order to serve others stood in sharp contrast to the cultural values of Jesus' time. Hutchison, "Servanthood," 54.

53. Hutchison, "Servanthood," 69.

54. Hutchison, "Servanthood," 69.

55. Hiebert, "Pauline Images of a Christian Leader," 227–28.

it is hard and he will face opposition, even suffering. Ready to pay the cost, the leader has the hope of reward and the gratefulness of his Savior.

Accountability in transformational leadership theory leans heavily toward the accomplishment of mutually held goals within the bounds of shared values. Accountability to God and his revealed Word has no place in transformational leadership theory except as a possible mode of moral evaluation. In practice, transformational leadership is accountable to the goals of the organization. Accountability in theology of Christian missions and accountability in transformational leadership theory have some areas of overlap. Both call for responsibility to followers, albeit for different reasons. Bass' leaders are accountable because of mutually held goals and, perhaps, a sense of morality and transcendental good. Mission leaders are accountable to followers because of God's direct command to love and serve them. The primary area of accountability in a missions theology is to God, and this notion has little if any place in transformational leadership theory as espoused by Bernard Bass and his colleagues.

Summary

Transformational leadership espouses that a leader's power is found in their character traits, a kind of referent power, and locates authority in the relationship in leader and follower dyad. Authority for Bass is primarily psychological and relational and related to intent, capacity, and felt needs. Similarly, Bass believes that accountability is tied to another relational factor, namely mutual goals. These aspects of transformational theory are not strongly aligned with those of a biblical theology of leadership. To be sure, referent power is found in the Scriptures along with legitimate and expert power, power by virtue of position and knowledge, respectively. Bass' theory is dependent on charisma, and though that is not at odds with power in the Scriptures, it is out of balance. The Bible places more weight on legitimate power, such as that in the role of elder or overseer, and expert power derived from knowledge and wisdom from God's Word. In regard to authority and the right to lead, in the Bible, that resides in the leader's calling and alignment with God's Word. Concerning the issue of responsibility, once again, the biblical view stands in stark contrast to that of transformational theory. The Bible assigns man's accountability to God, then others. Bass' theory has little place for a biblical understanding of capacity, authority, and responsibility.

Chapter 7

Analyze the Ethic Aspect

The Leader as Servant of God: How do Leaders Serve the Lord?

LEADERSHIP ETHIC REFERS TO the desired behaviors or principles of conduct that result from a particular leadership theory. Leadership in missions should transform communities, some argue.[1] Others claim that leadership behavior is identification with the will of those led.[2] Still others posit that leadership is about unity, through seeking the best interest of followers.[3] Commonly cast as servant leadership, these follower–oriented formulations of leadership represent a significant about–face from the modern view of leadership as power and authority.[4]

---

1. Bartz, "Leadership from the Inside Out," 90.

2. Spears, "Character and Servant Leadership," 27.

3. Ayers, "Toward a Theology of Leadership," 19–20, 24; Zscheile, "The Trinity, Leadership, and Power," 54–55.

4. Ayers, "Toward a Theology of Leadership," 20. Ever since Robert K. Greenleaf's book, *Servant Leadership*, pundits have relied heavily on a servant ethic. Greenleaf's ideas have been picked up by writers such as James Autry, Warren Bennis, Peter Block, Stephen Covey, Max De Pree, Parker Palmer, M. Scott Peck, and Peter Senge. Servant leadership theories are reflected in the popular leadership training series *Lead Like Jesus* by Ken Blanchard and Phil Hodges. Blanchard and Hodges, *Lead Like Jesus*. Greenleaf and Larry C. Spears, *Servant Leadership*.

Missionaries are messengers and their labor is predicated on the gospel of Christ. To substitute anything else in place of the gospel message is to cease practicing missions. A theology of leadership in missions grows out of that purpose, subsequent ontology, and biblical view of power and authority and results in a ranked ethic: missions leaders are servants of God, then servants to others.[5] By pleasing God first leaders serve others best, argues Jeanine Parolini, because "serving others is not the same as pleasing them."[6]

A missions leader must be God's servant. In reply to a question from the Pharisees about the priority of the commandments, Jesus taught his disciples that the greatest commandment is to "Love the Lord your God with all your heart, soul, and mind" (Matt 22:36–40). Jesus taught this concept of putting God first from a different perspective in his reply to the Pharisees:

> But you are not to be called rabbi, for you have one teacher, and you are all brothers. And call no man your father on earth, for you have one Father, who is in heaven. Neither be called instructors, for you have one instructor, the Christ. The greatest among you shall be your servant. Whoever exalts himself will be humbled, and whoever humbles himself will be exalted.[7]

Jesus taught that leaders should not seek to be called teacher, father, or leader, but that leaders should serve others, acknowledging that only God is truly the teacher, father, and leader of all.

Two other New Testament teachings help flesh-out the act of loving God as part of a leader's ethic. The first New Testament teaching is found in John 20:21, where Jesus said to his disciples "Peace be with you. As the Father has sent me, even so I am sending you." The Apostle John exhorts all Christians to be obedient to the Lord as Christ was obedient to the Father. Carson reasons from this verse that Jesus' complete obedience to the Father is the model for Christians. Some interpretations of John 20:21 suggest that to do missions is to do the things Jesus did—specifically heal the sick, tend to the poor—these interpretations appeal to Luke 4:18, 19; 7:22 for that understanding. Carson finds this interpretation methodologically unsound because it requires leaving the immediate context of

---

5. Wendell Jones, "A Theological Comparison between Social Science Models and a Biblical Perspective of Servant Leadership," 4.

6. Parolini, *Transformational Servant Leadership*, 78.

7. Matt 23:8–12.

the verse for the interpretation to work.[8] One needs only to look back to John 17 and see the emphasis of obedience in Jesus' prayer for his followers. Jesus prays that, though his followers no longer belong to the world, but must be sent back into it—risky as that sending may be—so that they can continue to witness to the glory of God. Christ modeled and taught obedience to the Father, and leaders in his church must do the same. The author of Hebrews taught the same idea: "Therefore, holy brothers, you who share in a heavenly calling, consider Jesus, the apostle and high priest of our confession, who was faithful to him who appointed him, just as Moses also was faithful in all God's house" (Heb 3:1–2). Faithful obedience is vital. This biblical theme and interpretation of John 20:21 fits John's Gospel and the Great Commission.[9]

A second passage to consider is 1 Peter 5:1–5.[10] In these verses, Peter clarifies important leadership behaviors:

> So I exhort the elders among you, as a fellow elder and a witness of the sufferings of Christ, as well as a partaker in the glory that is going to be revealed: shepherd the flock of God that is among you, exercising oversight, not under compulsion, but willingly, as God would have you; not for shameful gain, but eagerly; not domineering over those in your charge, but being examples to the flock. And when the chief Shepherd appears, you will receive the unfading crown of glory. Likewise, you who are younger, be subject to the elders.[11]

At least seven principles for leadership behavior emerge from this passage. First, leaders lead as one among peers.[12] Peter refers to himself as a fellow elder, witness to Christ, and participant in God's glory. Peter has already

---

8. Carson, *The Gospel According to John*, 648–49.

9. Jesus defines abiding in him and the father in terms of obedience to his word and will (John 15:15). Jesus commands his followers to love others. This love stems out of the new birth, as a natural overflow of love for God in response to his love (John 3:16; 13:34–35; 15:9, 12; 16:27; 1 John 3:1; 11; 4:9, 11, 19, 21; 5:3; 2 John 1:5–6). Those who love obey. Jesus loves the Father and obeys him. Loving obedience is the only appropriate ethic toward God (John 14:15, 21, 23–24, 31; 15:10, 17). See also Bartz, "Leadership from the Inside Out," 87; Blackaby, *Spiritual Leadership*, 164–67; Peters, *A Biblical Theology of Missions*, 142.

10. J. Louis Spencer takes the phrase "shepherd of the flock of God" as a metaphor for leadership and "serving as overseers" as a synonym for leadership. Spencer, "Peter: A Phenomenology of Leadership," 22.

11. 1 Pet 5:1–5.

12. 1 Pet 5:1.

referred to his apostolic authority, so his phrasing in 5:1 does not indicate any loss of authority for him. Clearly, he exhibits some level of authority in his readers' lives as demonstrated by the instructional nature of this letter, but when he addresses the leaders, he describes himself as a peer.[13] Second, leaders lead God's people, not their own.[14] Michaels argues that Peter may be thinking back to Jesus' command to feed his sheep and affirms that, in John's Gospel, the flock belongs to Christ or, as in Peter's letter, belongs to God.[15] Third, leaders exercise oversight.[16] The flock belongs to the Lord, the chief Shepherd, but he has entrusted his flock into the care of leaders in his physical absence.[17] Fourth, Peter specifically exhorts the leaders to care for those in their charge and younger believers should follow their leaders.[18] Clearly, biblical leadership involves authority over others. Oversight of the flock means the leader must tend to their direction as well as their needs. Fifth, leaders should lead willingly, not under compulsion.[19] A leader's motivation is at the heart of this principle. The Apostle charges leaders to serve out of a "free and joyous response to God's love," not self-serving compulsion. Sixth, leaders should lead by example and not be domineering.[20] Peter may recall Jesus warning not to lead as worldly rulers do.[21] In keeping with verse 2, Peter may be charging the leaders not to use their power and authority for personal benefit over those of their people.[22] Instead of abusing power and position, Peter urges them to lead by example. Seventh, leaders are accountable to Christ, who brings reward with him.[23] The unfading crown of glory rewarded to leaders is no different than that given to every believer. Michaels argues poignantly that difficult times do not require leaders to take on emergency powers, but to all-the-more

13. Michaels points out that this practice of "benevolence" by identifying oneself as a fellow elder is not exclusive to 1 Peter. An angel in Revelation 19:10 and 22:9 assures John that his is a fellow servant with John. Michaels, *1 Peter*, 280. Also Leahy, "A Study of Peter as a Model for Servant Leadership," 5.

14. 1 Pet 5:2

15. Michaels, *1 Peter*, 282.

16. 1 Pet 5:2.

17. Michaels, *1 Peter*, 283.

18. 1 Peter 5:2, 5.

19. 1 Peter 5:2.

20. 1 Peter 5:3.

21. Mark 10:42–45.

22. Michaels, *1 Peter*, 285.

23. 1 Peter 5:4.

continue to be examples for the flock of Christ.[24] Our will and desires must be overwhelmed by the Lord's ways and delight.

How do missions leaders serve the Lord? Mission leaders exercise humble authority as stewards of God's people in obedience to God. They provide oversight willingly, not under compulsion from internal or external motivations. They lead by example and are accountable to Christ, who brings reward with him for all believers, leaders and followers alike.

Analysis of Transformational Leadership.

How does Bass' transformational leadership theory measure up to the seven principles discussed above? His theory does not promote robust and authoritative behavior but does call for leaders to demonstrate confidence in their purpose, goals, and actions. Transformational leaders articulate a clear vision and communicate expectations and reasonable goals with a clear path for success—establishing a cognitive framework for implementation. These behaviors are in keeping with authority, but Bass never challenges leaders to be humble. Therefore, only a modified transformational leadership theory is compatible with leadership in Christian missions.

Transformational leadership theory champions that leaders serve mutual goals, not God. Obedience to God, or to any authority for that matter, is not a stated or implied aspect of Bass' theory. Bass' leaders are responsible people who emphasize moral values, but his approach does not include the principle of stewardship of God's people.

Bass' theory expects leaders to provide oversight by speaking truthfully to followers about expectations and mistakes. Transformational leaders coach and mentor followers to help them succeed out of the follower's strengths and abilities; they are not hesitant to correct in private and praise in public. As such, the theory is compatible with biblical leadership behavior.

Transformational leaders are tenacious and selfless, demonstrating confident self-control. These characteristics may indicate that they lead willingly and without compulsion. As with the previous behaviors, transformational leadership appears to be compatible, though not overtly affirming the biblical principle of willing service.

Modeling and coaching are primary means of influence for transformational leaders, consistent with the biblical principle to lead by example and

24. Michaels, *1 Peter*, 290–91.

not dominate others. The final principle in Paul's charge to Timothy, to serve God through his church leadership is accountability to Christ. Accountability in Bass' formulation is limited to a diffuse notion of transcendental values, a general altruistic morality, and mutually held purposes and goals. A clear, overt accountability to Christ is necessary for transformational leadership theory to work in the setting of the Christian mission.

The Leaders as Servant to Others: How do Leaders Serve Others?

A core biblical theme is that leaders serve others for Christ's glory. When the religious leaders asked Jesus to name the most important commandment, he replied that to love God is the foremost commandment and that a second like it is to love your neighbor as yourself.[25] Leaders of Jesus' day, arguably today, were known to exercise authority over their people. Jesus taught his disciples a new paradigm of leadership—one in which authority is used to serve others, for the Son of Man came to serve and give his life as a ransom.[26]

When Paul commended Timothy to the church at Philippi, he illustrated this leadership theme by serving others for Christ's glory. He noted that leaders like Timothy were hard to come by. Specifically, Paul notes that Timothy was genuinely concerned for the welfare of others, but when he does, Paul compares Timothy to others who look after their interests, not Christ's.[27] Timothy's leadership is not altruistic care but Christocentric care for others—the ultimate interest is Christ.

Service to others as taught to Timothy by Paul.

In 1 Timothy 3:1–7, Paul provides leadership selection criteria and gives insight into biblical leadership behavior toward others. Those who aspire to lead must prove themselves through personal discipline and display leadership ability.[28] The one skill requirement in the list of character requirements

25. Matt 22:36–40.

26. Matt 20:25–28.

27. Phil 2:20–22.

28. See Oginde, "Antecedents of Christian Leadership," 23–31. Leaders must exercise personal discipline: be above reproach, the husband of one wife, sober-minded, self-controlled, respectable, hospitable, able to teach, not a drunkard, not violent but gentle,

is the ability to teach.[29] In 2 Timothy 2:1–3:2, Paul is concerned about teaching and proper doctrine, just as Peter was in his epistle.[30] In his second letter to Timothy, Paul articulates profound teaching on the role of God's servant. He outlines eleven characteristics of God's servant who leads. First, God's servant is courageous in God's love, power, and self-control. Second, he obeys and guards God's Word, the good deposit that Paul terms "the oracles of God" in his letter to the church at Romans 3:2. Third, he teaches others, who are faithful to the Word of God and able to teach others. Fourth, God's servant is single-minded in his devotion to the Lord's commands, even in suffering. Fifth, he serves according to the rules; shortcuts do not tempt him to fame. Sixth, he works hard for future gain. Seventh, he endures with Christ. Eighth, God's servant rightly handles the Word of God. Ninth, he is God's vessel, sanctified and useful to the Lord. Tenth, he is a slave of Christ, humble toward others, firm in conviction and. Eleventh, God's servant is always ready to preach the Word.[31]

The eleven characteristics of leadership behavior from 2 Timothy can be summarized under the following four themes:

1. A servant of God: A leader is God's vessel, sanctified and, therefore, useful and to the Lord, a slave of Christ, humble toward others, firm in conviction, submits to the Lordship of Christ, obeys and guards God's Word, and is single-minded in his devotion to the Lord.

2. Courageous in God's love and power: A leader displays self-control, is compliant to God's ways; he is not tempted by short-cuts to fame.

3. Preaches and teaches the Word of God: A leader rightly handles the Word of God, is ready to preach the Word, and teaches others who are able to teach others.

---

not quarrelsome, not a lover of money (1 Tim 3:2–3). Leaders should display leadership ability: manage his own household well, not be a recent convert, and be well thought of by outsiders. 1 Tim 3:4–7.

29. 1 Tim 3:2.

30. 1 Tim 1:3–5. Schnabel insists that the leadership requirements listed by Paul in 1 Timothy 3 and Titus 1 are "fundamental . . . for the missionaries who establish churches." Schnabel, *Paul the Missionary*, 389.

31. Bredfeldt maintains that leaders lead best by teaching God's Word. Teachers exert significant influence, bring about change, and push followers to grow. Bredfeldt, *Great Leader, Great Teacher*, 18.

4. Works hard and endures with Christ: A leader serves according to God's ways and for future gain.

Leading as a teacher of God's word address the key elements of a theology of leadership. Teaching God's Word helps maintain awareness of God's purposes and is the primary means to accomplish the biblical directives to share the gospel and make disciples. The ontological aspect of leadership calling and character are firmly grounded in the Bible. Leading as a teacher of the word affirms the Bible as the central authority and brings the power of God's eternal Word to bear. Power in teaching relies on persuasion and less on positional power or charisma which a leader may or may not have. Finally, pertaining to ethic leading as a teacher of God's Word keeps the leader accountable to God.

Analysis of Transformational Leadership.

How does Bass' transformational leadership theory measure up to the four leadership themes from 2 Timothy enumerated above? Nowhere does Bass' work support the notion that leaders should be servants of God, submitted to his Lordship. Leaders in Bass' formulation model high moral standards. Bass' expectation that leaders follow a high moral standard is as close as he gets to the biblical expectation that leaders submit to God's will. Transformational leadership theory is committed to self–actualization, humanistic altruism, and an open view toward truth, which are antithetical to a leader submitted to the Lordship of Christ.

Confidence, self–control, responsibility, willingness to take risks, and dissatisfaction with the *status quo* are characteristics of transformational leadership behavior that are in line with courage. The biblical notion of courage, however, is rooted in God's character, not self–confidence. The discrepancy between biblical courage and transformational leadership confidence and risk taking may result in similar courageous behavior with different rationales.

Transformational leaders teach and coach, but Bass does not characterize this behavior as preaching. Bass' leaders articulate vision, teach moral standards, model behavior, speak truth, are persuasive, develop others, promote intellectual growth and rational problem–solving, correct mistakes, and question assumptions—all arguably consistent with the biblical theme that leaders preach and teach God's Word.

Transformational leaders work hard and are persistent. They demonstrate trustworthiness and responsibility, gain respect, inspire others, and are tenacious. The goal, or motivation, for perseverance in Paul's letter to Timothy is union with Christ and for his glory. Bass' scheme is insufficient in this area.

Summary

The theological examination of Bass' transformational leadership theory determined that areas of compatibility and incompatibility exist between Bass' theory and a biblically-based theology of leadership. The general core elements of Bass' theory—Idealized Influence, Inspirational Motivation, Intellectual Stimulation, and Individualized Consideration—are compatible with biblical theology. A biblical theology of leadership affirms that leaders articulate a compelling vision, are confident, hold to high moral standards, serve as role models, and are trustworthy, responsible, and ethical people respected by others—characteristics of Idealized Influence. The Bible teaches that leaders should inspire, teach, be optimistic and enthusiastic, work hard toward goals, speak the truth, persuade, be willing to take risks for the noble cause, and communicate expectations—characteristics of Inspirational Motivation. The Bible promotes intellectual growth, rational processing, and problem-solving, and commends that leaders confront people for their mistakes, question assumptions, and offer praise and encouragement—items associated with Intellectual Stimulation. A biblical theology of leadership challenges leaders to pay attention to individual gifting and skills, coach and mentor followers—as with Individualized Consideration.

Incompatibility between Bass' transformational leadership theory and a biblical theology of leadership can be categorized in two ways: first, those items that are incompatible with a biblical theology of leadership and, second, those items that are part of a biblical theology of leadership that are lacking in Bass' formulation.

Within the first category, this research concludes that four of Bass' requirements for transformational leadership are incompatible with a biblical theology of leadership. First, Bass requires that leaders adopt and demonstrate undefined *transcendent moral values*—an element of the Idealized Influence factor. Second, he contends that leaders develop others toward self-actualization—part of Inspirational Motivation. Third, transformational leaders maintain a transcendent open–mindedness by which to access truth—vital to Intellectual Stimulation. Fourth, Bass' theory expects that leaders live out a strong altruism—a component of Intellectual Stimulation. These four aforementioned items from each of Bass' four Factors of transformational leadership are incompatible with a biblical theology of leadership in missions as argued in chapter 3 of this study.

As to the second category of incompatibility, a biblical theology of leadership calls for elements that are not included in Bass' theory. A biblical theology of leadership in missions needs leaders who are committed to and dependent upon the revealed, objective truth of God. Such leaders should be motivated not out of a desire for self–actualization but out of a desire for God's glory through love and self–sacrifice. A biblical ontology of leadership requires leaders who are called to serve God's purposes and who model godly character. Biblical theology requires that leaders acknowledge the power of the Holy Spirit and the authority that comes from God's Word and submit to it. A biblical ethic of leadership extolls trust in God's provision, stewardship of God's people, the courage to stay the course in the midst of opposition, and hope in God's reward. These items are essential to a biblical framework of leadership and are not part of Bass' theory—even contradictory to his theory at some points.

Because of the serious nature of the discontinuity between Bass' transformational leadership theory and a biblical theology of leadership, I recommend a reformulation of transformational leadership theory with an explicit biblical foundation. Before that reformulation, we must also consider the effect and implications of culture on leadership theory and practice.

PART 3

Assess the Influence of Culture on the Leadership Theory

IN THIS SECTION, I describe how culture can influence leadership theory and practice. To begin, I will provide a succinct description and critique of the two primary research approaches to describing culture in leadership studies. Then, in chapter 8, I describe Hofstede's six dimensions of culture. In chapter 9, I provide a brief review of literature pertinent to the dimension of culture and transformational leadership and assess the integration of Bass' transformational leadership factors with Hofstede's dimensions of culture.

Intercultural leadership is growing into a distinct field of study. Significant research, such as that by Geert Hofstede, the GLOBE study, Richard Lewis, and Erin Meyer contribute to this specialized domain of academic research.[1] Academic organizations, such as the International Leadership Association and centers of study like the Regent University School of Business and Leadership, enhance the quality and consistency

1. Hofstede, *Culture's Consequences*; Hofstede et al., *Cultures and Organizations*; Chhokar et al., *Culture and Leadership across the World*; House et al., *Culture, Leadership, and Organizations*; Meyer, *Culture Map*; Lewis, *Cultural Imperative*; Lewis, *When Cultures Collide*.

of leadership studies. These efforts to build up the science of leadership are furthered by journals such as *The Leadership Quarterly*, *Advances in Global Leadership*, the *Journal of Perspectives in Biblical Leadership*, and *The International Journal of Leadership Studies*. Cultural influence assessment of leadership theory is needed because many individuals and organizations harness leadership theories and practices developed from a particular cultural perspective and apply them with little or no cultural assessment. When it comes to research in field of business and leadership, two approaches stand above the rest.

The first is Geert Hofstede's work on the dimensions of culture, and the second is the GLOBE study by Robert House. Culture in these instances refers to the cognitive, affective, and behavioral patterns within a given group of people—the rules by which members of a society interact.[2] This learned pattern or "collective programming of the mind," as Hofstede refers to it, is what sets one culture apart from another.[3]

Culture helps people interpret the world around them, express themselves to others in meaningful ways, and identify who is part of a society and who is not. Culture is a function of a society. Societies are units of social organization bound together by the cognitive, affective, and behavioral patterns called culture. Nations, on the other hand, are political entities and may consist of more than one culture. Hofstede recognizes that nations are not societies but argues that strong forces, such as national pride, a common language, and commercial and educational systems, help unify several cultures under a single national identity—a national culture.[4] He measures cultural expression at the level of society, but to make research manageable, Hofstede and many other researchers refer to cultural expressions as typical of one nation. This simplification of phenomena makes it possible for researchers to deal with large data and highly complex human interactions. The resulting nomenclature gives us handholds for otherwise unwieldy ideas, but we must guard against using descriptive work in an overly predictive, fixed way. Whereas the cultural categories and tags identified and made by Hofstede and many others are

---

2. For more definitive work on the topic of culture see: Grunlan and Mayers, *Cultural Anthropology*, 39; Hesselgrave, *Communicating Christ Cross-Culturally*, 164; Hiebert, *Anthropological Reflections on Missiological Issues*, 30; Kraft, *Anthropology for Christian Witness*, 38; Van Rheenen, *Communicating Christ in Animistic Contexts*, 81; Spradley, *Participant Observation*, 24.

3. Hofstede et al., *Cultures and Organizations*, 6.

4. Hofstede et al., *Cultures and Organizations*, 5–6, 20–22, 24.

helpful, they are not intended to be used as restrictive categories. Even with these stipulations, these systems are important means to help us understand complex interpersonal engagements.

In his work, Hofstede argued against the universality of psychological, sociological, and managerial theories and his early research identified four cultural dimensions that differentiate cultures in such a way as to influence management practices.[5] His study was done in 1968 and 1972 with over 116,000 predominantly non–managerial IMB employees in fifty countries and later corroborated by the Rokeach Value Survey.[6] Both the IBM survey and the Rokeach Value Survey are findings of western researchers. Consequently, Hofstede was concerned that the resulting cultural dimensions, although validated by another completely independent set of data, are the product of Western—oriented questions given to non–Westerners. Michael Bond, another Westerner, resolved the problem by asking a group of Chinese researchers to develop a set of values questions for Chinese people. The results of this Chinese Value Survey (CVS) correlated with Hofstede's research at IBM and the Rokeach Value Survey, with one exception. The CVS research had no equivalent to *uncertainty avoidance* and demonstrated a fifth dimension of culture, which Hofstede labeled *long–term orientation versus short–term orientation.*[7] Ronald Inglehart added a sixth dimension, *indulgence versus restraint,* as a result of examining the World Values Survey.[8] Hofstede's six cultural dimensions help define cultural differentiation. The dimensions are Power Distance, Individualism and Collectivism, Masculinity and Femininity, Uncertainty Avoidance, Long–Term Orientation versus Short–Term Orientation, and Indulgence versus Restraint. Table 5 depicts Hofstede's dimensions that form the backbone of a cultural assessment of transformational leadership theory.

5. Hofstede et al., *Cultures and Organizations*, xi.

6. Hofstede et al., *Cultures and Organizations*, 37.

7. Hofstede et al., *Cultures and Organizations*, 37–38.

8. Hofstede et al., *Cultures and Organizations*, 44–45.

Table 5. Hofstede's Dimensions of Culture

Hofstede's Dimensions	Description
Power Distance (PDI)	What is the general perception of dependence on others?
Individualism–Collectivism (IDV)	How do people see themselves in relation to others?
Masculinity–Femineity (MAS)	What is the attitude toward assertiveness and roles?
Uncertainty Avoidance (UAI)	What is the level of tolerance of ambiguity?
Long–Term vs. Short–Term Orientation (LTO)	What time–related values are important?
Indulgence vs. Restraint (IDR)	What is the importance of personal liberty, leisure, and happiness?

The Global Leadership and Organizational Behavior Effectiveness (GLOBE) study is a comprehensive work that identifies leader behaviors, attributes, and organizational practices both universal and distinct across the global spectrum. Robert J. House and his team at the Wharton School of Business started with Hofstede's dimensions of culture to develop a system of understanding leadership throughout the world. The GLOBE research began with an investigation of 17,000 managers in 951 companies in 62 societies from 1994–1997.[9] The work resulted in a system of nine categories. Table 6 displays Hofstede's dimensions alongside the GLOBE categories. The GLOBE system appears to have created several categories to describe singular dimensions in Hofstede's approach. At face value, it appears that the GLOBE nomenclature intentionally avoids Hofstede's gender–associated labels. For example, Hofstede ascribes assertiveness and performance orientation ascribed as masculine characteristics and caring and nurturing as feminine qualities.

---

9. House et al., "Project GLOBE: An Introduction." 489–505.

Table 6. Comparing Hofstede's Dimensions to the GLOBE Categories

Hofstede's Dimensions	GLOBE Categories
Power Distance	Power Distance
Individualism—Collectivism	Institutional Collectivism
	In–Group Collectivism
Masculinity—Femininity	Gender Egalitarianism
	Assertiveness
	Humane Orientation
	Performance Orientation
Uncertainty Avoidance	Uncertainty Avoidance
Long–Term vs. Short–Term Orientation	Future Orientation
Indulgence vs. Restraint	

The GLOBE study delves into the acceptability and effectiveness of leadership behavior in various societies and organizational cultures, and how society and organizational cultures affect those behaviors. House and his team identify six culturally–endorsed implicit leadership dimensions: Charismatic/Value–based, Team–oriented, Self–protective, Participative, Humane–oriented, and Autonomous.[10] I considered using Project GLOBE's dimensions for this research but believe that Hofstede's emic approach to culture and the smaller number of cultural dimensions is more appropriate for this study.[11]

---

10. House et al., *Culture, Leadership, and Organizations*, 19.

11. See Jagdeep S. Chhokar et al., *Culture and Leadership across the World.*

Chapter 8

Six Dimensions of Culture

HOFSTEDE'S CULTURAL DIMENSIONS ARE a useful tool to gauge the universality of a leadership theory. Some research indicates that many transformational and charismatic leadership features are transferable between cultures. The argument goes, for example, that integrity, justice, and honesty are transferable leadership concepts welcome in any or most cultures.[1] Followers in numerous cultures enjoy charismatic, encouraging, positive, motivating, dynamic and visionary leaders who build confidence.[2] Despite these universals, some aspects of leadership show variation between cultures, the argument continues.[3] The apparent universality of concepts notwithstanding, many researchers distinguish between *levels of universality*. Two such levels are *simple universal*—in which the construct in question is consistent throughout the world and *variform universal*—in which the general principle is consistent throughout the world, but the expression of the principle is culturally influenced.[4] Leadership features such as independence, risk-taking, avoiding conflict, a subdued personality, status

---

1. Hartog et al., "Culture Specific and Cross-Culturally Generalizable Implicit Leadership Theories," 237.

2. Hartog et al., "Culture Specific and Cross-Culturally Generalizable Implicit Leadership Theories," 240.

3. Hartog et al., "Culture Specific and Cross-Culturally Generalizable Implicit Leadership Theories," 231.

4. Lonner, "The Search for Psychological Universals," 143–204.

consciousness, self–effacing behaviors, sensitivity, and individualism are very important in some cultures but not at all important in others. Leadership features not associated with transformational leadership, such as evasiveness, provocation, domineering attitude, elitism, and a ruling style, are abhorred in some cultures but are only a slight infraction in others.[5] Therefore, we must take care to understand the impact of culture of expressions of leadership theories and practices.

Before assessing a theory or practice culturally, we need to understand some of the categories and perms that aid such as evaluation. Following are brief descriptions and explanations of power distance, individualism and collectivism, masculinity and femineity, uncertainty avoidance, long–term and short–term outlook, and indulgence restraint from the work of Geert Hofstede and his colleagues.

Power Distance

Every society displays power inequity. The manner by which people manage power inequity, however, differs from one culture to another. Power may be associated with physical strength, wealth, position, or some other measure. Power in one aspect of life may or may not be associated with power in another. For example, the village chief may not demonstrate power as an agile hunter. Hofstede defines power distance as "the extent to which the less powerful members of institutions and organizations within a country expect and accept that power is distributed unequally."[6]

Power distance is measured from the perspective of the less powerful, not the more powerful. Usually, power is discussed from the viewpoint of the powerful, which makes the Power Distance Index (PDI) unique. The PDI defines a society's general perception of dependence. Subordinates in societies with a low power distance have little dependence on their managers and prefer consultation and interdependence in their work relationships. The emotional distance between subordinate and boss is small, and their perception of reality and their preferred reality are closely related. Subordinates in low power distance societies are not afraid of their managers, feel their managers are not autocratic and prefer it that way.[7]

5. Hartog et al., "Culture Specific and Cross–Culturally Generalizable Implicit Leadership Theories," 241.

6. Hofstede et al., *Cultures and Organizations*, 54, 61.

7. Hofstede et al., *Cultures and Organizations*, 61. Hofstede finds that managers'

In contrast, subordinates in societies with a high power–distance report a high degree of dependence on their bosses.[8] The emotional distance in these cultures is large, meaning subordinates are not likely to approach, much less contradict their managers. A significant polarization shows up in these instances. Subordinates in high power distance societies either prefer the dependence, which they acknowledge exists in their relationships with their managers, or they reject that dependence outright. Many subordinates in high power distance societies are afraid of their managers and believe that their managers are autocratic. Some prefer the emotional gap that exists between themselves and their supervisors, while others disdain it.

The national perception of power distance is strongly related to cultural values. Bond's Chinese Values Survey reports that high power distance societies tend to believe that ordinary people should have few desires and live moderate, disinterested, and "pure" lives.[9] Adaptability, carefulness, and problem–solving are important values in low power distance societies. The data from Hofstede's study is drawn primarily from middle–class people with at least a secondary education who were employed in sales or service at IBM. The researchers argue that middle–class values represent the country inasmuch as they have a direct effect on the institutions of a society. Interestingly, high power distance countries display little socioeconomic differentiation, but in low power distance countries, lower–status, lower–educated segments display high power distance scores and hold more authoritarian values.[10]

Cultural norms and their associated values are learned early in life and family values, therefore, may have a powerful influence on culture and broadly held values.[11] Values set at early stages in life are very strong and hard to change. Children in high power distance societies are expected to obey their parents and show respect to elders. This respect frequently means

---

self–ratings closely match the leadership style they prefer in their bosses, but their subordinates' ratings do not match their manager's self–rating or preferred style. He claims further that the best predictor of subordinate ratings is to look at the manager's rating of his boss.

8. Hofstede et al., *Cultures and Organizations*, 61.

9. Bond's work was published under the nickname of his research team. Chinese Culture Connection, "Chinese Values and the Search for Culture–Free Dimensions of Culture," 143–64.

10. Hofstede et al., *Cultures and Organizations*, 63–64.

11. Hofstede et al., *Cultures and Organizations*, 67–68.

that children will care for their aging parents and grandparents, often taking them in as they become unable to care for themselves.

The situation in low power distance societies is quite different. Children are treated as equals and parents encourage them to make decisions and experiment with many different things. Formal respect is rarely a cultural norm in low power distance societies. Independence is highly valued.[12] Once in school, teachers join parents as important influencers in a child's life. Values learned in childhood remain fairly constant, even after the child goes to school. In high power distance societies, that which a teacher transmits is personal wisdom, not impersonal truth.[13] In low power distance societies, students may argue with teachers and are expected to carve out their own paths to the future. Teachers pass on truth as an impersonal notion—unrelated to the teacher.[14]

Power distance, well–established early in life, continues into the workplace. Hofstede reports that high power distance workplaces manifest a widely accepted inequality in pay, benefits, status symbols, and privileges.[15] Supervisors are abundant in such societies and work within a centralized system dependent on rules to accomplish the desires of the boss. Subordinates are expected to behave as directed, and the ideal boss is a benevolent dictator. Relationships are laden with emotion—typically, subordinates either admire or loathe their manager.

Low power distance workplaces are characterized by the inequity of roles, not people. People, therefore, can move up and down within an organization's hierarchy.[16] Workers are highly qualified in low power distance workplaces, and highly skilled labor is seen as important as lower–skilled office work. Supervisors are few and work in a decentralized system dependent on the manager's experience and the subordinate's input. Subordinates expect to be consulted, and the ideal boss is resourceful and democratic, although the boss makes the final decision. Supervisory relationships are practical—to ensure that work runs smoothly.

Hofstede remarks that management techniques from the United States, a middle–range power distance society, are likely to fail in high power distance societies because they require manager-employee bargaining that

12. Hofstede et al., *Cultures and Organizations*, 67–68
13. Hofstede et al., *Cultures and Organizations*, 69.
14. Hofstede et al., *Cultures and Organizations*, 70.
15. Hofstede et al., *Cultures and Organizations*, 73–74.
16. Hofstede et al., *Cultures and Organizations*, 74.

is out of character for high power distance societies.[17] The temptation to export management techniques from one culture to another is strong when a society is perceived to be successful. For example, many management techniques, especially quality management processes, were imported from Japan to the United States in the 1970s. Hofstede argues that no research backs up the claim that methods from either end of the PDI spectrum are more effective than the other.[18] The critical notion is that leaders understand how to maximize the host society's values and norms for the organization's benefit. For example, high power distance workers may be embarrassed or feel let down by a boss who steps out of his role to ask an employee's opinion. In the same light, a low power distance worker may feel oppressed by a manager who gives direction without asking for input.

Individualism–Collectivism

How do the members of a given society see themselves in relation to other members? Some societies tend toward a sense of *I* and other toward a feeling of *we*, but all have ways of defining who is in and who is out—*us* and *them*. Cultural anthropologists and sociologists refer to societies as collectivist or individualist to understand and identify these notions of who is in one's group and who is out. Individualism is common in societies in which a person's core responsibilities to self and his immediate family. Collectivism expresses as a strong pattern of belonging to the group, normally beyond the family where protection or the reward of loyalty.[19] The IBM survey identifies a society's tendency toward individualism or collectivism by asking questions designed to measure an employee's feelings of independence from or dependence on the organization. The degree of individualism or collectivism is scaled on the Individualism Index (IDV).

The level of analysis is critical to the individualism–collectivism dimension. Individuals can hold a mix of individualist and collectivist values. An individual can score high for both individualist and collectivist, low for both and any mix thereof.[20] Therefore, the two dimensions must be assessed separately when measuring individual people. Societies tend toward one end of the IDV scale or the other is evident at the level of

17. Hofstede et al., *Cultures and Organizations*, 74

18. Hofstede et al., *Cultures and Organizations*, 75.

19. Hofstede et al., *Cultures and Organizations*, 92.

20. Hofstede et al., *Cultures and Organizations*, 102.

society. For example, a society that reflects mostly individualist values will reflect few collectivist values and vice versa.

The Individualism Index shows a strong negative correlation to PDI. Societies that have a high power distance are most likely to have an IDV rating of similar intensity but in the opposite direction.[21] Societies with a low power distance will most likely show a high IDV of similar intensity as their power distance rating. If one plots national PDI scores against national IDV scores, the result is close to a 1:1 negative correlation. If the correlation is so strong, why measure the two as distinct from one another? Costa Rica, Switzerland, Belgium, and France completely break the PDI–IDV correlation. Costa Rica is a very low individualism society, quite collectivist, and with a very low power distance. Because several societies break the strong negative correlation pattern, Hofstede and his colleagues maintain IDV as a distinctive measure of culture.

People in individualist societies tend to look after themselves and their immediate families. Children are taught to stand on their own and think in terms of *me*. Communication is direct and low context in individualist societies. In these societies, direct speech is associated with honesty, and individuals tend to be more self–reliant. Low–context communication is more verbal, information is passed along in explicit terms, and business contracts are longer.

Sin leads to guilt and loss of respect. Guilt is an aspect of an individually held conscience and occurs when one breaks a rule. One feels guilty, even in secret.[22] Students from individualist societies expressed values such as tolerance, harmony, non–competitiveness, trustworthiness, solidarity, and conservatism according to the Chinese Value Survey, presumably because relationships with others are not set by family lines but must be fostered.[23]

Collectivist societies guard the in–group—usually the extended family. Children are taught to think in terms of *we*. Communication is high–context in these societies, less is spoken, and more is implied, and business contracts are shorter. Harmony is a high social value. The family expects individuals to chip–in and support the family. Students from collectivist societies rate the values of familial fidelity, female chastity, and

---

21. Hofstede et al., *Cultures and Organizations*, 102–5.

22. Hofstede et al., *Cultures and Organizations*, 106–13.

23. Hofstede et al., *Cultures and Organizations*, 100.

patriotism as important values. These values are those that shore–up and protect the in–group relationship.[24]

The differences between individualist and collectivist societies extend into school and the workplace. Hofstede relates how a teacher from an individualist society might be frustrated in a classroom of students from a collectivist society when the teacher asks the class a question and no one answers.[25] From the students' point of view, it would be improper for them to self–select to be the class spokesperson. The solution is for the teacher to ask a particular student to reply. Students from collectivist societies are reluctant to speak up from the crowd so breaking the class into small groups for discussion often solves the problem. Another distinction is that members from collectivist societies expect preferential treatment by teachers, judges, or referees from their own society when in heterogeneous cultural contexts. Nepotism, a seriously immoral act in an individualist society, is expected and viewed as proper. In a collectivist society, a teacher should avoid conflict and inadvertently shaming a student in low IDV societies.

Students from individualist societies expect to be treated individually and impartially.[26] Education in individualistic societies is primarily designed to teach students how to learn. However, education is a rite of passage in collectivist societies. Completing an education bestows honor on the graduate and his family. Therefore, it is not unusual for a student to get a diploma by any means necessary.

Employees in individualist societies are expected to operate on their self–interest. Employers look for and manage toward some kind of intersection of the employee's and corporation's interests. Hiring is best done based on a person's individual skill or ability. Nepotism is frowned upon. Workplace relationships are contractual and performance appraisals, individual work objectives, and training methods that involve asking participants to share their feelings about one another are common. Management in an individualist society is about managing the individual.[27]

In collectivist societies, employees are usually hired from within the in–group and, therefore, tend to act in the group's best interests. Managers do well to hire family members because their sense of loyalty comes ready–made. Direct confrontation over performance may cause serious

24. Hofstede et al., *Cultures and Organizations*, 100.

25. Hofstede et al., *Cultures and Organizations*, 117.

26. Hofstede et al., *Cultures and Organizations*, 118–19.

27. Hofstede et al., *Cultures and Organizations*, 119–23.

shame. Sometimes an intermediary is necessary to deliver bad news or frank talk about poor performance. Management in a collectivist society is about managing the group and *particularism*—honoring in-group members—is culturally appropriate.[28]

Masculinity–Femininity

Hofstede's third cultural dimension concerns assertiveness. The Masculinity Index (MAS) is the only dimension in which men's and women's scores were consistently different, with the notable exception of societies with extremely low MAS scores. Societies scoring high in masculinity demonstrate more concern for earnings, recognition for a job well done, the opportunity to advance, and appreciate challenging work. Societies scoring low in masculinity, tending toward the feminine pole, show more interest in positive work relationships, cooperation, a living situation that is good for the family, and job security. In a masculine society, "gender roles are clearly distinct: men are supposed to be assertive, tough, and focused on material success, whereas women are supposed to be more modest, tender, and concerned with the quality of life."[29] In a feminine society, "emotional gender roles overlap: both men and women are supposed to be modest, tender, and concerned with the quality of life."[30]

Masculinity–Femininity and Individualism–Collectivism are often confused. Individualism–Collectivism is a measure of independence or dependence on the in-group, but the Masculinity–Femininity dimension is about personal assertiveness versus relationship maintenance.[31]

The development and stability of gender roles is a volatile issue. This cultural dimension is laden with values and morals which, from Hofstede's perspective, are completely dependent values. He claims that there can be no moral standard—that morality is in the "eye of the beholder" and that acts are judged according to their associated cultural norms.[32] Although I reject Hofstede's stance on the particular nature of morality,

28. Hofstede et al., *Cultures and Organizations*, 118–19

29. Hofstede et al., *Cultures and Organizations*, 140. The most masculine societies measured by Hofstede were Slovakia, Japan, Hungary, Austria, and Venezuela.

30. Hofstede et al., *Cultures and Organizations*, 139. The most feminine societies measured by Hofstede were Sweden, Norway, Latvia, the Netherlands, and Denmark.

31. Hofstede et al., *Cultures and Organizations*, 146.

32. Hofstede et al., *Cultures and Organizations*, 158.

Hofstede's insights into this domain remain important because he reflects a commonly held post–modern view of morality. The family is a critical part of determining and stabilizing the patterns of gender roles in society. An interesting experiment reported by Hofstede demonstrated that boys and girls in higher masculinity societies choose games different from the other gender, whereas they choose the same kinds of games as one another in societies higher in femininity. In the United States, boys choose competitive games and girls choose games that emphasize relationships and inclusiveness. In much more feminine Holland, boys and girls choose the same, more feminine games.[33]

Plotting power distance and masculinity–femininity indices against each other helps explain some cultural differences in parenting. High power distance and high masculinity societies tend to encourage dominant fathers and submissive mothers—Slovakia and Venezuela are examples of such countries. High power distance and low masculinity usually means both parents are dominant, yet tender—Russia and Thailand exemplify this mix. Low power distance and high masculinity societies have two non–dominant parents in families in which fathers are tough and deal with the facts and mothers are less tough and deal with feelings—in the United States for example. Finally, low power distance and low masculinity results in equal and tender parenting in which both parents are concerned with nurturing relationships—such as in Sweden and the Netherlands.[34] Remember that these are broad–sweeping generalizations and individuals do not always display the same norms and dimensions of their society or to the same degree.

The social constructs learned in childhood are reinforced in school.[35] Teachers are more likely to encourage and praise weaker students rather than highlight better students in low masculinity societies. Average performance is considered normal in low masculinity societies and assertive students may become the objects of ridicule. Things are quite the opposite in masculine cultures. Excellence, considered by some to be a masculine term, is the rule of the day in high masculinity societies. In high masculinity societies, teachers praise and award excellence, students compete openly, and the majority of students believe themselves to be among the best.

---

33. Hofstede et al., *Cultures and Organizations*, 153.
34. Hofstede et al., *Cultures and Organizations*, 151–52.
35. Hofstede et al., *Cultures and Organizations*, 158–63.

The general work ethos in feminine societies is "work to live," but in masculine societies the tenant is "live to work."[36] Reward in low masculinity societies tends to be based on equality—according to need, whereas in high masculinity societies the rewards tend to be based on equity—according to performance. Low masculinity in a culture does not mean that women will not work outside the home or family setting. The role of women in the workplace has more to do with opportunity and necessity than the issue of masculinity versus femininity. The more masculine a culture is, the more it tends to hold different standards of behavior for men and women. Feminine cultures tend to have a single standard of behavior, and that standard may be strict or loose.[37] All these generalizations are mediated by other dimensions, especially power distance and IDV.

Uncertainty Avoidance

Ambiguity left unchecked leads to anxiety.[38] Societies develop measures to manage extreme ambiguity, but the level of ambiguity that a society can tolerate varies greatly across the globe. The range of ambiguity tolerance in a culture can be quantified by the Uncertainly Avoidance Index (UAI). Uncertainty is "the extent to which the members of a culture feel threatened by ambiguous or unknown situations."[39] Hofstede and his colleagues measure uncertainly avoidance by assessing the level of: 1) job stress—feeling nervous or tense at work, 2) rule orientation—feeling toward rule–keeping at work, and 3) intent toward long–term careers with a company. Survey responses to these three issues do not measure individual uncertainly avoidance, but societies whose majority of people answered positively to the diagnostic questions are societies that express much higher need for explicit written and unwritten rules. Societies that share similar scores for PDI, IDV, and MAS do not necessarily share similar scores in UAI; therefore, the Uncertainly Index stands out as a distinct cultural dimension.

High uncertainly avoidance societies tend to be more expressive. Members of high uncertainly avoidance societies tend to talk with their hands, pound the table, or raise their voices. Low uncertainly avoidance society members tend not to demonstrate aggression, and people from

36. Hofstede et al., *Cultures and Organizations*, 164–70.

37. Hofstede et al., *Cultures and Organizations*, 156–57, 167.

38. Hofstede et al., *Cultures and Organizations*, 190–95.

39. Hofstede et al., *Cultures and Organizations*, 191.

high uncertainly avoidance societies appear to be emotional and aggressive. All societies teach their children what is clean and dirty, safe and dangerous, but the definition of clean and safe differs greatly from culture to culture. The terms "dirty" and "dangerous" have tight definitions in high uncertainly avoidance societies, but loose, general definitions in low uncertainly avoidance societies. Parents from high uncertainly avoidance societies are likely to wipe dirt off a child who falls in the public square, but less so in low uncertainly avoidance societies. Dirt and danger categories extend to feelings about people and ideas. Notions of good and bad show up in cultural taboos and definitions of truth, both of which are elements of this dimension. Extreme feelings of uncertainty avoidance may be expressed as xenophobia. High uncertainly avoidance societies are concerned with truth as an absolute. Ideas that differ from the truth are considered dangerous in high uncertainly avoidance societies—summarized by the sentiment that *different is dangerous*.

Low uncertainly avoidance societies face each day as it comes. They tend to be less stressed, even laid back, and are comfortable with ambiguity. Rules for children about matters of cleanliness and dirtiness tend toward leniency, and family life tends to be relaxed. The general sentiment toward others in low uncertainly avoidance societies is that *different is interesting*.[40]

Teachers are expected to be experts in high uncertainly avoidance societies. Students want teachers who have all the answers. In some cases, such as in Germany, highly respected teachers write in difficult-to-understand language with complicated sentence structure. Hofstede's group reports that German students believe that if a subject is not hard to understand, it is probably unscientific and, therefore, suspect. Members of very high uncertainly avoidance societies often view good performance in school as circumstantial—simply fortunate for the student, according to Hofstede. Teachers are viewed as experts and, therefore, parents should not get involved in education. Parents expect to be informed of that which the teacher deems necessary for them to know. On the other end of the spectrum are low uncertainly avoidance societies. Students in low uncertainly avoidance societies will accept that a teacher does not know everything. Student effort and ability leads to good results in the low uncertainly avoidance mindset. Parents are a welcome part of the educational team in societies with a high tolerance for uncertainty avoidance.[41]

40. Hofstede et al., *Cultures and Organizations*, 200–204.
41. Hofstede et al., *Cultures and Organizations*, 205–08.

Policy and procedure are vital to the workplace in societies with a low tolerance for ambiguity—high UAI. This cultural aspect expresses itself as a busy society. People like to work hard with little idle time; after all, time is money and marks progress. Detailed job descriptions are important in these societies and organizational structure is expected to be clear and neat. Organizations tend to be made up of experts in their areas of specialty with the educational backgrounds matching their fields. Executives in high uncertainly avoidance societies occupy themselves with strategic issues, leaving operations to lower-level managers. Low uncertainly avoidance societies tend to desire few rules. People in such societies certainly work hard, but not out of an internal drive to be busy. Work is necessary because of what it produces, not as a value in-and-of-itself. Time in these societies is not a specific marker of progress, but gives one orientation or general context. Organizations are full of generalists—many hold a Liberal Arts degree. Britain is a prime example of the level of societal comfort with a general education.[42]

The characteristics of high and low uncertainly avoidance societies lead some researchers to theorize that innovation and entrepreneurialism are expressed differently according to the uncertainly avoidance orientation of a society. Hofstede did not find any correlation between uncertainly avoidance and creativity. Surprisingly, he found that self-employment is positively related to UAI—societies with high uncertainly avoidance have higher self-employment rates.[43] This result presses the point that avoiding uncertainty and ambiguity is not the same as avoiding risk because striking out on one's own and being self-employed certainly involves an element of risk. Hofstede and his fellow researchers also discovered that creativity looks different across the UAI spectrum. Low uncertainly avoidance societies tend to be good suppliers of ideas, but poor at putting those ideas into action. The opposite is true for high uncertainly avoidance societies. High uncertainly avoidance societies tend to supply fewer new ideas than low uncertainly avoidance societies, but tend to put more new ideas into action. Therefore, innovation is expressed differently at the two ends of the UAI spectrum—low uncertainly avoidance societies supply ideas and high uncertainly avoidance societies implement those ideas.

Hofstede's UAI dimension sheds light on motivation, an issue important to transformational leadership. Motivation theory in Bass' transformational

42. Hofstede et al., *Cultures and Organizations*, 210–16.
43. Hofstede et al., *Cultures and Organizations*, 211–13.

leadership relies on Abraham Maslow's needs construct ascending from physiological, to safety and security, belongingness, esteem, and finally, to self-actualization. Hofstede argues that a culture's individuality–collectivism orientation may skew Maslow's hierarchy.[44] When UAI is plotted against MAS, Hofstede finds that though Maslow's categories of need remain important, the order of needs changes according to the MAS–UAI relationship. For example, feminine societies with high uncertainly avoidance value security and belongingness—the polar opposite of masculine societies with low uncertainly avoidance, which value achievement and esteem. According to Hofstede, Maslow's hierarchy order matches those of China, Britain, the United States, South Africa, and Switzerland, but not Portugal, Russia, Costa Rica, Suriname, and Thailand. Other countries, such as Indonesia, low masculinity and low uncertainly avoidance, seek achievement and belongingness. Still others, like Japan, seek security and esteem.

Long–Term vs. Short–Term Orientation

Many behaviors relate to time. Societies demonstrate a generally short–term or generally long–term outlook on life. This outlook about time shapes behavior. Hofstede's original work with IBM did not address cultural perceptions of time. The long–term versus short–term orientation dimension did not arise out of their research because the questions were formulated by westerners for use in western societies. Later, when Hofstede looked at the Chinese Value Survey (CVS), he noted this dimension missing in his work. The CVS research was limited to twenty–three countries, so Hofstede worked with Michael Minkov to gather long–term versus short–term orientation data from a much broader population with the World Values Survey (WVS). Long–term orientation (LTO) is found in societies that foster "virtues oriented toward future rewards—in particular, perseverance and thrift." Short–term orientation (STO) is found in societies that foster "virtues related to the past and present—in particular, respect for tradition, preservation of 'face,' and fulfilling social obligations."[45] Long–term orientation and short–term orientation represent the two poles of cultural expression in this dimension. East Asian countries—South Korea, Taiwan, Japan, and China—hold the highest positions in this dimension. Except for Malaysia, Thailand, and the Philippines, South and Southeast Asian countries have a

44. Hofstede et al., *Cultures and Organizations*, 213–16.
45. Hofstede et al., *Cultures and Organizations*, 236–39, 252.

long-term view of time. Africa; The Middle East; and Central, South, and North America are more short-term in their orientation.[46]

In long-term orientation societies, parents and teachers teach children to save money and things and to persevere through hardships for a better tomorrow. Pragmatism is an important value; therefore, the society tends to be open in order to learn from other societies and countries. This pragmatic outlook also means that success and failure are viewed as a result of effort or, with regard to failure, a lack thereof. Knowledge and education, seen as providing a long-term benefit, are highly esteemed in long-term orientation societies.[47]

Parents and teachers in short-term orientation countries stress service to others as a high cultural value. Children learn that tradition is as important as is pride in one's family. Good luck brings success and bad luck results in failure. Many short-term orientation societies maintain strong traditions of folk wisdom and practice witchcraft. Hofstede argues that these societies are prone to fundamentalism, especially in the three monotheistic religions: Christianity, Islam, and Judaism. Societies with long-term orientation are focused more on virtue than revealed truth. Confucianism, for example, plays a significant role in developing the rational basis for many long-term orientation virtues such as pragmatism and thrift. Societies with short-term orientation tend to emphasize truth, especially revealed truth. Virtue is important in short-term orientation societies, argues Hofstede, but this virtue is derived from truth as revealed in the holy books. Hofstede is quite biased against short-term orientation cultural reliance on these "old holy books" and complains that such societies cannot cope with the modern world. In the face of "backwardness and poverty," some subsets within short-term orientation societies resort to harsh forms of fundamentalism such as Sharia Law. Hofstede does not hide his preference for long-term orientation and claims that the future is strongly dependent on "responsible thinking about the long term" as it relates to limitations on population and sustainable economic growth. His vigorously pragmatic perspective is based in research, but the research with which he warrants these claims comes from East Asian and Nordic societal studies—societies deeply imbedded with a long-term outlook.[48]

46. Hofstede et al., *Cultures and Organizations*, 255–59.

47. Hofstede et al., *Cultures and Organizations*, 260–75.

48. Hofstede et al., *Cultures and Organizations*, 260–76.

Indulgence vs. Restraint

The final dimension in Hofstede's system is related to happiness. The World Values Survey (WVS) attempts to measure happiness and its related components: (1) control over life and (2) the importance of leisure. The perception that one has control over one's life—that a person has the ability to live as he or she chooses—and the significance one places on leisure, are positively and strongly correlated to happiness. The indulgence versus restraint index (IVR) measures this aspect of culture. Indulgence refers to "a tendency to allow relatively free gratification of basic and natural human desires related to enjoying life and having fun."[49] Restraint refers to "a conviction that such gratification needs to be curbed and regulated by strict social norms."[50] The results of the ninety–three country survey rank Egypt and Pakistan as the saddest countries on earth. Pakistan has an IVR index of zero.[51]

Indulgent societies have higher percentages of very happy people. Thrift is not as important in high indulgence versus restraint societies when compared to low indulgence versus restraint societies.[52] The WVS reveals that people in high indulgence versus restraint societies are more likely to remember positive emotions than negative emotions. Members of more indulgent societies enjoy less discipline and tend to be more extroverted, expressing high optimism. Indulgent societies enjoy a more satisfying family life, and gender roles are poorly defined. Civil order is not a priority, and these societies tend to have fewer policemen per capita. Restrained or low indulgence versus restraint societies have low percentages of very happy people. A general feeling of helplessness and the power of fate reigns strong. Leisure and friends are not highly valued in low indulgence versus restraint societies. Thrift is important and moral discipline is high. Generally, people are cynical and pessimistic—smiles are often suspect. Gender roles are well–defined. Law and order are vital to these societies.

With the descriptions above it is clear that significant differences exist between cultures—something we needed no research to know. The advantage of a system like Hofstede's is that by it we can pin–point specific aspects of culture and have a vocabulary with which to assess leadership theory and practice in an intercultural setting. Put another way, now we have a tool to guide your leadership in a culture other than your own.

49. Hofstede et al., *Cultures and Organizations*, 281.
50. Hofstede et al., *Cultures and Organizations*, 281.
51. Hofstede et al., *Cultures and Organizations*, 285.
52. Hofstede et al., *Cultures and Organizations*, 288–98.

Chapter 9

Culture and Transformational Leadership

RESEARCH RELATING HOFSTEDE'S CULTURAL dimensions to transformational leadership is sparse. The newness of the field of study and the popularity of the GLOBE approach to intercultural leadership assessment may explain the scant research on transformational leadership and Hofstede's work.[1] The rising interest in intercultural leadership will surely result in more study in this domain. In this section, I review research relevant to transformational leadership from two perspectives. First, reviewing research on culture and transformational leadership as a whole, then second, reviewing research on distinct transformational leadership factors and culture.

---

1. Examples of research that apply the GLOBE study to analyze transformational leadership include Chhokar et al., , *Culture and Leadership across the World*; House et al., *Culture, Leadership, and Organizations*; Mark Green et al., "Assessing the Leadership Style of Paul," 3–28; Dastmalchian et al., "Effective Leadership and Culture in Iran," 532–58; Abdalla and Al-Homoud, "Exploring the Implicit Leadership Theory in the Arabian Gulf States," 503–31; Javidan et al., "In the Eye of the Beholder" 67–90; House et al., "Project GLOBE: An Introduction," 489–505; Winston and Ryan, "Servant Leadership as a Humane Orientation," 212–22.

Transformational Leadership and
the Dimensions of Culture

Culture influences leadership in at least three ways. First culture may *mediate* leadership practices. Culture mediates a leadership practice when culture serves to implement or facilitates a particular leadership behavior. Second, culture may *modify* leadership practices. A culture modifies a leadership practice when culture changes or influences the expression of leadership. Third, culture may *moderate* leadership practices. Culture moderates a leadership practice when it enhances or diminishes of a leadership behavior. Culture can influence the means, expression, or result of leadership behaviors. Research has demonstrated the effect of power distance, individualism–collectivism, masculinity-femininity, and long-vs.-short term orientation on transformational leadership. The results provide us with a good opportunity to consider culture's influence on leadership theory and practice.

Power Distance and Transformational Leadership.

The Power Distance Index measures how much a society accepts power inequity. Sherwood Lingenfelter argues that control and power issues are essential to understanding intercultural leadership.[2] Collaborative behaviors are common in transformational leadership decision–making in low power distance societies such as the Netherlands and Australia, but transformational leadership decision–making in high power distance societies takes a more directive approach. Similarly, in low power distance United States, referent power is highly related to effectiveness, but in high power distance Bulgaria, legitimate power is more common. Policy and procedure are important in high power distance societies and followers are likely to gain the support of those in authority before attempting something new.[3] These examples demonstrate how aspects of culture can modify transformational leadership behaviors.

China offers a clear example of how power distance affects transformational leadership. Sheng–Min Liu and Jian–Qiao Liao measured the effect of transformational leadership across power distance and structural distance. Structural distance refers to the formal gap between people in

---

2. Lingenfelter, *Leading Cross-Culturally*, 8.

3. Dickson et al., "Research on Leadership in a Cross–Cultural Context," 729–68.

organizational hierarchy and work units within an organization. For example, structural distance is greater between an employee and the president of his organization than between an employee and his immediate supervisor. Structural distance is also greater between an employee in the Finance department and another in Human Resources as opposed to two employees in the same division. Transformational leadership was positively linked to employees speaking up in front of their leaders in Liu and Liao's study. The lower the power distance, the more likely employees were to speak up to their leaders. Transformational leadership had a more positive influence when the structural distance was higher than in contexts where the structural distance was lower. Liu and Liao argue that this result may have more to do with the type and length of communication in high structural–distance relationships rather than transformational leadership *per se.* Liu and Liao conclude that power distance was the greater determinant of the likelihood of employees to speak up compared to structural distance and that the likelihood of employees to speak up was enhanced by transformational leaders.[4] In other words, transformational leadership was moderated by culture.

High power distance may be positively related to leadership development. Kyung Kyu Kim and Richard L. Starcher demonstrate that leaders report a strong motivation to grow as leaders after meeting exceptional, high–status leaders such as Foreign Minister Byun, John F. Kennedy, and Billy Graham. It appears that the heroes of these Korean leaders were all of a rather high status and the researchers believe this motivation may relate to the high power distance dimension of their culture.[5]

Individualism–Collectivism and Transformational Leadership.

Individualism and Collectivism refer to the manner in which people understand themselves in relation to groups in their society. Fred O. Walumbwa and John J. Lawler build on previous research in allocentrism and transformational leadership and demonstrate that transformational leadership is more impactful among allocentrics than idiocentrics in collectivist cultures.[6] Allocentrism refers to a tendency to base one's behavior

4. Liu and Liao, "Transformational Leadership and Speaking Up," 1747–56.

5. Kim and Starcher, "Cultivating Intercultural Leaders," 75.

6. Walumbwa and his colleagues studied 825 bank tellers and clerks in China, India, Kenya, and the United States and used questions from the MLQ. Walumbwa and Lawler,

on the expectations of other people. Allocentrics view themselves as part of the in–group and are, therefore, concerned with group goals whereas idiocentrics are more concerned with individual goals over those of the group. The researchers conclude that collectivism moderates the positive effect of transformational leadership on employee commitment to the organization and job satisfaction.[7] The research strengthens the arguments that understanding the cultural–anthropological aspects of leadership theory is vital to intercultural implementation of that theory, transformational leadership is viable in collectivist cultures, and that collectivism may positively moderate the effect of transformational leadership.

Trust, value congruence, and loyalty are possible follower outcomes of transformational leadership.[8] These positive feelings and associations on the part of those led toward their leader are part of that which enables the leader to draw followers toward a noble cause. Dongil Jung, Francis J. Yammarino, and Jin K. Lee demonstrate that collectivistic cultures positively moderate transformational leadership.[9] Jung and his associates report that collectivistic followers are "more likely to accept a leader's challenge to put organizational objectives ahead of their personal ones, focus on teamwork, and embrace a collective vision and identity," compared to followers in high individualism societies.[10] The researchers go so far as to argue that the association between transformational leadership and collectivism is so strong that transformational leadership practice would have a positive influence on work outcomes no matter the followers' opinion of their leader. Strong group orientation is conducive to transformational leadership because followers are expected to shift their interests from self to that of others—an aspect of collectivism.[11] In more individualistic cultures, the leader must pay particular attention to the organizational climate—how individualistic or collectivistic the work unit is. A transformational leader's influence may

---

"Building Effective Organizations," 1083–101.

7. Walumbwa and Lawler, "Building Effective Organizations,"1096–97.

8. C. S. Burke et al., "Trust in Leadership," 606–32; Philip M. Podsakoff et al., "Transformational Leader Behaviors and Their Effects on Followers' Trust," 107–42.

9. Jung et al., "Moderating Role of Subordinates' Attitudes," 600.

10. Jung et al., "Moderating Role of Subordinates' Attitudes," 598.

11. Jung et al., "Bridging Leadership and Culture." Charismatic leadership tends to function at a higher level when values are shared between the leader and followers—also a characteristic of collectivistic cultures. Pillai and Meindl, "Context and Charisma," 643–64.

be somewhat limited in high individualism contexts coupled with work units where individualism is highly valued.[12]

This association between transformational leadership and low individualism societies extends into Christian circles. For example, collectivism is an important facet of the South Korean expression of the Christian faith. Jeong–We Son demonstrates the dimension of collectivism in Christian work environments in his study of Korean pastors. One of the pastors in the study expressed a well–developed theology of respecting parents linked to the Korean cultural practices and rituals of parental honor called "Hyo."[13] This aspect of Korean Christian culture is strongly collectivistic because it expresses the deep sense of connection and reliance on the family common in low individualism societies. Son identifies this pastor's leadership style as transformational leadership, indicating that the pastor's collectivism modifies the pastor's transformational leadership.

Masculinity and Femininity and Transformational Leadership.

South Korea is a low masculinity, more Feminine society. Research by Jeong–We Son applies a case study approach to assess the transformational leadership of six Korean senior pastors.[14] This study of transformational leaders as role models illustrates the sacrifice transformational pastors make for the sake of the church through simple living and even giving away personal property. The pastors in this study serve as role models for junior pastors and staff, often mentoring and teaching them. The pastors give individual attention to the gifting of their junior pastors and provide opportunities for them to preach and teach. The group of pastors in this study were formed and influenced through personal Bible study and by mentors—usually family members, or high–profile Christian leaders, seminary professors, or very successful Korean pastors. The low masculinity culture—characterized by consensus, negotiation, and cooperation—appears to mediate transformational leadership in this study.[15]

12. Junget al., "Moderating Role of Subordinates' Attitudes," 599. For more on how to identify and modify individualistic work unit culture in organizations, see Logan et al., *Tribal Leadership*.

13. Son, "An Analysis of Leadership Styles," 115.

14. Son, "An Analysis of Leadership Styles," 115.

15. Hofstede et al., *Cultures and Organizations*, 164–70. The South Korean pastors' low MAS behavior is couched in their philosophy of ministry. One pastor wrote that his

In another example of transformational leadership modification by femininity, a pastor reports that church ministry must focus on people, not achievement. This philosophy bears out in the pastor's care of a member who was "cheating the church out of its offerings."[16] Realizing that the family of the offending member would be terribly hurt by any public action against the offender, the pastor advised the church elders to punish the sin quietly but to protect the person. Arguably, one could interpret this incident as an example of collectivism, but the pastor, in this case, attributes his actions to his desire to care for the individual—an expression of low masculinity. After the pastor's intervention, the church grew by seven hundred members, which the pastor interpreted as an indicator that his decision was correct.

Long–Term vs. Short–Term Orientation and Transformational Leadership.

Values are set early in life. In societies with a long–term orientation, these values can contribute to individuals successfully developing as transformational leaders. In a study of twenty Indian leaders recognized for their outstanding contribution to organizational growth, Punam Sahgal and Anil Pathak completed in–depth interviews to investigate leadership development, the effect of life–experiences on leaders, and the leaders' self–perception of drivers for success.[17] They find that these leaders attribute part of their success to the inspiration of their fathers and their pursuit of values learned early in childhood. The research highlights the importance of fathers in establishing values in children in India, although childrearing is considered a mother's work. Long–term outlook characteristics such as respect for others, adaptability, contentment, sacrifice to achieve, and sense of duty were among the values the leaders reported as significant to their success. The respondents assert that they persist in striving toward these values. The authors find that these early experiences developed core values that helped the subjects develop as transformational leaders later in life.

---

philosophy was that "My church was late in preparing [for] this media ministry so there was some time lost in the ministry, but I did not lose any people. God does not want to lose people in the ministry." Son, "An Analysis of Leadership Styles," 79.

16. Son, "An Analysis of Leadership Styles," 102.

17. Sahgal and Pathak, "Transformational Leaders," 263–79.

Values learned at a young age are stable. Research, as published in a position paper from the Center for Creative Leadership, demonstrates no significant differences across four generations of Indians with regard to certain work–related values. The team researched attitudes of workers from urban middle and upper socio–economic strata and sought out responses regarding effective leadership styles. The report indicates that Indian workers believe that hierarchical and autonomous leadership styles are the least effective and that humane, participative, team–oriented, and charismatic leadership are the most effective leadership styles in increasing order.[18] Transformational leadership fits this description of a leadership style reported to be preferred by workers in a long–term outlook culture.

Values learned at home are replaced, modified, or strengthened by workplace practices.[19] Figure 3 displays the declining balance of values and rising balance of practices as differentiating factors in culture at the level of home, school, and work

Figure 3. Values and Practices in Levels of Culture.

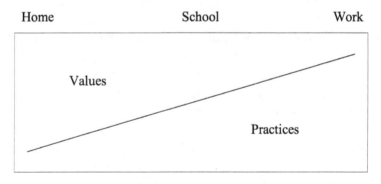

Modified from Hofstede, Hofstede, and Minkov, *Cultures and Organizations*, 347.

Hofstede makes the argument that the higher the congruence between home values and work practices, the more stable and satisfying work will be because of the cultural symmetry between home and work

18. Deal et al., "What Makes an Effective Leader?" a white paper for the Center for Creative Leadership, January 20, 2014, http://insights.ccl.org/?post_type=articles&article–type=white–papers.

19. Hofstede et al., *Cultures and Organizations*, 347.

cultures. If this argument holds up, then long–term orientation societies like India should prove to be fertile ground for transformational leadership because of the positive association between long–term orientation and transformational leadership. Clearly, culture affects the reception, expression, and results of a leadership practice. Culture mediates, modifies, and moderates leadership practices.

The Transformational Leadership Factors and Culture

General principles of leadership theory may be transferable between cultures, but not without some changes. Peter B. Smith examined moderated transferability and demonstrated that emic correlates of etic leadership styles occur in different cultures.[20] For example, a researcher might pose a question such as, does your supervisor support your efforts at work? The reply may measure the presence of an aspect of transformational leadership but indicates nothing about how that transformational leadership factor is displayed. In other words, how does a supervisor in a particular context display support? Smith and his team report that British supervisors display support when they measure performance at a work–unit or team level.[21] Supervisors in the United States tend to press for performance by demonstrating job processes and dressing like their subordinates to show support. In Hong Kong, supervisors rate high in performance when they engage in lengthy discussion about employee's personal difficulties—even in the employee's absence—and spend time together with subordinates after hours. The conclusion is that transformational leadership can be modified or expressed by different means according to the local culture. Therefore, researchers and leaders must employ a means by which to understand culture if they are going to understand transformational leadership in different cultures. Hofstede's dimensions of culture is one means of assessing these cultural differences. In the previous section, we have seen how culture affects the implementation of a leadership theory. The following section explores the relationship between Bass' four transformational leadership factors and Hofstede's six domains of culture. Assess culture and the four factors, Idealized Influence, Inspirational Motivation,

20. Smith et al., "On the Generality of Leadership Style Measures across Cultures," 97–109.

21. Smith et al., "On the Generality of Leadership Style Measures across Cultures," 107.

Intellectual Stimulation, and Individualized Consideration, give a more granular look and examine the implementation level of leadership where most leaders find themselves at the level of implementation.

Culture and Idealized Influence.

Leaders demonstrate Idealized Influence when they live out their values. As previously mentioned, such leaders are concerned with and speak often about their beliefs, especially those beliefs that support the organization's purpose and goals. Followers see these leaders as moral people who pay attention to the means by which they achieve their ends.

The inequity of power in high power distance societies, such as Saudi Arabia, Mexico, and China, may be a good fit for transformational leaders who show Idealized Influence. The key will be a close fit between the leader's values and beliefs and those of his followers. In high power distance contexts, the dependence that followers have on leaders requires a high degree of similarity of value and belief—a key characteristic of leaders who lead with Idealized Influence. Without such similarity, a constant strain will run beneath the surface of all relationships. Followers are not likely to speak or behave against the wishes and direction of the leader in a high power–distance culture, but the opposing beliefs and values may build up to a breaking point. Common beliefs and values in a high power–distance context can result in very strong leadership. In the case of common–ground values and beliefs, the leader in a high power–distance culture will find his leadership enhanced by the culture's acceptance of hierarchy and power inequity.

Individualist cultures are not necessarily good hosts for leaders who display Idealized Influence. People tend to consider value–decisions a private matter. More collectivist societies with strong loyalty to in–groups can be fertile ground for this factor of transformational leadership. Societies with high collectivism, such as those in Columbia, Indonesia, and Pakistan, are likely to produce very strong followership for leaders with Idealized Influence and beliefs held in common with followers due to the influence of the in–group.

If the leader values hard work, personal performance, goal–setting, and time–management systems, high masculinity societies such as Japan and Mexico will be a good fit for their leadership. If a leader's values include quality of life, service to others, and rely on intuition—low masculinity societies such as Thailand, Peru, and France will be a good fit. Both high and low masculinity societies can be suitable contexts for transformational leadership. The deciding factor for how to apply transformational leadership with regard to this cultural dimension is the nature of the high or low-MAS values held by the society in question.

Uncertainty and ambiguity are feared in high uncertainty avoidance societies. Leaders who are strong in the Idealized Influence factor are a good match for high uncertainty avoidance context because they are able to establish a firm moral foundation. Japan, Peru, and Turkey exemplify high uncertainty avoidance societies.

China is the standard–bearing country for long–term orientation. High long–term orientation societies tend to be more pragmatic and future–oriented. China as a nation also tends toward restraint overindulgence—low indulgence. Values that may be important in these societies are those that benefit the group, be it family or society. In high long–term orientation low indulgence societies, Idealized Influence may not be a powerful factor; however, some of these societies, those in China and Indonesia, are also high power–distance societies that should support Idealized Influence.

At first glance, it appears that this assessment of transformational leadership factors in light of Hofstede's dimensions of culture renders contradictory data—Idealized Influence is a good fit by one measure of culture and a poor fit by another measure. The key is to be aware of how each transformational leadership factor is likely to be perceived in the host culture. This research demonstrates the importance of considering dimensions of culture in leadership theory and application. Subtle differences may make a world of difference such that Idealized Influence in China and Indonesia may rest more on issues of power distance and less on holding to a particular moral or ethical stance. In other words, the better a leader understands why followers react the way they do, the potentially more effective his leadership will be.

Culture and Inspirational Motivation.

Charisma can be a powerful influence. When leaders draw followers together to accomplish a common vision, they exhibit Inspirational Motivation. High power distance may serve to highlight the inspirational-charismatic quality of a leader. In high power distance societies, superiors live a privileged life, inaccessible to common folk. This distance may enhance the hero stature of some leader figures.

Inspirational Motivation is likely to be a very important leadership factor in both individualistic and collectivistic societies (high and low IDV respectively). The nature of the follower's needs—fuel for motivation—is a critical distinctive between societies. Hofstede argues that need for security, belongingness, esteem, and achievement can be measured and used as a means by which to understand motivation across cultures.[22] Charting MAS against UAI can clarify these distinctions in motivation in different cultures. Figure 4 depicts motivational need pairs for MAS and UAI indices.

Low uncertainty avoidance, high masculinity societies such as China, India, the United States, Great Britain, and the Philippines tend to place achievement and esteem at the pinnacle of needs.[23] Safety and security are not as important in these societies—low uncertainty avoidance—and they have a lower need for belonging when compared to the need for recognition and esteem—high MAS. Heroes in these societies are decisive achievers who struggled against all odds to make it.

Figure 4. Need Pairs Related to MAS and UAI.

High UAI	Security and Belongingness	Security and Esteem
Low UAI	Achievement and Belongingness	Achievement and Esteem
	Low MAS	High MAS

Adapted from Hofstede, Hofstede, and Minkov, *Cultures and Organizations*, 214.

Low UAI, high MAS societies such as China, India, the United States, Great Britain, and the Philippines tend to place achievement and esteem at

22. Hofstede et al., Cultures and Organizations, 214.
23. Hofstede et al., Cultures and Organizations, 213–16.

the pinnacle of needs.[24] Safety and security are not as important in these societies—low UAI—and they have a lower need for belonging when compared to the need for recognition and esteem—high MAS. Heroes in these societies are decisive achievers who struggled against all odds to make it.

Maslow's hierarchy of needs, with safety and security at the base of his pyramid and personal achievement at the top, comes from this kind of culture.[25] In low UAI, high MAS societies, Inspirational Motivation is based on an optimistic outlook full of opportunity for self–development and personal success.

Portugal, Slovenia, Guatemala, and Russia represent the polar opposite of Maslow's world. These strongly feminine societies tend to seek out belongingness—epitomized in the notion of Mother Russia. The strong need to belong, coupled with high UAI, results in motivation based on the need pair of security and belongingness.[26] Inspirational Motivation in these societies comes in the form of the image of a caring group with a leader strong enough to provide security.

Other countries with high UAI, like Japan, Mexico, Hungary, and Greece, share the need for security, but have a high MAS index. This particular mix results in a need pair of security and esteem.[27] Esteem is important in these societies, but this need comes with a discomfort for ambiguity. Therefore, these societies tend to make laws to help people feel safe and avoid conflict. The higher motivators in such societies are security and esteem.

The opposite of security–esteem is the achievement–belongingness pair. Denmark, Sweden, Vietnam, and the Netherlands occupy this quadrant. Quality of life and service to others are important and matched with a desire for self or group achievement.[28] In Vietnam, achievement takes on a group–oriented nuance in keeping with its collectivist view of life.

Inspirational Motivation in cultures with a long term orientation (high LTO) tends to be more focused on a possible future. The future looks good and achievable. Quickly achieving the right outcome tends to be important in short–term orientated societies (low LTO). Inspirational

---

24. Hofstede et al., Cultures and Organizations, 213–16.

25. Hofstede et al., Cultures and Organizations, 215–16.

26. Hofstede et al., Cultures and Organizations, 213–16.

27. Hofstede et al., Cultures and Organizations, 213–16.

28. Hofstede et al., Cultures and Organizations, 213–16.

Motivation in these societies may center on truth, convention, and tradition as opposed to a distant goal.

The more indulgent a society is, the more likely people express happiness. Examples of high IVR societies are Venezuela, Nigeria, Sweden, and the United States. Motivation may be stimulated by giving personal control, reducing rules, and an emphasis on personal fulfillment. Indulgence is generally associated with a short–term outlook. Therefore, motivational goals and images must be obtainable within a relatively short span of time. Societies with low IVR are more restrained and tend to appreciate order, moral discipline, and thrift. Pakistan, Iraq, Hong Kong, India, and South Korea are examples of low IVR countries.

Culture and Intellectual Stimulation.

Some leaders have the ability to spur others on to engage their critical apparatus and analyze problems and design innovative solutions. Bass refers to these abilities as Intellectual Stimulation. How can one expect Intellectual Stimulation to fare in societies outside the west, where transformational leadership was developed?

Countries with high PDI may pose a bit of a problem for Intellectual Stimulation. The power associated with knowledge may prohibit some leaders from creating an intellectually free environment required for innovative thinking. In high PDI societies, change comes by revolution. Intellectual Stimulation may be perceived as a threat to high–level leaders if a mid or low–level manager pursues this leadership factor. If leaders are transformational, the latitude given to followers to draw from outside sources and to consider novel approaches to problems may seem foreign and strange to individuals from high PDI societies. A transformational leader with Intellectual Stimulation skills should proceed with caution and awareness of the challenges of Intellectual Stimulation in a high PDI environment. Low PDI societies seem tailor–made for Intellectual Stimulation. The lack of power distance is fertile ground for this transformational leadership factor.

Individualist cultures promote personal achievement and the open challenging of authority and ideas. These notions are supported by leaders with a high Intellectual Stimulation factor. Theoretically, education and intellectual growth is open to everyone in high IDV societies. Skill and competency is the path toward self–improvement and financial gain; therefore, Intellectual Stimulation appears to be a good fit.

Harmony is important in collectivist societies, and so, challenging the *status quo*, an important aspect of Intellectual Stimulation is likely taboo. Educational systems in collectivist societies focus on how to accomplish tasks rather than how to learn—possibly a limiting factor on the self-growth promoted in transformational leadership. Being part of the in-group may have more influence on promotion than ability or insight. Because of the above limitations, Intellectual Stimulation may need to be individually focused behavior to keep from appearing to go against the collectivist grain.

Uncertainty avoidance—managing fears and ambiguity—will modify the manner in which a leader expresses Intellectual Stimulation. Very high UAI societies tend toward the "different is dangerous" extreme.[29] Such societies accept familiar or managed risks but tend to stay away from the unknown. Innovation is difficult to encourage in these societies in which learning tends to be structured, and the goal is getting the answer right as opposed to free discussions and intellectual exploration. Followers of transformational leaders tend to be more imaginative and inventive in collectivist cultures, but idea generation is more common among followers of transactional leaders in individualist cultures.[30] Awareness of these distinctions is key to implementing transformational leadership.

High UAI societies normally manage behaviors with rules. Rules describe the proper place and way for things. Rules can be explicit or implicit, codified or imbedded in tradition—which one depends on how individualistic a society is. More collectivist societies tend to manage uncertainty with implicit rules based in tradition, whereas more individualist societies tend to write explicit laws.[31]

Long-term versus short-term orientation and Intellectual Stimulation is a complicated mix. High LTO societies value learning, adaptability, accountability, self-discipline, and synthetic thinking.[32] Low LTO societies value freedom, rights, achievement, independent thinking, possessing the truth, and axiomatic, abstract, and analytical thinking.[33] Both extremes of the LTO scale are compatible with Intellectual Stimulation, but by very

---

29. Hofstede et al., Cultures and Organizations, 201.

30. Dickson et al., "Research on Leadership in a Cross-Cultural Context," 743.

31. The high UAI—low IDV (collectivist) quadrant tends to respond to otherness—minorities—by denying they exist, assimilating them, or quelling then. Dicksonet al., "Research on Leadership in a Cross-Cultural Context," 225.

32. Hofstede et al., Cultures and Organizations, 246–51.

33. Hofstede et al., Cultures and Organizations, 246–51.

different means. The transformational leader outside his own LTO context must be aware of these differences and strive to encourage creative thought in culturally appropriate ways.

Masculinity–Femininity may not provide any particular advantage or disadvantage to Intellectual Stimulation. The range of societal differences in Indulgence versus Restraint does not appear to have a significant effect on Intellectual Stimulation either.

Culture and Individualized Consideration.

Leaders show Individualized Consideration when they teach, coach, and train for their followers' personal betterment. Structurally, high PDI societies would appear to have an advantage over low PDI societies. High PDI societies commonly set up centralized organizations with more supervisors per workers whereas low PDI societies tend toward decentralized hierarchies with fewer supervisory personnel. Centralization and a high supervisor to worker ratio would appear to make for a better environment for Individualized Consideration, but high PDI comes with a price—managers are predisposed to rely on rules and processes and subordinates expect to be told what to do.

High PDI societies may offer better organizational structures for Individualized Consideration, but functionally, low PDI societies have the advantage over high PDI societies. Students and learners are more likely to be treated as equals in low PDI societies than in high PDI contexts. These societies show more interdependence between leaders and followers.

Hofstede deals with individualism and collectivism as a function of society, but cautions that if one changes the level of analysis to the individual level, this single cultural dimension should be considered as two separate aspects.[34] Leaders who give individual attention in collectivist societies will always need to be aware that all the teaching, coaching, and supporting they give to the individual follower will be filtered through the followers' collectivism. The recipient of individual attention will factor in the question of how this new information or skill, even the attention itself, will be interpreted by his group. The followers' evaluations of the leader's help will be all the more critical if the leader is not part of the followers' in–group.

Encouragement to act against the will of the in–group may not result in the transformational leadership that the leader intends. Individualized

34. Hofstede et al., Cultures and Organizations, 102.

attention may be rare in collectivist societies but may remain valuable. Leaders can guide individual followers toward better ways of being a part of the group, of improving the group, or even change the group's value system. Any such expectation of a transformational leader in a low IDV society must be checked with the expectation that such deep–level changes will likely be slow, especially for the first person to change.

Another important aspect of collectivism that related to Individualized Consideration is shame. Shame is based in collective obligation and occurs when one infringes on the social rules of the group.[35] The individualist counterpart to shame is guilt, which is the feeling associated with breaking one's conscience. Shame is felt when the infringement is known by the group. Guilt is felt whether others know about it or not. Face is related to shame but deals more specifically with loss of status as a result of an infringement of social norms. Saving face in the CVS is a kind of "self–enhancing feeling," like pride.[36] When leading in a collectivist society, the transformational leader needs to be cognizant of possible shame issues and causing someone to lose face.

As with Intellectual Stimulation, Masculinity versus Femininity does not appear to have a significant role in Individualized Consideration beyond the point of attending to the MAS needs mentioned in the section on Inspirational Motivation.

A society's PDI score reveals who has power, and its UAI score reveals something about how rules and procedures will influence its goals. Together, these two indices can help explain organizational structures in a given culture. Hofstede expands the work of Owen James Stevens to give four organizational models based on cultural values of power distance and uncertainty avoidance.[37] Figure 5 displays Hofstede's organizational models.

France is home to the high UAI, high PDI model—the *pyramid*. This model depends on both highly structured rules and a strong top–level manager to deal with problems in the organization. The *machine* model, found in Germany, features an organization that relies on rules and procedures to fend off and resolve problems. In dire circumstances, management can step in to solve exceptional problems. Structure—because of a high UAI—is the dominant factor. Indonesia has many examples of the *family* model. With a low UAI, rules and procedures are not as important

35. Hofstede et al., Cultures and Organizations, 110.

36. Hofstede et al., Cultures and Organizations, 252.

37. Hofstede et al., Cultures and Organizations, 302–6.

as relationships. When this relationship–oriented society is combined with strong power distance, the top man in the family, known as the *Bapak*, becomes a very powerful figure. Even in banks and oil companies, the chief executive or board chairman is often viewed as a powerful father–figure, permanent and with no need of any supporting rule or activities. The *market* model is found in Great Britain and the United States. Here, rules and procedures are not as vital as with the family model and, because of a low PDI, the relationships are more often on the same level. Therefore, the organization is often more like a village market where negotiation, not rules or hierarchy, is the rule of the day.

Figure 5. Organizational Structures by UAI and PDI.

High UAI Machine	Pyramid
Low UAI Market	Family
Low PDI	High PDI

Adapted from Hofstede, Hofstede, and Minkov, *Cultures and Organizations*, 303.

Long–term orientation in Individualized Consideration centers on the search for virtue; in other words, right moral behavior.[38] Leaders enacting Individualized Consideration in societies with high LTO should be responsive to the needs of followers to grow in virtue and to the reality that even mundane tasks or skills can be accomplished virtuously. Leaders in low LTO societies can concentrate more on knowledge and skill transfer without particular regard to virtue, unless of course their core purpose calls for it, as does the core purpose in missions.

High IVR societies tend to express optimism and enjoy control over personal life. Low IVR societies report they are less satisfied with family

---

38. Hofstede et al., *Cultures and Organizations*, 247.

life and more pessimistic than high IRV societies. These aspects may be helpful to transformational leaders, but do not pose any particular advantage or hindrance.

Transformational leadership in high PDI cultures should recall that followers in these societies display a high dependence on their bosses and emotional distance between leaders and followers is great. Therefore, subordinates are unlikely to oppose their managers and, instead, followers may prefer consultation and interdependence. Therefore, a leader used to working in more independent work environments will have to adjust his expectations and behaviors accordingly. Management techniques from middle and low–range PDI contexts are likely to fail in high PDI societies because they require manager–employee bargaining. Bargaining requires a degree of manager–employee equity that is foreign to most high PDI contexts.

Collectivist cultures think in terms of *we*, not *me*. Harmony is a high social value. Instead of verbal communication, where information is explicit and direct speech is associated with honesty, communication is high–context—less is spoken and more is implied. People expect preferential treatment by leaders from their own society, honoring the in–group members. Therefore, management is about managing the in–group and employees are usually hired from within the in–group. Transformational leaders who reward according to performance may run into trouble and create dissatisfaction because they are not caring for the in–group. Tools such as management by objectives are foreign and difficult to implement in some high collectivist cultures.

A transformational leader might expect a high motivation for work that may be missing in low MAS cultures with high cultural femininity. In these cultures, people tend to work to live, not live to work. Furthermore, the reward is based on need in low MAS contexts, not performance.

Both the high and low extremes of uncertainty avoidance may pose problems for transformational leadership. On one hand, high UAI societies tend to believe that truth is absolute. Often these societies view new and different things with suspicion and may even believe that different is dangerous. Governments and organizations in high UAI societies often use policy and procedure to manage ambiguity. Transformational leadership in these societies may find it difficult to innovate and implement new ideas. On the other hand, low UAI societies take one day at a time, tend to be more laid–back, and less stressed than high UAI societies. People in these societies often view differences as interesting. Goal–setting and transformational leadership activities that press for performance may not be successful in low UAI societies.

Summary

Culture—the socially grounded ways of thinking, feeling, and behaving that mold our perception of the world around us, our expectations of others, the confines of our actions, how we measure things as good or bad, acceptable or rejected, and how we express and communicate—influences, regulates, enhances and impedes leadership, especially leadership practice imported from another culture. We often take culture for granted, in part because we absorb and acquire culture more than we actively learn it. Our culture feels right, it is comfortable to us. The leadership practices we are used to are part of our culture for the most part. No wonder these practices seem universal to us, they are part of us and seem to be second nature. But upon closer examination, we find that leadership theory and practice is culturally bound. All theories and practices developed in a culture and if they are successful, it is in large part because they work within the bounds of cultural rules and expectations.

The good news is that culture is not static and the Lord has given us the ability to observe, think, and change. When we bring a leadership approach into a different cultural setting, we must be mindful that the receiving culture is no blank slate; neither is it likely to be the same as the culture from which we imported the ideas. But there is hope. Researchers like Hofstede, House, Lewis, and Meyer have given us tools by which we can examine our culture and that of our host. With the differences in mind, we can assess and anticipate how the host culture may mediate, modify, or moderate a theory, it's expression and results. Knowing this, we can determine a leadership theory's suitableness in a given cultural setting.

PART 4

Determine the Appropriateness of the Leadership Theory

LEADERS IN MISSIONS NEED a way to think about leadership and evaluate leadership theories and methods. Missions leadership frequently occurs in an intercultural context where the people of God need to be led to accomplish his purposes for his glory. Therefore, three domains of study—leadership philosophy, theology, and cultural anthropology—are vital components for a proper evaluation of leadership theory and practice. We must analyze any leadership theory we hope to implement and understand the *philosophy and practice* of that theory. We must evaluate the theory and practice *theologically*, appraise it in light of Scripture to ensure that it is in keeping with the Lord's revealed purposes and means. We must measure the *cultural influences* on a leadership theory or practice and identify potential effects caused by importing a leadership approach. These effects may show up in how the theory is expressed or received. To accomplish this purpose, I designed the Leadership Assessment Matrix displayed in Table 7.

Table 7. A Leadership Assessment Matrix

Tier 1: Philosophical Aspect	Elements to Assess
Development and Description of the Theory	Historical context, theory development and description.
Exercise of the Theory	Purpose, locus of leadership, influence mechanisms, and stewardship orientation.
Outcomes of the Theory	The theory's performance measures, meta–relationships, contextual influences, and universality.

Tier 2: Theological Aspect	Elements to Assess
Teleology	A leader's purpose, motivation, and objectives.
Ontology	A leader's calling, character, and competency.
Authority	A leader's capacity, authority, and responsibility
Ethic	The leader as servant of God and servant to others.

Tier 3: Cultural Aspect	Elements to Assess
Power Distance	The degree of existence and acceptance of hierarchy.
Individualism vs. Collectivism	Emphasis on personal and family goals and needs vs. that of the group.
Masculinity vs. Femininity	Assertiveness, competition, distinct gender roles vs. quality of life, cooperation, and overlap in roles.
Uncertainty Avoidance	Response to volatility, uncertainty, complexity, and ambiguity.
Long–term vs. Short–term Orientation	Patience and preparation vs. immediate gratification.
Indulgence vs. Restraint	Satiating desires vs. compliance with social norms.

I used Bass' transformational leadership theory as an example to demonstrate my Leadership Assessment Matrix. In this final tier, I will summarize the key findings of my evaluation and draw final conclusions on the appropriateness of Bass' theory and the usefulness of my Leadership Assessment Matrix. In chapter 10, I draw conclusions about transformational leadership theory in missions and ministry settings. In chapter 11, I will share my conclusions about the Leadership Assessment Matrix and share some recommendations about leaders and leading.

Chapter 10

Conclusions about Transformational Leadership Theory

Is Bass' TRANSFORMATIONAL LEADERSHIP theory right for Christian missions? That is the primary question at hand. To answer, I will draw conclusions according to my Leadership Assessment Matrix that evaluates a theory in its philosophical, theological, and cultural domains. Leadership theory can be quite complex, and intercultural missions are no less multifaceted. The Leadership Assessment Matrix is a useful tool to examine and assess any leadership theory and make a reasonable, biblically faithful, culturally appropriate determination about the theory's rightness and usefulness in the context of intercultural missions.

Philosophical Conclusions

At the level of philosophy and practice, The Leadership Assessment Matrix delves into the development and description of the theory or practice at hand and evaluates the exercise and expected outcomes of the theory or practice. My assessment brings to light some concerns regarding purpose and values, the locus of leadership, the exercise of authority, and the universality of transformational leadership theory.

Shared purpose and values.

Shared purpose is critical to transformational leadership. In Bass' theory, purpose arises out of the free choice of those involved and that it serves their common needs and values. Revealed objective purpose is not a concern for Bass and his colleagues, but it is vital to Christian missions. The influence of mutually held purposes and values serves to differentiate between transactional and transformational leadership. Transactional methods keep followers on track by policy and procedure. Similar to Paul Hiebert's bound-set theory, a transactional approach delineates who is in and who is out, what is acceptable and what is unacceptable.[1] Conversely, transformational methods draws followers together through values and purpose, much like Hiebert's centered-set theory.[2] In other words, transformational leadership practices tend to be attractional, behaviors that appeal to followers' motivations, purpose, and sense of oughtness. Attracting followers to a purpose has merit as a strong motivational factor that is well-established in Western academic circles.

Locus of leadership.

Hernandez contends that the locus of leadership in transformational leadership is dyadic or located within the leader-follower relationship. Bass and Steidlmeier support her view, but Bass recognizes the need for leaders to lead and stands firm on the idea that someone must have the authority and responsibility for an organization at the end of the day. Singular leadership is not necessarily self-indulgent, and neither is a group of leaders necessarily noble-minded. In the Bible, a single individual is frequently called upon to correct the group. The key is not in a singular or plurality of leadership but in righteous leadership.

In terms of transformational theory, the locus of leadership lies in the leader who guides and encourages the group toward mutually held purposes in keeping with shared needs and values. In other words, transformational leaders can be considerate of others yet determined and steadfast in their role. John Adair's Three Circle model of intersecting needs of task, team, and individual is helpful at this juncture.[3] Adair refers

1. Hiebert, *Anthropological Reflections on Missiological Issues*, 122–31.
2. Hiebert, *Anthropological Reflections on Missiological Issues*, 122–31.
3. Adair, *How to Grow Leaders*, 19–26.

to this model as the group or functional approach to leadership and states that leaders attend to the need to accomplish the shared goal, the need for unity in work, and the needs of the individuals of the group. In his postulation, the leader is not a self-serving individual but one who is attentive to the needs and abilities of the group and the task set before them. Therefore, it appears there is room for a clear leader in transformational leadership, but researchers seem to capitulate to a dyadic form of authority in some cases. The locus of leadership is unclear.

Exercise of authority.

Influence or the exercise of authority is a complicated affair. Hernandez maintains that the core mechanisms of influence in transformational leadership are behavior and cognition. Hernandez's conclusion that transformational leadership's influence mechanisms are primarily behavioral and cognitive is supported by a wide body of research. She correctly argues that behaviors alone do not differentiate transformational leadership from other theories. The distinctiveness of transformational leadership theory lies in the whole—the sum of its parts—not in the parts themselves. The effects of transformational leadership factors are difficult to isolate in research. The theory works only when taken in its entirety because of the highly meta-relational aspect of the system. One factor is dependent upon or mediated by another such that clean, direct factor-to-response data is illusive. As a system, the correlation of transformational leadership theory to individual and group confidence, satisfaction, engagement, and productivity is well established by a significant body of qualitative and quantitative research.

Universality of the theory,

Bass and colleagues theorized that transformational leadership has universal application. Many studies, including the massive and ongoing GLOBE study, warrant the claims of transformational leadership's universality. From the beginning, Bass argued that universality does not mean that culture and context do not mediate the interpretation and application of his theory, but that the basic system holds up in other, non-western, cultures.

Summary of philosophical conclusions.

Bass's transformational leadership theory is a conceptual schema that provides leaders and followers with a system by which to process leadership notions, behaviors, and effects. As such, the theory provides users with a path forward and clear markers of successful leadership, and the theory is well–tested. This assessment reveals a few difficulties in the philosophy of transformational leadership theory.

In the arena of purpose, two examples illustrate the occasional need for a directive style of leadership. First, there are occasions when a leader sets the agenda and calls people to it. In this case, he persuades others to join the cause, and it becomes a mutual cause. Unfortunately, history is full of organizations that experience mission drift. Sometimes, the drift is led by the leader, but sometimes, the drift occurs because the leader is simply following the crowd in their mutual agreement to let go of their previous commitment to the cause. Leaders must be committed to their organization's cause even when others oppose it or are willing to let the cause drift. In these cases, the cause is not mutual, and inspirational motivation may be largely ineffective. Second, a leader must be able to guide his organization by policy and procedure. In the life of every organization, there are times in which the leader must be able to rely on good policy and right procedure to guide the activities and responses of the organization. If a leader applies Bass' Full Range of Leadership theory, which includes transactional and even laissez–faire leadership approaches, this aspect should be protected. However, if a leader is restricted to transformational leadership, the leader loses a significant leadership tool.

The locus of leadership is another problematic area for transformational leadership theory. A leader may lead with clear direction in transformational leadership, but the theory authors capitulate to a dyadic locus of authority that would cloud matters of authority when the situation calls for a stronger, more directive form.

Theological Conclusions

At the level of theology, The Leadership Assessment Matrix evaluates the teleological, ontological, power and authority, and ethic aspects of a given theory, answering questions such as what should leaders do and what drives them, what are the roles of character, gifting, and experience in leadership, how should leaders exercise power and authority, and how do leaders serve the Lord and others? My assessment of transformational leadership theory uncovers concerns in the four primary areas of my theological assessment.

Great confusion about leadership persists. Writing in a popular magazine for leaders, Polly LaBarre claims:

> There's a terrible defect at the core of how we think about people and organizations today. There is little or no tolerance for the kinds of character–building conversations that pave the way for meaningful change. The average person is stuck, lost, riveted by the objective domain. That's where our metrics are; that's where we look for solutions. It's the come–on of the consulting industry and the domain of all the books, magazines, and training programs out there.[4]

The world of leadership is looking for ground on which to stand. LaBarre's thoughts reflect a general frustration with leadership models fixated on performance and outcomes while paying little attention to the nature of the leader and to character. In Christian missions and ministry circles, the problem is no less severe. Oversimplified formulations of leadership are insufficient, yet they abound. Typically, scholars take one of three basic approaches: they reject transformational theory outright with little substantive evaluation, they accept the theory wholeheartedly with little correction, or they design a blended theory.

Jacqueline Faulhaber's work is an example of the first approach. She proclaims that Bass's theory is "typical of Confucian and Socratic typologies" and dismisses the theory's basic principles rather quickly.[5] The second approach—accepting the theory wholeheartedly with little correction—is more common. For example, Jerry Wofford argues that Jesus was a transformational leader because he advocated and modeled a set of high values, articulated a vision that the kingdom of God is at hand and accessible through faith, confronted the status quo, stimulated hearts and minds, and was a charismatic leader. Wofford asserts that these five characteristics of Jesus' leadership—values, vision, change, inspiration, and

---

4. LaBarre, "Do You Have the Will to Lead?" 222. *Fast Company* is a magazine that focuses on how companies change and compete, showcases new business practices and innovative teams, and individuals.

5. Faulhaber, "Virtue Development and Authentic Transformational Leadership," 9.

charisma—make him a transformational leader in line with Bass' model.[6] The third approach, taking up a blended theory, is rare. Jeanine Parolini provides an example of this approach. She makes the case for a blended theory called transformational servant leadership.[7]

Bass' transformational leadership theory holds promise as a viable theory for leadership in missions, and leaders may be tempted to accept and apply Bass' theory as is. But, if researchers and practitioners ignore theological evaluation of the theories they espouse, they run the risk of misapplying a secular theory for a sacred task. For this reason, I created the theological assessment grid for leadership theory consisting of teleology, ontology, authority, and ethic. Following is a summary of the most important points of tension resulting from a theological assessment of Bass' theory.

Teleological problems.

Two problems plague the teleology of transformational leadership theory. The most significant issue is Bass' articulation concerning purpose. Bass' theory has no mention of revealed, objective truth, morality, or purpose. Quite the opposite, transformational leadership theory rests on entirely subjective purpose and morality dictated by the group, modulated by context, and bounded only by a vague sense of altruism. Bass and Steidlmeier insist that transformational leaders display core transcendental values, but they do not explain what those values might be and appear to suggest that the standard is subjective. The subjective nature of transformational theory's value system is troubling. Transformational leadership can only be healthy if purpose and values are established in God's Word. Christian leaders must explicitly reject Bass and Steidlmeier's presuppositions, founded on a common–ground approach, and replace them with a biblically founded teleology and morality—righteousness.

The second significant teleological problem with transformational leadership theory is the source of motivation. Bass relies on Maslow's hierarchy of needs for motivation, with self–actualization as the highest goal

---

6. Wofford, *Transforming Christian Leadership*, 21–33. Also see Lewis, *Transformational Leadership*; Ford, *Transforming Leadership*; Brown, "The Building of a Virtuous Transformational Leader," 6–14; Cooper, "The Transformational Leadership of the Apostle Paul," 48–61; Gray, "Christological Hymn: The Leadership Paradox of Philippians 2:5–11," 3–18; McCabe, "Jesus as Agent of Change," 32–43.

7. Parolini, *Transformational Servant Leadership*, 13.

through altruism where the leader moves beyond himself for the greater good. Leadership in Christian missions calls for a self–sacrificing leadership, but with the goal of God's glory and out of love for him.

Neither of these two problems spell the end for transformational leadership as a useful theory for Christian leadership. Once scholars and practitioners are aware of these problems, they can take steps to develop and maintain a proper theological trajectory. Explicit attention to the primary purpose, motivation, and goals of missions can establish a biblical and reasonable path for transformational leadership theory application. The burden for adjustment rests upon the leader.

Ontological problems.

Calling, character, and competency are vital in a biblical understanding of the leader. Calling in transformational leadership ontology is little more than self–awareness. Bass argues that self–efficacy and self–worth are measurable predictors of the likelihood that a person will naturally develop transformational leadership characteristics and behaviors. His approach to identify those who may become leaders primarily relies on psychological factors. While psychological factors should not be ignored, the Bible is replete with examples of surprisingly unlikely leaders such as Jacob, Moses, David, and Peter, whom God called to lead his people. Jacob was a cunning, selfish manipulator who spent most of his time and energy protecting himself—hardly a selfless leader, Moses was reluctant to lead, David was young, inexperienced, and appeared weak, and Peter was rash and over–confident in his own strength though sometimes, cowardly.[8] Yet, the Lord used all of these men to lead his people.

Character is important to both transformational leadership and a biblical conception of leaders. Transformational leaders maintain high moral standards and are trustworthy, responsible, and respectable. Bass insists that leaders be optimistic, and truthful, exhibit self–control, and listen well. The Bible teaches that leaders should demonstrate these characteristics, but the Bible's emphasis on the fruit of the Spirit renders unnecessary Bass' requirement for a humanistic worldview of self–development and altruism.

Competency in transformational leadership refers to those which are commonly referred to as soft skills or interpersonal skills. These same skills

8. Gen 25:29–34; 27:36;31; Exod 3:11; 4:13; 1 Sam 16:11–12; 17:26–43; John 18:10; 15–27.

are important to biblical leadership in missions with the vital addition of the ability to teach. Calling, character, and competency are essential to an ontology of leadership and form a rigorous ontology for transformational leadership in missions and ministry.

Authority problems.

Bass' transformational leadership establishes power in a leader's referent and expert power bases. Power themes in a theology of leadership are very similar to those espoused by Bass and his colleagues. Referent power arises out of this desire to imitate the best in a leader's character and behavior. A leader's displayed and attributed character moves followers to trust and emulate their leader. The apostle Paul relies on referent power when he asks the church to follow his example.

Expert power is also a theme in theology of leadership. In this case, the area of cognitive ability is not technology or commerce, but the Word of God. Teaching and the ability to teach are well-established requirements for leaders in the Bible and therefore, vital to missions leadership. The referent and expert power bases are important to transformational leadership theory and theology of missions alike.

A theologically accurate take on leadership power must account for the work of the Holy Spirit. Bass' theory has no place for the Holy Spirit because his system is utterly dependent on human effort. His theory fails to meet the standard of a theology in missions because it has no room for a theology of the Holy Spirit. Only a reformulation of Bass' theory can make up for this error.

A second concern is that accountability in a leadership theology is owed to God. Bass' transformational leadership theory has no mention of accountability to anything beyond human structures. A framework for accountability is already in place in Bass' theory, but any leadership theory for missions and ministry must include an explicit statement of accountability to God.

Ethic problems.

The theological assessment reveals five areas of concern under the ethic aspect of Bass' theory. First, humility—trusting in God's provision and putting others first—is not an explicit concern in transformational leadership theory. Second, a leader is a steward of God's people; Bass' theory has no place for this ethic. Third, leaders may need to initiate change—a behavior at the heart of transformational leadership—but leaders may also need to stay the course. For example, leaders are called to maintain orthodoxy and orthopraxy. This behavior is not addressed in transformational leadership theory, which concentrates on leaders as agents of change. Fourth, leaders should demonstrate courage in God's sovereign care. Conversely, Bass' leaders have courage in their own strengths and abilities. Courage is related to the ability to initiate change. Both change and steadfastness require courage in the face of opposition. Fifth, leaders in the Bible articulate hope for God's presence, provision, care, and reward. Bass' transformational leadership does not have a place in its theory for divine reward or accountability.

Summary of theological conclusions.

In conclusion, transformational leadership theory is a reasonable basis for leadership, as argued in part 1. The theological research in part 2 concludes that Bass' theory is suitable for missions and ministry only after a thorough reformulation based on an explicitly theological foundation of biblical principles, guidelines, and teachings.

Cultural Conclusions

The effectiveness of a theory is not the only issue to consider when evaluating a theory for leadership in missions. A reasonable theory for leadership in missions must also include a theological critique of the theory, as argued in the previous chapter. Because of the intercultural aspect of missions, cultural assessment of leadership is also necessary.

Case studies by Sherwood Lingenfelter illustrate the importance of evaluating leadership theory and practice. In Lingenfelter's case study of South Korean churches with large memberships, pastoral succession was determined by either pastor–driven succession in a very Confucian–patriarchal leadership style or by elder–driven succession in which younger pastors then relied heavily on an authoritarian role as God's chosen leader. In the former case, churches embraced the culturally–endorsed norm of a father–figure who clearly leads the church. He gives authority to his associates who lead various ministries in the church. Many such churches have large mission budgets and support 50–100 missionaries. In the latter case, churches and their leaders spent a great deal of time and energy to gain and maintain positional power. Lingenfelter concludes that the second, elder–driven model is one of the reasons that church growth in Korea has nearly ground to a halt.[9] Lingenfelter's Korean case serves to illustrate the notion of variform universality. Both types of churches relied on a hierarchy to lead the church, but the pastor as father–figure was an emic form that resounded with the local culture.

In post–communist Hungarian churches, Lingenfelter reports that churches employed authoritarian and hierarchical leadership.[10] Lingenfelter concludes that the variable which determined the level of the church's missions activity and success was not organizational structure but the vision of the church and the pastor teaching, empowering, and releasing or authorizing the church body in missions. When the pastors worked within the cultural norms of the society and used position and authority to prepare and encourage the members to serve the mission of God, the church proved to be active and successful in missions.[11]

Lingenfelter argues that "the problem is not one of the 'right social structure,' but rather of the relationship of leaders and people to Christ, and their commitment to the mission of God."[12] He is correct to argue that faith in Jesus and the church's desire to participate in God's missions are factors in their success in following God's will. His cases reveal, however, that culturally appropriate leadership made a difference in both the Korean and Hungarian cases.

At the level of culture, The Leadership Assessment Matrix applies Hofstede's dimensions of culture to assess the impact of a theory or practice. The matrix includes power distance, individualism–collectivism, masculinity–femininity, uncertainty avoidance, time orientation, and indulgence versus restraint.

9. Lingenfelter, "The DNA of the Church," 439–41.

10. Lingenfelter uses a system of *social games* borrowed from Mary Douglas to identify groups as authoritarian, hierarchical, egalitarian, or individualist. Mary Douglas, "Cultural Bias," in *In the Active Voice* (London: Routledge and Kegan Paul, 1982), 183–254; Lingenfelter, "The DNA of the Church," 436.

11. Lingenfelter, "The DNA of the Church," 441–44.

12. Lingenfelter, "The DNA of the Church," 4

Transformational Leadership assumptions of Power Distance and Individualism.

Leadership theories are not without cultural bias. For example, most servant leadership theories assume an individualist and egalitarian worldview.[13] Bass' transformational leadership theory was developed in the United States. The United States tends to score a medium level on the Power Distance Index, high in Individuality, medium–high on the Masculinity scale, medium on the Uncertainty Avoidance Index, a Short–Term Outlook, and medium–high with regard to Indulgence versus Restraint.[14] Leaders who attempt to implement transformational leadership outside of the cultural mix in which Bass developed his theory may encounter difficulties. While these biases and potential areas of mismatch do not disqualify the intercultural application of transformational leadership theory, they shed light on potential problem areas.

For example, transformational leaders expect that their followers will respond positively when the leader suggests the subordinates set their own work goals. In a low power distance, highly individualistic culture, the leader's expectation would be seen as appropriate and correct. That same latitude for individual planning can be very disconcerting to a follower from a high PDI, low IDV (collectivistic) culture. In this case, the follower is likely to be bewildered at how he should respond to a suggestion from the leader. Questions likely to run through the follower's mind include: What goals does the leader want me to articulate? How will the leaders respond if I suggest the wrong goal? Why is he putting me in this difficult position? Does he want to get rid of me or show others that I am inept?

Transformational Leadership as a variform universal.

Unless the leader considers the cultural views of his followers, he is unlikely to see the desired result from his leadership efforts. He may even go so far as to believe that his efforts at transformational leadership are a failure and resort to a different leadership style or theory. Transformational leadership is applicable across cultures but as a variform universal. In other words, the general principles of transformational leadership are consistent throughout the world, but local culture influences and changes

13. Lingenfelter, *Leading Cross-Culturally*, 100.

14. Hofstede et al., *Cultures and Organizations*, 59, 95, 141, 194, 240, 257.

the expression of the principle. To overcome these difficulties, the leader must be cognizant of how different cultures will mediate, modify, and moderate transformational leadership behaviors and outcomes.

Missions leadership theory must consider the needs and influences of the leader's host culture in order to provide appropriate leadership for God's mission. As I have argued, a host culture will mediate, modify, or moderate the practice, expression, and outcome of transformational leadership theory. Culture may facilitate (mediate) transformational leadership in a new context. Culture may change the expression (modify) of transformational leadership or enhance or inhibit its outcomes (moderate). Table 8 summarizes the manner in which Hofstede's dimensions of culture are likely to influence Bass' four transformational leadership factors.

Table 8. Transformational Leadership Factors and the Dimensions of Culture

TL factors	Mediators	Modifiers	Moderators (+/−)
Idealized Influence	High PDI, Low IDV, High MAS, and High UAI	IVR	
Inspirational Motivation		IDV, MAS, LTO, and IVR	High PDI (+)
Intellectual Stimulation	Low PDI, High IDV	UAI, IDV, LTO	Low IDV (−)
Individualized Consideration		IDV, PDI, UAI, LTO	Low IDV (−), High IVR (+)

As far as mediating factors go, cultures with high Power Distance, Masculinity, and Uncertainty Avoidance, as well as those with low Individualism, are likely to facilitate or positively influence the implementation of Idealized Influence. Conversely, cultures with low Power Distance may experience a mediating boost in Intellectual Stimulation and Individualized Consideration.

In other cultures, the leader can expect that the expression of certain transformational leadership factors will need to be adjusted to suit the recipient norms. For example, in low IVR settings, where the outlook tends toward pessimism and expects highly structured systems and leadership, successful factors of influence and motivation will look different than in more indulgent societies (high IVR). Different societies require different motivators. The modifications are unique to the culture and difficult to predict. Leaders must pay close attention to their host culture and observe what influences, motivates, stimulates, and shows proper consideration. These differences may even play out from region to region in the same society. Relying on what worked in a leader's home culture is a dangerous pattern.

Finally, leaders can expect that some cultural dimensions enhance or diminish leadership outcomes. It is reasonable to expect that high Power Distance has an enhancing effect on the Inspirational Motivation factor and that high IVR enhances the outcome of Individualized Consideration. However, low IDSV, or more collectivistic cultures may diminish the power of Intellectual Stimulation and Individualized Consideration.

Summary of cultural conclusions.

Transformational leadership theory is a reasonable basis for leadership in missions and ministry but not apart from careful consideration of the influence of Power Distance and Individualism. Therefore, leaders must be aware of the likely complications of implementing a transformational leadership approach in high Power Distance and more Collectivistic cultures and societies. Culture will mediate, modify, and moderate the results of leadership behaviors to a degree such that the leader must understand his home cultural dynamics and those of his host culture in order to lead. A host society's culture will determine how leadership is perceived and, to some degree, should be implemented. Therefore leaders should adjust their leadership outputs and expectations accordingly. One final important caveat. Though we are creatures of culture, culture does not dictate individuals. The stereotyping required for cultural analysis helps us understand people in a general way, but individuals are just that–individuals. Whereas the dimensions of culture help us understand people of our host culture, we must pay close attention to the individuals we lead and where they fall on these dimensional spectra. In the final analysis, leaders can have a reasonable hope that transformational leadership will be an effective and appropriate leadership theory for use in intercultural contexts when we lead with the awareness that people are more than the society of which they are a part.

Summary Evaluation

Transformation leadership theory can be a useful leadership approach if we understand the philosophical, theological, and cultural limitations and errors of the theory and make the adjustments I have outlined above.

Chapter 11

Conclusions on the Leadership Assessment Matrix.

THE PROCESS OF EXAMINING leadership theory from the perspective of theory, theology, and cultural anthropology leads to a better understanding of its missiological applicability. Better, because missionary and ministry leaders must understand the theories they put into practice, evaluate them theologically, and assess their intercultural applicability. Missiologists, missionaries, and ministers need a way to weigh leadership ideas from the perspectives of leadership philosophy, missions theology, and cultural anthropology. But, up to now, no one has designed a system for a missiological assessment of leadership theory or practice. Therefore, I hope that the Leadership Assessment Matrix and analytical process used in this research will aid the study of other leadership theories and practices in missions and ministry.

My purpose has been to design a usable system for evaluating a leadership theory. I call this system the Leadership Assessment Matrix. In this work I attempted to answer four research questions. 1) How should I fundamentally understand and analyze a leadership theory or practice? 2) What is essential in evaluating leadership theory and practice theologically? 3) What is a reasonable approach for understanding culture's effect on a leadership theory or practice? 4) What are the implications of a missiological assessment of transformational leadership theory in missions? In conclusion, here are my concluding answers to those questions.

How should I fundamentally understand and analyze a leadership theory or practice?

Understanding and analyzing any leadership approach, whether practice or theory, requires taking that theory at face value. We must strive to understand the theory or practice in its own right. The temptation to solve problems and just get on with work is overwhelming, and many leaders just reach for the current leadership bestseller, hoping that it will solve their problems. Over and over again, this approach fails. It fails, not because the theory at hand is necessarily wrong, but, most often, because it is misunderstood and misapplied. First, many misunderstand the intended audience and misapply it to their level of leadership. For example, many leadership books aim at the top levels of leadership and corporate executive officers and are not designed for teams or font-line work groups. Second, many misunderstand the occasion of a leadership theory, the background and the context or data driving the theory, and misapply it to their situation. A clear example was Jim Collins' bestseller, *Good to Great* which celebrated a very small number of companies out of a massive pool drawn from the Fortune 500 who managed massive success during one of the most economically positive runs in U.S. history. The Fortune 500 are all mature, stable companies by definition, and only eleven were identified by Collins as great. But even these elite eleven did not make it through the economic downturn of 2008 unscathed. Third, many misunderstand the worldviews that uphold certain theories and misapply them despite substantial differences of perspective on the world, how it operates, and how it should. Fourth, many misunderstand the cultural context in which theories develop and misapply them abroad. The United States has been a leadership theory-producing machine creating theories and practices well suited for that culture.

Therefore it is incumbent upon every leader to understand the theories or practices they exercise. That bestseller in your hands may have something to offer, but you need to be able to analyze it fairly and accurately, That means, understanding how it came to be, in what context, based on what ideals, for what purpose, and how it does the things it purports to do. The Leadership Assessment Matrix can guide you through that process.

What is essential in evaluating leadership theory and practice theologically?

To my surprise, when I set out on this journey, I found no typology, assessment grid, or system of evaluation for leadership in missions and ministry and very little systematic study of leadership theory in missions. Therefore, I constructed a typology for based on the work of Michale Ayers, James E. Plueddemann, and several studies in theology of missions. I proposed and demonstrated that the essential theological elements of a leadership evaluation include four aspects: teleology, ontology, authority, and ethic.

Each of the four main aspects of a theology of leadership consists of sub-categories or elements. The purpose, motivations, and goals of missions leadership are essential elements of leadership theory under the aspect of teleology. Under the ontology aspect, a leader's calling, character, and competency, especially competency in teaching, are vital. The capacity to lead, the right to lead, and responsibility are necessary elements of authority in leadership theory. Finally, under the aspect of ethic, serving the Lord and serving others are crucial behavioral elements in leadership. These elements of the Leadership Assessment Matrix constitute important biblical themes related to leadership in missions and ministry.

What is a reasonable approach for understanding culture's effect on a leadership theory or practice?

Many leaders lead with little or no regard for the nature of their leadership and lead without a really understanding the theories and methods they apply. Few give much attention to the theological implications of their leadership theories and methods. Some uncritically impose their home cultural forms of leadership in their host culture, while others simply adopt the local leadership practices uncritically. None of the above approaches is healthy; none are reasonable, responsible ways of leading.

Fortunately, research in intercultural leadership is growing. As businesses continue to grow more and more global and interconnected, the study of intercultural leadership has grown accordingly. Several good models for understanding culture exist, and the classic work by Geert Hofstede is a good example. Hofstede's model in the Leadership Assessment Matrix can help us understand the influence of culture on our leadership, how it is perceived and received, how it is mediated, modified, and moderated by views of power distance, individualism versus collectivism, masculinity versus femininity, uncertainty avoidance, long-term versus short-term orientation, and indulgence restraint.

What are the implications of a missiological assessment of transformational leadership theory in missions?

Leadership is important. Christian missions needs a philosophically sound, biblically grounded, and anthropologically informed leadership theory. This research on Bass' transformational leadership resulted in three implications for leadership in missions. First, leaders in mission need a biblically based theory of leadership. Bass' transformational leadership is clearly not suitable for missions leadership in its current form. This research concludes that transformational leadership theory can be a reasonable basis for leadership in missions, but only with an explicitly theological foundation and clear biblical guidelines in the theory's teleological, ontological, authority, and ethic aspects. Transformational leadership for missions must be reformulated to meet these vital requirements.

Second, researchers in this field of study need a systematic approach to leadership theory in order to achieve the biblically based leadership theory argued for above. Perhaps the most difficult aspect of this research was that I did not have a roadmap to guide the research. Missiological thinking about leadership often begins in the Bible, but such efforts tend to produce character studies or anecdotal descriptions of favorite leadership practices instead of comprehensive leadership theories. Missions leaders need a process to effectively study leadership from philosophical, theological, and cultural-anthropological perspectives. I submit the two typologies presented in this research, Hofstede's six dimensions of national cultures, and the roadmap displayed in Figure 6, as a path to this end.

Figure 6. A Roadmap to Missiological Thinking about Leadership.

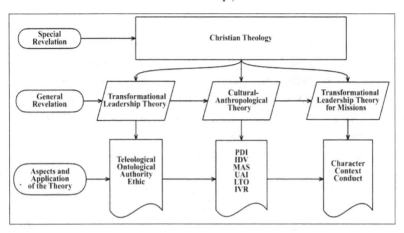

Third, researchers and leaders in missions and ministry need a theology of leadership. Leadership theory for missions and ministry must come from leadership themes or principles drawn from the Bible. Any leadership theory or practice should be defined from a clear theological perspective. In order for such an examination and modification to occur, researchers and leaders require a theology of leadership in missions.

Something I did not expect was to discover that this biblical and reasoned approach to evaluating leadership in missions and ministry would be a useful tool in general. I have come to believe that the Leadership Assessment Matrix is not only a powerful missiological assessment model but a means by which we can evaluate leadership in many settings.

Scholars and practitioners of leadership in Christian missions need to think and, subsequently, lead with greater attention to the philosophical, theological, and cultural anthropological assumptions that stand behind their leadership theories and practices. The analytical tools developed during the process of this study will be a great help to formulate a new way of thinking and behaving as leaders for the sake of God's glory displayed among the nations. The biblical framework for leadership presented here serves as the basis for a biblically–transformed leadership theory. Such a theory must begin with a biblical philosophical perspective and express a biblical purpose, nature, and ethic for Christian leadership. To assist the reader, I made a list of thirty questions in Appendix 2 that walk through the tiers and elements of the Leadership Assessment Matrix. A leader can use the questions to guide their study and evaluation of any leadership theory or practice.

The Leadership Assessment Matrix gives missionaries and ministry leaders the assessment power they need to evaluate leadership. Even better would be a model of leadership built on the foundation established here. The Bible teaches that leadership at a fundamental level, leadership is about being, knowing, and doing. For example, Ezra demonstrated these three aspects of leadership: *be* "the good hand of his God was on him," *know* "Ezra had set his heart to study the law of the LORD," *do* "to do it and to teach his statutes and rules in Israel," (Ezra 7:9-10). Peter's second epistle also demonstrates the three aspects to the churches in Asia Minor, teaching that they should strive for faith and moral excellence—*be*, knowledge—*know*, with self-control, perseverance, godliness, brotherly kindness, and love—*do* (2 Pet 1:5-7). Of all Bible passages, Psalm 78 depicts these three themes most clearly. Out of righteous character, with knowledge and skill, David led God's people.

> He chose David his servant and took him from the sheepfolds; from following the nursing ewes he brought him to shepherd Jacob his people, Israel his inheritance. With upright heart he shepherded them and guided them with his skillful hand. (Ps 78:70-72)

Furthermore, leadership established in the Bible is an intentional effort to guide and influence others for God's purposes and in God's ways. Leadership established in the Bible models Christ-like character. Leadership established in the Bible affirms the individual in Christ. Leadership established in the Bible acknowledges our interdependence of Christ's body. Leadership established in the Bible aims to be for Christ's mission. Leadership established in the Bible is active. Leadership established in the Bible is gracious to all. I call this essential leadership.

Soli Deo gloria.

Appendix 1

Outline of a Theology of Leadership

THE FOLLOWING IS A simple theology of leadership—themes pertaining to leaders and leadership drawn directly from the Word of God. The themes included in this theology are purpose, the nature of leadership, authority, and ethic.

The Purpose of Leadership: The Teleological Aspect

Leaders follow, teach, and model God's Word so that others may know God's purpose and will (Deut 6:1–9; Josh 1:1–9). God's people are emissaries of Christ to all peoples, proclaiming the good news and making disciples in the name of the Father, Son, and Holy Spirit for the glory of God (Matt 24:14; 28:18–20; Mark 16:15–16; Luke 24:46–48; Acts 1:8). The purpose of missions is to preach the gospel of salvation in Jesus among peoples where the church has not yet been established to bring about the obedience of faith for his name's sake (Rom 1:5; 15:18–21).God has gifted his church with leaders to lead for his purposes, namely to bring glory and praise to himself (Eph 4:11–14; Rom 12:6–8; John 16:13–15).

Motivation for Leadership

All of humanity are lost in sin, dead in our trespasses and objects of wrath (2 Kgs 22:13; Ps 90:1–11; John 3:36; Rom 1:18). The Apostle Paul writes of his strong motivation to reach the lost so that they might be saved (Rom 9:1–3; 11:13–15; 1 Cor 9:19, 22). Leaders are motivated by the power of the gospel, which compelled the apostles to forsake all others and become men who "turned the world upside down" (Acts 17:6). The apostles were motivated by their view of Jesus as Savior and Lord to obey and follow his commands. The gospel brings together two basic Christian concepts—faith and obedience. One is never present without the other (1 John 2:3–4, 29; 3:7, 24; 5:2–4).

Leaders are motivated by the greatness of God's glory. Part of the motivation for missions is the desire to know Christ (1 John 4:9–11). Christians are encouraged to missions out of love for the lost in the same manner that God demonstrated his saving love in Christ. This noble cause, God's glory—that God should be worshipped because he is worthy of our complete adoration, is the deepest of motivations.

None of the above motivations—the plight of the lost, the awesomeness of God's glory, and the power of the gospel to propitiate God's wrath, redeem sinners, and reconcile us to God—are mutually exclusive. Mission leaders will express their motivation to lead in various ways, but the biblical root motivation in missions leadership is that God is worthy. God is supremely worthy of worship and praise because of his love powerfully expressed in Christ's substitutionary atonement (Rev 5:6–14). God's worthiness is the essential motivation for missions.

Objectives in Leadership

Christian leadership has a two-fold goal: to make disciples and to promote disciple-making to all peoples. Jesus assured his followers of the certainty and scope of his mission and missions, teaching that the gospel would be preached throughout the world to all nations before the end comes (Matt 24:14, Rom 10:11–15).

The Nature of Leadership: The Ontological Aspect

Mission leaders are called men of character and capability (Ps 78:70–72). God's calling to reach the nations is a specific call (Acts 13:2; Rom 1:1; Gal 2:8–9). The Apostle Paul recognized the need for other leaders to be called. He instructs the church to seek the man who aspires to lead (1 Tim 3:1). God gifts those whom he calls. God gifts leaders to the church to fulfill this role (1 Cor 12:28; Rom 12:6–8; 1 Tim 4:14; 2 Tim 1:16). Churches affirm the calling, gifting, and authority of leaders in the church, but it is the Holy Spirit that makes them leaders (Acts 20:28). Authority lies in God's Word. The requirements for church leaders in 1 Timothy and Titus include the need for both biblical knowledge and character worth following. Followers may attribute authority to organizational leaders because of the leader's presumed or demonstrated character, teaching skill, or wisdom that comes from God and his Word. Most importantly, power and authority in leadership are for God's glory, not for personal gain (Matt 20:25–28).

Leaders are People of Exemplary Character.

Three foundational characteristics: integrity, humility, and courage, are vital to leadership (Deut 8:1–3, 11–20; Ps 56; Ps 78:70–72; Job 2:3; 1 Sam 14:6–15; Phil 2:1–16; 1 Tim 3:2, 10; Jas 1:12, 1 Pet 1:7). Leaders are people of integrity. The Bible bases integrity on righteousness—adherence to God's standards (Deut 17:18–19; Ps 101, 1 Kgs 9:4 and Job 2:3, Ps 7:8; 25:21, Prov 10:9; 11:3;28:6; Titus 2:7). Leaders are humble toward God and others. Humility is, ultimately, dependence on God (Deut 8:1–3, 11–20; 17:19–20; 2 Kgs 22:11–13, 18–19; 1 Pet 5:5–7). Humility is not ascetic self-abasement, for such is false wisdom (Col 2:23). Humility is putting others first in service to Christ for the glory of God (Col 2:23; Phil 2:1–16; Eph 4:2). Leaders are courageous—faithful to the Lord amidst danger and temptation (1 Pet 5:8–9). Courage is trusting in God and his care (Ps 56; 1 Sam 14:6–15; 16:1–13; Dan 3:17–18). Courage in God remains steadfast despite circumstances (Ps 119:46; Matt 14:26–31; Mark 8:38; 2 Tim 1:8–12).

Leaders have the Capability to Lead.

The ability to teach is the most common skill required of leaders, according to the New Testament (1 Tim 3:2–3; 2 Tim 2:2, 24; Titus 1:9; Jude 1:3). The

Apostle Peter warns us that unscrupulous teachers can lead believers astray from the faith (2 Pet 2:1–3). The preventative measure to defend the church from false teachers is to remember good teaching, even difficult doctrines (2 Pet 3:1–3, 14–16). Leaders who teach are necessary so the church is not thrown off-point by false teaching and clever deceit (Eph 4:11–14). Many ought to be teachers, but some continue in immaturity and discount themselves as teachers and leaders (Heb 5:12).

The Authority to Lead.

The parable of the talents depicts three essential aspects of authority. The servant was given *capacity*—the power to do the master's will, *right*—the authority to do the master's will, and *responsibility*—held accountable for the results of doing the master's will (Matt 25:13–30). Leaders exert the power of a good example, "Remember your leaders, those who spoke to you the Word of God. Consider the outcome of their way of life and imitate their faith" (Heb13:7. Also 1 Cor 4:16; 11:1; Phil 3:17; 4:9; 1 Thess 1:6–7; 2 Thess 3:7, 9; 1 Tim 4:12; Titus 2:7; 1 Pet 5:3, 8).

The Capacity to Lead.

Leaders exert power through knowledge of God's Word. Leaders are commanded to teach (Lev 10:11; Deut 4:10, 14; 5:31; 6:1, 7; 11:19; 31:19; 33:10; Ezra 7:25; Ps 78:5) and inspired to teach (Exod 35:34; Ps 51:13; 94:12; 119:171; Mic 4:2; John 14:26). Teaching is sought for in prayer (Judg 13:8; 1 Kgs 8:36; 2 Chr 6:2; Ps 25:4, 5; 27:11; 32:8; 45:4; 51:6; 86:11; 90:12; 119:12, 26, 29, 33, 64, 66, 68, 108, 124, 135; 143:10), directed by earthly leaders (2 Chr 17:7; Ezra 7:10; Ps 34:11; Prov 9:9; Isa 2:3; 28:9; Jer 9:20), exemplified by Jesus (Matt 11:1; 22:16; Mark 4:1; 6:2, 34; 8:31; 12:14; Luke 11:1; 20:21; Acts 1:1), and modeled and commanded by the apostles (Acts 5:21; 1 Cor; 1 Tim 3:2; 4:11; 6:2; 2 Tim 2:2; 24; Titus 2:3; Heb 5:12; Jas 3:1).

The Right to Lead.

Authority is the right to lead and comes from God. Paul, in Romans 13, teaches that God has established governments and civic authorities. Jesus asserted that his authority came from God (John 5:7; 7:17; 8:28; 10:18; 12:49;

14:10; 17:2). In the Old Testament, God's servants minister in the name of the Lord (Deut 18:5–7; 21:5). God's servants stand/walk/live in the name of the Lord (1 Sam 17:45; Mic 4:5; Ps 118:26; Zep 3:12). God's servants bless others in the name of the Lord (2 Sam 6:18; 1 Chr 16:2). God's servants speak in the name of the Lord (1 Chr 21:19; 2 Chr 33:18; Ezra 5:1; Jer 26:16, 20; 44:16). Jesus gave his church the authority to carry out his mission and make disciples of all the nations. Jesus' disciples assemble and teach in the name of the Lord (Matt 28:18–20; 1 Cor 5:4; Acts 4:18; 5:40; 9:27–28; Acts 19:5; Col 3:17). Jesus has all authority and gave the right for disciples to teach and live out his will. Leaders teach, exhort, and rebuke with all authority (Titus 2:15). Leaders instruct and correct the church as part of being a good servant of God (1 Tim 1:3; 4:6; 4:16; 6:17–18; 2 Tim 4:2).

Responsibility in Leading.

Leaders are responsible to God. Leaders are stewards of their gifts, including the gift of leadership. The Apostle Peter reminds his readers that the purpose of the gifts is to serve to serve others in order that God may be glorified (1 Pet 4:10–11). With the power and authority in leadership comes responsibility (1 Cor 8:9–13). Because of this responsibility, teachers and leaders are subject to stricter judgment—accountable to God for their behavior and that which they teach others, by word and deed (Jas 3:1–4).

Leaders are responsible to followers. Jesus taught his disciples that the path to spiritual leadership was paved with suffering and sacrifice and demonstrated through servanthood. Seeking position for the sake of honor is not the way of spiritual leadership, but sacrificial service is (Matt 16:24–25, Mark 8:34–35, Luke 9:23–25).

Leadership Behavior

A missions leader is God's servant. The greatest commandment is to love the Lord God with all your heart, soul, and mind. A second commandment is to love your neighbor as yourself (Matt 22:36–40). Leadership behavior is to love God and love others. Therefore, leaders lead following Jesus path of loving obedience to the father (John 3:16; 13:34–35; 15:9, 12, 15; 14:15, 21, 23–24, 31; 15:10,17; 20:21; 16:27; Heb 3:1–2; 1 John 3:1; 11; 4:9, 11, 19, 21; 5:3; 2 John 1:5–6).

Leaders are genuinely concerned for the welfare of others in service to Christ (Phil 2:20–22). The leadership that Timothy exhibited is not altruistic care for humanity, but Christocentric care for others—the ultimate interest is Christ. Subsequently, leaders lead as one among peers—leading God's people, not their own. Leaders exercise oversight, care for those in their charge, lead willingly, not under compulsion. Leaders should lead by example and not be domineering and are accountable to Christ, who brings reward with him (1 Pet 5:1–4).

A leader is a servant of God: God's vessel, sanctified and, therefore, useful to the Lord. A leader is a slave of Christ, humble toward others, and firm in conviction. Submits to the Lordship of Christ. Obeys and guards God's Word. Single-minded in his devotion to the Lord (1 Pet 1:13–14; 2:3–4, 20–21, 21). A leader is courageous in God's love and power and displays self-control. Compliant to God's ways–not tempted by shortcuts to fame (1 Pet 1:6–7). He preaches and teaches the Word of God. He rightly handles the Word of God. Ready to preach the Word and teaches others who are able to teach others (1 Pet 2:2, 15; 3:2). Finally, a leader works hard and endures with Christ: Serves according to God's ways, not tempted by shortcuts to fame (1 Pet 2:5, 6, 11–13).

Appendix 2

Thirty Leadership Theory
Assessment Questions

To FACILITATE IMPLEMENTING THE Leadership Theory Matrix, I prepared a list of questions to guide your assessment of a leadership theory or practice. Following the assessment matrix, the questions fall into four tiers relating to the philosophy of the theory, the theology of the theory, the theory and culture, and the final assessment. The questions all refer to *theory*, but most leadership *practices* can be evaluated by the same set of questions.

Tier 1: Philosophical questions.

1. What is the pertinent historical or situational context of the theory—what are the relevant theoretical antecedents or social phenomena surrounding the theory's development?

2. How did the theory take form and improve?

3. How would you summarize the theory? Describe the central tenants and any norms or values that are part of the theory.

4. What does the theory attempt to do, or what goal does it seek to accomplish?

5. Where does leadership reside in the theory?

6. In practice, how does the theory exert leadership or influence others?

7. Whom or what group does the theory serve?

8. How do you know the theory is working—what are appropriate measures of performance for the theory? Look for relationships between the theory, behaviors (output), and results (impact).

9. How do the internal aspects or elements of the theory interrelate or affect one another?

10. What in the context can affect the theory's implementation or outcomes?

Tier 2: Theological questions.

In your theology of leadership:

11. What is the biblical purpose of leadership?

12. What should motivate leaders?

13. Where do leaders come from (nature, nurture, and calling)?

14. What sort of character should we expect from leaders?

15. What kinds of gifts, abilities, or experience are necessary for leadership?

16. How should we define or determine a person's capacity to lead?

17. What is a leader's source of authority, to whom are they responsible, and whom should they serve?

18. What should be the code of conduct for leaders?

19. How does the leader serve God and man?

20. How does the theory stand up to your theology of leadership?

Tier 3: Culture questions.

21. Power Distance: What is the degree of existence and acceptance of hierarchy in the host culture?

22. Individualism vs. Collectivism: Does the host culture place emphasis on personal/immediate family goals and needs or more toward those of the group/society?

23. Masculinity vs. Femininity: How are assertiveness, competition, and distinct gender roles viewed in the culture versus quality of life, cooperation, and overlap in gender roles?

24. Uncertainty Avoidance: What are the cultural views or responses to volatility, uncertainty, complexity, and ambiguity?

25. Long–term vs. Short–term Orientation: Does the host culture value patience and preparation or immediate gratification?

26. Indulgence vs. Restraint: What is the host culture's perspective on satiating desires versus compliance with social norms?

27. How is the theory in question mediated by the host culture?

28. How is the theory in question moderated by the host culture?

29. How is the theory in question modified by the host culture?

Tier 4: Appropriateness of the leadership theory.

30. The final question: Is the leadership theory appropriate for your work in your setting?

Bibliography

Abdalla, Ikhlas A., and Moudi A. Al-Homoud. "Exploring the Implicit Leadership Theory in the Arabian Gulf States." *Applied Psychology: An International Review* 50, no. 4 (2001): 503–31.

Adair, John. *How to Grow Leaders: The Seven Key Principles of Effective Development.* London: Kogan Page, 2009.

Allen, Bill. "Pathways to Leadership." In *Creative Church Leadership*, edited by John Adair and John Nelson, 32–47. Norwich, England: Canterbury, 2004.

Anderson, Justice. "An Overview of Missiology." In *Missiology: An Introduction*, edited by John Mark Terry and Ebbie C. Smith. Nashville: Broadman and Holman Academic, 1998.

Army Center for Leadership. *The U.S. Army Leadership Field Manual.* New York: McGraw-Hill, 2004.

Avey, James B., Bruce J. Avolio, and Fred Luthans. "Experimentally Analyzing the Impact of Leader Positivity on Follower Positivity and Performance." *The Leadership Quarterly* 22 (2011): 282–94.

Avolio, Bruce J. *Full Leadership Development: Building the Vital Forces in Organizations.* Thousand Oaks, CA: SAGE Publications, 1999.

Avolio, Bruce J., and Bernard M. Bass. "Individual Consideration Viewed at Multiple Levels of Analysis: A Multi-Level Framework for Examining the Diffusion of Transformational Leadership." *Leadership Quarterly* 6 (1995): 199–218.

———. "Re-Examining the Components of Transformational and Transactional Leadership Using the Multifactor Leadership Questionnaire." *Journal of Occupational & Organizational Psychology* 72, no. 4 (1999): 441–62.

Avolio, Bruce J., and William L. Gardner. "Authentic Leadership Development: Getting to the Root of Positive Forms of Leadership." *The Leadership Quarterly* 16 (2005): 315–38.

Ayers, Michale. "Toward a Theology of Leadership." *Journal of Biblical Perspectives in Leadership* 1, no. 1 (Fall 2006): 3–27.

Banks, Robert. *Reviewing Leadership: A Christian Evaluation of Current Approaches.* Grand Rapids: Baker Academic, 2004.

Baron, Reuben M., and David A. Kenny. "The Moderator-Mediator Variable Distinction in Social Psychological Research: Conceptual, Strategic, and Statistical Considerations." *Journal of Personality and Social Psychology* 51, no. 6 (1986): 1173–82.

Bartz, James P. "Leadership from the Inside Out." *Anglican Theological Review* 91, no. 1 (2009): 81–92.

Bass, Bernard M, and Bruce J. Avolio. *Multifactor Leadership Questionnaire.* Palo Alto, CA: Consulting Psychologists, 1990.

Bass, Bernard M. "From Transactional to Transformational Leadership: Learning to Share the Vision." *Organizational Dynamics* 18, no. 3 (1990): 19–32.

———. "Theory of Transformational Leadership Redux." *Leadership Quarterly* 6 (1995): 463–78.

———. *Assessment of Managers.* New York: Free, 1979.

———. *Bass and Stogdill's Handbook of Leadership: Theory, Research and Managerial Applications.* 2nd ed. New York: Free, 1981.

———. *Leadership and Performance beyond Expectations.* New York: Free, 1985.

———. *Leadership, Psychology, and Organizational Behavior.* New York: Harper & Row, 1960.

Bass, Bernard M., and P. Steidlmeier. "Ethics, Character, and Authentic Transformational Leadership." *Leadership Quarterly* 10 (1999): 181–217.

Bass, Bernard M., and Ronald E. Riggio. *Transformational Leadership.* 2nd ed. Mahwah, NJ: Psychology, 2005.

Bass, Bernard M., and Ruth Bass. *The Bass Handbook of Leadership: Theory, Research, and Managerial Applications.* 4th ed. San Francisco: Free, 2008.

Bennis, Warren. *On Becoming a Leader.* 4th ed. Philadelphia: Basic, 2009.

Berson, Yair, and Bruce J. Avolio. "Transformational Leadership and the Dissemination of Organizational Goals: A Case Study of a Telecommunication Firm." *The Leadership Quarterly* 15 (2004): 625–46.

Blackaby, Henry, and Richard Blackaby. *Spiritual Leadership: Moving People on to God's Agenda.* Nashville: Broadman and Holman Academic, 2011.

Blanchard, Ken, Patricia Zigarmi, and Drea Zigarmi. *Leadership and the One Minute Manager: Increasing Effectiveness through Situational Leadership.* New York: William Morrow, 1999.

———. *Situational Leadership II.* San Diego: The Ken Blanchard Companies, 2007.

Blanchard, Kenneth H. *Ken Blanchard's Situational Leadership II: The Article.* San Diego: Blanchard Training and Development, 1994.

Blanchard, Kenneth H., and Phil Hodges. *Lead Like Jesus: Lessons from the Greatest Leadership Role Model of All Time.* Nashville: Thomas Nelson, 2008.

Bolton, Robert. *People Skills: How to Assert Yourself, Listen to Others, and Resolve Conflicts.* New York: Simon & Schuster, 1986.

Bommer, William H., Robert S. Rubin, and Timothy T. Baldwin. "Setting the Stage for Effective Leadership: Antecedents of Transformational Leadership Behavior." *The Leadership Quarterly* 15 (2004): 195–210.

Bredfeldt, Gary. *Great Leader, Great Teacher: Recovering the Biblical Vision for Leadership.* Chicago: Moody, 2006.

Brown, J. Brock. "The Building of a Virtuous Transformational Leader." *The Journal of Virtues and Leadership* 2, no. 1 (2011): 6–14.

Burke, C. S., D. E. Sims, E. H. Lazzara, and E. Salas. "Trust in Leadership: A Multi-Level Review and Integration." *The Leadership Quarterly* 18 (2007): 606–32.

Burns, James MacGregor. *Leadership*. New York: Harper and Row, 1978.

———. *Transforming Leadership*. New York: Grove, 2004.

Carson, D. A. *The Gospel According to John*. Pillar New Testament Commentary. Grand Rapids: William B. Eerdmans, 1991.

———. "Conclusion: Ongoing Imperative for World Mission." In *The Great Commission: Evangelicals and the History of World Missions*, edited by Martin Klauber and Scott M. Manetsch, 176–95. Nashville: Broadman and Holman Academic, 2008.

Carter, John F. "Power and Authority in Pentecostal Leadership." *Asian Journal of Pentecostal Studies* 12, no. 2 (2009): 185–207.

Chhokar, Jagdeep S., Felix C. Brodbeck, and Robert J. House, eds. *Culture and Leadership across the World: The GLOBE Book of In-Depth Studies of 25 Societies*. New York: Psychology, 2007.

Christiano, Tom. "Authority." Edited by Edward N. Zalta. *The Stanford Encyclopedia of Philosophy*, 2013.

Clark, Kenneth E., Miriam B. Clark, and Robert R. Albright. *Measures of Leadership*. West Orange, NJ: Leadership Library of America, 1990.

Clinton, Robert. *The Making of a Leader: Recognizing the Lessons and Stages of Leadership Development*. Colorado Springs: NavPress, 1988.

Collins, Jim. *Good to Great: Why Some Companies Make the Leap... and Others Don't*. New York: HarperCollins, 2001.

Conger, Jay A. "Charismatic and Transformational Leadership in Organizations: An Insider's Perspective on These Developing Streams of Research." *Leadership Quarterly* 10 (1999): 145–79.

Cooper, Michael T. "The Transformational Leadership of the Apostle Paul: A Contextual and Biblical Leadership for Contemporary Business and Ministry." *Christian Education Journal* 2, no. 1 (2005): 48–61.

Dastmalchian, Ali, Mansour Javidan, and Kamran Alam. "Effective Leadership and Culture in Iran: An Empirical Study." *Applied Psychology: An International Review* 50, no. 4 (2001): 532–58.

Deal, Jennifer, Sarah Stawiski, Menna Wilson, and Kristin Cullen. "What Makes an Effective Leader? Generations in India Weigh In." A white paper for the Center for Creative Leadership, January 20, 2014, http://insights.ccl.org/?post_type=articles& article-type=white-papers.

DeYoung, Kevin, and Gregory D. Gilbert. *What Is the Mission of the Church?* Wheaton, IL: Crossway, 2011.

Dickson, Marcus W., Deanne N. Den Hartog, and Jacqueline Mitchelson. "Research on Leadership in a Cross-Cultural Context: Making Progress, and Raising New Questions." *The Leadership Quarterly* 14 (2003): 729–68.

Douglas, Mary. "Cultural Bias." In *In the Active Voice*, 183–254. London: Routledge and Kegan Paul, 1982.

Downton, James V. *Rebel Leadership: Commitment and Charisma in the Revolutionary Process*. Thousand Oaks, CA: SAGE, 1973.

DuBrin, Andrew J. *Leadership: Research Findings, Practice, and Skills*. Mason, OH: South-Western Cengage Learning, 2011.

Elliston, Edgar J. "Leadership Theory." In *Evangelical Dictionary of World Missions*, edited by A. Moreau, 567–68. Grand Rapids: Baker Academic, 2000.

Faulhaber, Jacqeline. "Virtue Development and Authentic Transformational Leadership: A Social-Cultural Analysis of 2 Peter 1:1–11." *Biblical Perspectives* May (2007): 1–39.

Fee, Gordon D. "Laos and Leadership under the New Covenant." *Crux* 25, no. 4 (1989): 3–13.

Ford, Leighton. *Transforming Leadership: Jesus' Way of Creating Vision, Shaping Values and Empowering Change.* Downers Grove, IL: Intervarsity, 1993.

Ford, Paul R. *Your Leadership Grip: Assessment Process.* Edited by Robert Rummel. 2nd ed. St. Charles, IL: Churchsmart Resources, 2007.

French, John R. P., and Bertram Raven. "The Bases of Social Power." In *Group Dynamics: Research and Theory,* 2nd ed., 259–69. New York: Harper & Row, 1959.

Gardner, Howard E. *Leading Minds: An Anatomy of Leadership.* New York: Basic, 1995.

Gay, Larry, and Susan Gay. *The Servant Leader's Handbook.* Singapore: unpublished, 2008.

Gay, Larry. "LEAD360 Rollout Plan 2009." unpublished, February 11, 2009.

Gill, Roger. *Theory and Practice of Leadership.* 2nd ed. London, England: SAGE, 2011.

Gray, David R. "Christological Hymn: The Leadership Paradox of Philippians 2:5–11." *Journal of Biblical Perspectives in Leadership* 2, no. 1 (2008): 3–18.

Green, Mark, Stephanie Kodatt, Charles Salter, Phyllis Duncan, Diana Garza-Ortiz, and Esther Chavez. "Assessing the Leadership Style of Paul and Cultural Congruence of the Christian Community at Corinth Using Project GLOBE Constructs." *Journal of Biblical Perspectives in Leadership* 2, no. 2 (2009): 3–28.

Greenhouse, Robert K. *Servant Leadership: A Journey into the Nature of legitimate Power and Greatness.* Edited by Larry C. Spears. New York: Paulist, 2002.

Grunlan, Stephen A., and Marvin K. Mayers. *Cultural Anthropology: A Christian Perspective.* 2nd Edition. Grand Rapids: Zondervan, 1988

Habecker, Eugene B. *Rediscovering the Soul of Leadership.* Wheaton, IL: Victor, 1996.

Hackman, Michael Z., and Craig E. Johnson. *Leadership: A Communication Perspective.* Long Grove, IL: Waveland, 2013.

Hartog, Deanne N. Den, Robert J. House, Paul John Hanges, S. Antonio Ruiz-Quintanilla, and Peter W. Dorfman. "Culture Specific and Cross-Culturally Generalizable Implicit Leadership Theories: Are Attributes of Charismatic/Transformational Leadership Universally Endorsed?" *Leadership Quarterly* 10 (1999): 219–56.

Harvey, J. B. *The Abilene Paradox and Other Meditations on Management.* San Francisco: Jossey-Bass, 1996.

Hatter, J. J., and Bernard M. Bass. "Supervisor's Evaluations and Subordinates Perceptions of Transformational and Transactional Leadership." *Journal of Applied Psychology* 73 (1988): 695–702.

Hemphill, Ken. *You are Gifted: Your Spiritual Gifts and the Kingdom of God.* Nashville: Broadman and Holman, 2009.

Hernandez, Morela, Marion B. Eberly, Bruce J. Avolio, and Michael D. Johnson. "The Loci and Mechanisms of Leadership: Exploring a More Comprehensive View of Leadership Theory." *The Leadership Quarterly* 22 (2011): 1165–85.

Hersey, Paul, Kenneth H. Blanchard, and Dewey E. Johnson. *Management of Organizational Behavior: Leading Human Resources.* 8th ed. Upper Saddle River, NJ: Prentice Hall, 2000.

Hesselgrave, David J. *Communicating Christ Cross-Culturally.* 2nd ed. Grand Rapids: Zondervan, 1991.

Hiebert, D. Edmond. "Pauline Images of a Christian Leader." *Bibliotheca Sacra* 133, no. 531 (September 1976): 213–28.

Hiebert, Paul G. *Anthropological Reflections on Missiological Issues*. Grand Rapids: Baker Academic, 1994.

———. *Transforming Worldviews: An Anthropological Understanding of How People Change*. Grand Rapids: Baker Academic, 2008.

Higginson, Richard. *Transforming Leadership: A Christian Approach to Management*. London: SPCK, 1996.

Hofstede, Geert, Gert Jan Hofstede, and Michael Minkov. *Cultures and Organizations: Software for the Mind*. 3rd ed. New York: McGraw-Hill, 2010.

Hofstede, Geert. "A European in Asia." *Asian Journal of Social Psychology* 10 (2007): 16–21.

———. "Cultural Constraints in Management Theories." *Academy of Management Executive* 7, no. 1 (1993): 81–94.

———. *Culture's Consequences: Comparing Values, Behaviors, Institutions and Organizations across Nations*. 2nd ed. Thousand Oaks, CA: SAGE Publications, 2001.

Horner, David. *When Missions Shapes the Mission: You and Your Church Can Reach the World*. Nashville: Broadman and Holman, 2011.

House, Robert J. *A 1976 Theory of Charismatic Leadership*. Toronto: Faculty of Management Studies, University of Toronto, 1977.

House, Robert J., Mansour Javidan, and Peter W. Dorfman. "Project GLOBE: An Introduction." *Applied Psychology: An International Review* 50, no. 4 (2001): 489–505.

House, Robert J., Paul John Hanges, Mansour Javidan, Peter W. Dorfman, and Vipin Gupta, eds. *Culture, Leadership, and Organizations: The GLOBE Study of 62 Societies*. Thousand Oaks, CA: SAGE Publications, 2004.

Howell, Don. *Servants of the Servant: A Biblical Theology of Leadership*. Eugene, OR: Wipf & Stock, 2003.

Howell, Jane M., Derrick J. Neufeld, and Bruce J. Avolio. "Examining the Relationship of Leadership and Physical Distance with Business Unit Performance." *The Leadership Quarterly* 16 (2005): 273–85.

Huizing, Russell L. "Leaders from Disciples: The Church's Contribution to Leadership Development." *Evangelical Review of Theology* 35, no. 4 (2011): 333–44.

Hunt, J. G. "What Is Leadership?" In *The Nature of Leadership*, edited by John Antonakis, T. Cianciolo, and R. J. Sternberg, 19–47. Thousand Oaks, CA: Sage, 2004.

Hur, YoungHee, Peter T. van den Berg, and Celeste P.M. Wilderom. "Transformational Leadership as a Mediator between Emotional Intelligence and Team Outcomes." *The Leadership Quarterly* 22 (2011): 591–603.

Hutchison, John C. "Servanthood: Jesus' Countercultural Call to Christian Leaders." *Bibliotheca Sacra* 166, no. 661 (2009): 53–69.

Iorg, Jeff. *The Character of Leadership: Nine Qualities That Define Great Leaders*. Nashville: Broadman and Holman, 2007.

Jago, A. G. "Leadership: Perspectives in Theory and Research." *Management Science* 28, no. 3 (1982): 315–36.

Javidan, Mansour, Peter W. Dorfman, Mary Sully de Luque, and Robert J. House. "In the Eye of the Beholder: Cross Cultural Lessons in Leadership from Project GLOBE." *Academy of Management Perspectives* 20, no. 1 (2006): 67–90.

Johns, G. "The Essential Impact of Context or Organizational Behavior." *Academy of Management Review* 31 (2006): 386–408.

Johnson, Andrew M., Philip A. Vernon, Julie M. McCarthy, Mindy Molson, Julie A. Harris, and Kerry L. Jang. "Nature vs Nurture: Are Leaders Born or Made? A Behavior Genetic Investigation of Leadership Style." *Twin Research* 1, no. 4 (1998): 216–23.

Jones, Galen Wendell. "A Theological Comparison between Social Science Models and a Biblical Perspective of Servant Leadership." PhD diss., The Southern Baptist Theological Seminary, 2012.

Jung, D. I., B. M. Bass, and J. J. Sosik. "Bridging Leadership and Culture: A Theoretical Consideration of Transformational Leadership and Collectivistic Cultures." *Journal of Leadership and Organizational Studies* 2, no. 4 (1995): 3–18.

Jung, Dongil, Francis J. Yammarino, and Jin K. Lee. "Moderating Role of Subordinates' Attitudes on Transformational Leadership and Effectiveness: A Multi-Cultural and Multi-Level Perspective." *The Leadership Quarterly* 20 (2009): 586–603

Kellerman, Barbara. *The End of Leadership.* New York: Harper Business, 2012.

Khanin, Dmitry. "Contrasting Burns and Bass: Does the Transactional-Transformational Paradigm Live up to Burns Philosophy of Transforming Leadership?" *Journal of Leadership Studies* 1, no. 3 (2007): 7–25.

Kim, Kyung Kyu, and Richard L. Starcher. "Cultivating Intercultural Leaders." *International Journal of Leadership Studies* 7, no. 1 (2012): 71–86.

Kirkpatrick, Shelly A., and Edwin A. Locke. "Leadership: Do Traits Matter?" *Academy of Management Executive* 5, no. 2 (1991): 48–60.

Köstenberger, Andreas J., T. Desmond Alexander, and D. A. Carson. *Salvation to the Ends of the Earth: A Biblical Theology of Mission.* Second edition. London, Downers Grove, IL: IVP Academic, 2020.

Köstenberger, Andreas J. "The Challenge of a Systematized Biblical Theology of Mission: Missiological Insights from the Gospel of John." *Missiology: An International Review* 23, no. 4 (1995): 445–64.

Kowske, Brenda J., and Kshanika Anthony. "Towards Defining Leadership Competence around the World: What Mid-Level Managers Need to Know in Twelve Countries." *Human Resource Development International* 10, no. 1 (2007): 21–41.

Kraft, Charles H. *Anthropology for Christian Witness.* Maryknoll, NY: Orbis, 1997.

Kraybill, Ron. *Style Matters: The Kraybill Conflict Response Inventory.* Harrisonburg, VA: Riverhouse, 2005.

LaBarre, Polly. "Do You Have the Will to Lead?" *Fast Company*, March 2000.

Ladkin, Donna. *Rethinking Leadership: A New Look at Old Leadership Questions.* New Horizons in Leadership Studies. Northampton, MA: Edward Elgar, 2010.

Latta, Gail F. "A Process Model for Organizational Change in Cultural Context (OC3 Model)." *Journal of Leadership and Organizational Studies* 16, no. 1 (2009): 19–37.

Lawless, Chuck. "Paul and Leadership Development." In *Paul's Missionary Methods: In His Time and Ours,* edited by Robert L. Plummer and John Mark Terry, 216–34. Downers Grove, IL: IVP Academic, 2012.

Lawrenz, Melvin E. *Spiritual Influence: The Hidden Power behind Leadership.* Grand Rapids: Zondervan, 2012.

Leahy, Kevin. "A Study of Peter as a Model for Servant Leadership." *Inner Resources for Leadership* 2, no. 4 (2010): 1–10.

Lewis, Phillip V. *Transformational Leadership: A New Model for Total Congregational Involvement.* Nashville: Broadman and Holman, 1996.

Lewis, Richard D. *Cultural Imperative: Global Trends in the 21st Century.* London: Intercultural, 2002.

————. *When Cultures Collide: Leading across Cultures,* 3rd ed. Boston: Nicholas Brealey, 2006.

Lingenfelter, Sherwood G. *Leading Cross-Culturally: Covenant Relationships for Effective Christian Leadership.* Grand Rapids: Baker Academic, 2008.

————. "The DNA of the Church: Anthropological Reflections on the Missionary Structure of the Church." *Swedish Missiological Themes* 93, no. 3 (2005): 434–47.

Liu, Shang-Min, and Jian-Qiao Liao. "Transformational Leadership and Speaking up: Power Distance and Structural Distance as Moderators." *Social Behavior and Personality* 41, no. 10 (2013): 1747–56.

Logan, Dave, John King, and Halee Fischer-Wright. *Tribal Leadership: Leveraging Natural Groups to Build a Thriving Organization.* New York: Harper Business, 2011.

Lonner, W. J. "The Search for Psychological Universals." In *Perspectives Handbook of Cross-Cultural Psychology,* edited by H. C. Triandis and W. W. Lambert, 1:143–204. Boston: Allyn and Bacon, 1980.

Lowe, Kevin B., K. Galen Kroeck, and Nagaraj Sivasubramaniam. "Effectiveness Correlates of Transformational and Transactional Leadership: A Meta-Analytic Review of the MLQ Literature." *Leadership Quarterly* 7 (1996): 385–425.

Luthans, Fred, Carolyn M. Youssef, and Bruce J. Avolio. *Psychological Capital Developing the Human Competitive Edge.* New York: Oxford University Press, 2007.

Lyons, Joseph B., and Tamera R. Schneider. "The Effects of Leadership Style on Stress Outcomes." *The Leadership Quarterly* 20 (2009): 737–48.

Malphurs, Aubrey. *Being Leaders: The Nature of Authentic Christian Leadership.* Grand Rapids: Baker, 2003.

McCabe, Laurie. "Jesus as Agent of Change: Transformational and Authentic Leadership in John 21." *Journal of Biblical Perspectives in Leadership* 2, no. 1 (2008): 32–43.

McClough, A. C., S. G. Rogelberg, and G. G. Fisher. "Cynicism and the Quality of an Individual's Contribution to an Organizational Diagnostic Survey." *Organization Development Journal* 16 (1998): 31–41.

McCrae, R. R., and P. P. Costa. "Validation of the Five-Factor Model of Personality across Instruments and Observers" *Journal of Personality and Social Psychology* 52 no. 1 (1987): 81–90.

Merkle, Benjamin L. "Paul's Ecclesiology." In *Paul's Missionary Methods: In His Time and Ours,* edited by Robert L. Plummer and John Mark Terry, 56–73. Downers Grove, IL: IVP Academic, 2012.

Meyer, Erin. *The Culture Map: Decoding how People Think, Lead, and get Things Done across Cultures.* New York, NY: PublicAffairs, 2014.

Michaels, J. Ramsey. *1 Peter.* Word Biblical Commentary: Vol. 49. Waco, TX: Thomas Nelson, 1988.

Miley, George. *Loving the Church . . . Blessing the Nations: Pursuing the Role of Local Churches in Global Mission.* Waynesboro, GA: Authentic, 2005.

Mohler, Albert. *The Conviction to Lead: 25 Principles for Leadership That Matters.* Bloomington, MN: Bethany House, 2012.

Nohria, Nitin, and Rakesh Khurana, eds. *Handbook of Leadership Theory and Practice.* Boston: Harvard Business Review, 2010.

Northouse, Peter G. *Leadership: Theory and Practice.* 6th ed. Thousand Oaks, CA: SAGE Publications, 2012.

Oginde, David A. "Antecedents of Christian Leadership: A Socio-Rhetorical Analysis of 1 Timothy 3:17." *Journal of Biblical Perspectives in Leadership* 3, no. 2 (2011): 23–31.

Ott, Craig. *Encountering Theology of Mission: Biblical Foundations, Historical Developments, and Contemporary Issues*. Grand Rapids: Baker Academic, 2010.

Parolini, Jeanine. *Transformational Servant Leadership*. Maitland, FL: Xulon, 2012.

Patrick, Darrin. *Church Planter: The Man, the Message, the Mission*. Wheaton, IL: Crossway, 2010.

Pekerti, A. A., and S. Sendjaya. "Exploring Servant Leadership across Cultures: Comparative Study in Australia and Indonesia." *The International Journal of Human Resource Management* 21, no. 5 (2010): 754–80.

Peters, George W. *A Biblical Theology of Missions*. Chicago: Moody, 1984.

Peterson, Suzanne J., Fred Ochieng Walumbwa, Bruce J. Avolio, and Sean T. Hannah. "The Relationship between Authentic Leadership and Follower Job Performance: The Mediating Role of Follower Positivity in Extreme Contexts." *The Leadership Quarterly* 23 (2012): 502–16.

Pillai, R., and J. R. Meindl. "Context and Charisma: A 'Meso' Level Examination of the Relationship of Organic Structure, Collectivism, and Crisis to Charismatic Leadership." *Journal of Management* 24 (1998): 643–64.

Piper, John. *Let the Nations Be Glad! The Supremacy of God in Missions*. Grand Rapids: Baker, 1993.

Plueddemann, James E. "Theological Implications of Globalizing Missions." In *Globalizing Theology: Belief and Practice in an Era of World Christianity*, edited by Craig Ott and Harold A. Netland, 250–66. Grand Rapids: Baker Academic, 2006.

———. *Leading across Cultures: Effective Ministry and Mission in the Global Church*. Downers Grove, IL: IVP Academic, 2009.

Podsakoff, Philip M., Scott B. MacKenzie, Robert H. Moorman, and Richard Fetter. "Transformational Leader Behaviors and Their Effects on Followers' Trust in Leader, Satisfaction, and Organizational Citizenship Behaviors." *The Leadership Quarterly* 1 (1990): 107–42.

Prime, Derek and Alistair Begg. *On Being a Pastor: Understanding Our Calling and Work*. Chicago: Moody, 2004.

Pratt, Zane G., Michael David Sills, and Jeffrey Kirk Walters. *Introduction to Global Missions*. Nashville: Broadman and Holeman, 2014.

Purvanova, Radostina K., and Joyce E. Bono. "Transformational Leadership in Context: Face-to-Face and Virtual Teams." *The Leadership Quarterly* 20 (2009): 343–57.

Rheenen, Gailyn Van. *Communicating Christ in Animistic Contexts*. Pasadena, CA: William Carey Library, 1996.

Rost, Joseph C. *Leadership for the Twenty-First Century*. Westport, CT: Praeger, 1993.

Sahgal, Punam, and Anil Pathak. "Transformational Leaders: Their Socialization, Self-Concept, and Shaping Experiences." *International Journal of Leadership Studies* 2, no. 3 (2007): 263–79.

Sanders, J. Oswald. *Spiritual Leadership: Principles of Excellence for Every Believer*. Chicago: Moody, 2007.

Schein, Edgar H. *Organizational Culture and Leadership*. 4th ed. San Francisco: Jossey-Bass, 2010.

Schnabel, Eckhard J. "Paul the Missionary." In *Paul's Missionary Methods: In His Time and Ours*, edited by Robert L. Plummer and John Mark Terry, 29–43. Downers Grove, IL: IVP Academic, 2012.

———. *Early Christian Mission*. Downers Grove, IL: InterVarsity, 2004.

————. *Paul the Missionary: Realities, Strategies and Methods.* Downers Grove, IL: IVP Academic, 2008.

Seltzer, Joseph, and Bernard M. Bass. "Transformational Leadership: Beyond Initiation and Consideration." *Journal of Management* 16 (1990): 693–703.

Shaw, Perry W. H. "The Missional-Ecclesial Leadership Vision of the Early Church." *Evangelical Review of Theology* 37, no. 2 (2013): 131–39.

Sills M. David Sills. *The Missionary Call: Find Your Place in God's Plan for the World.* Chicago: Moody, 2008.

Smith, Peter B., Jyuji Misumi, Monir Tayeb, Mark Peterson, and Michael Bond. "On the Generality of Leadership Style Measures across Cultures." *Journal of Occupational Psychology* 62, no. 2 (1989): 97–109.

Son, Jeong-We. "An Analysis of Leadership Styles and Practices among Korean Senior Pastors." PhD diss., The Southern Baptist Theological Seminary, 2003.

Sosik, John J., Veronica M. Godshalk, and Francis J. Yammarino. "Transformational Leadership, Learning Goal Orientation, and Expectations for Career Success in Mentor-Protege Relationships: A Multiple Levels of Analysis Perspective." *The Leadership Quarterly* 15 (2004): 241–61.

Spears, Larry C. "Character and Servant Leadership: Ten Characteristics of Effective, Caring Leaders." *Journal of Virtues and Leadership* 1, no. 1 (2010): 25–30.

Spencer, J. Louis. "Peter: A Phenomenology of Leadership." *Biblical Perspectives*, May 2008, 2–35.

Spradley, James P. *Participant Observation.* New York: Rinehart and Winston, 1980.

Steffen, Tom. *Passing the Baton: Church Planting That Empowers.* La Habra, CA: Center for Organizational & Ministry Development, 1993.

Stoker, Janka I., Hanneke Grutterink, and Nanja J. Kolk. "Do Transformational CEOs Always Make the Difference? The Role of TMT Feedback Seeking Behavior." *The Leadership Quarterly* 23 (2012): 582–92.

Stott, John R. W. *The Cross of Christ.* Downers Grove, IL: IVP, 1986.

Strawbridge, Jennifer. "The Word of the Cross: Mission, Power, and the Theology of Leadership." *Anglican Theological Review* 91, no. 1 (2009): 61–79.

Taylor, Richard. "Interpretation of the Correlation Coefficient: A Basic Review." *Journal of Diagnostic Medical Sonography* 6 (1990): 35–39.

Tidball, Derek. "Leaders as Servants: A Resolution of the Tension." *Evangelical Review of Theology* 36, no. 1 (2012): 31–47.

Tims, Maria, Arnold B. Bakker, and Despoina Xanthopoulou. "Do Transformational Leaders Enhance Their Followers' Daily Work Engagement?" *The Leadership Quarterly* 22 (2011): 121–31.

Tippett, Alan Richard. *Introduction to Missiology.* Pasadena, CA: William Carey Library, 1987.

Tse, Herman H.M., Xu Huang, and Wing Lam. "Why Does Transformational Leadership Matter for Employee Turnover? A Multi-Foci Social Exchange Perspective." *The Leadership Quarterly* 24 (2013): 763–76.

Van Engen, Charles. *God's Missionary People: Rethinking the Purpose of the Local Church.* Grand Rapids: Baker, 1991.

Van Rheenen, Gailyn. *Communicating Christ in Animistic Contexts.* Pasadena: William Carey Library, 1996.

Van Gelder, Craig. "Defining the Issues Related to Power and Authority in Religious Leadership." *Journal of Religious Leadership* 6, no. 2 (2007): 1–14.

BIBLIOGRAPHY

Vogelgesang, Gretchen, Hannes Leroy, and Bruce J. Avolio. "The Mediating Effects of Leader Integrity with Transparency in Communication and Work Engagement/Performance." *The Leadership Quarterly* 24 (2013): 405–13.

Vogelgesang, Gretchen, Rachel Clapp-Smith, and Noel Palmer. "The Role of Authentic Leadership and Cultural Intelligence in Cross-Cultural Contexts: An Objectivist Perspective." *International Journal of Leadership Studies* 5, no. 2 (2009): 102–17.

Waldman, D. A., Bernard M. Bass, and E. Y. Yammarino. "The Augmenting Effect of Transformational Leadership." In *Measures of Leadership*, edited by Kenneth E. Clark and Miriam B. Clark, 151–69. West Orange, NJ: Leadership Library of America, 1990.

Walls, Andrew F., and Cathy Ross, eds. *Mission in the Twenty-First Century: Exploring the Five Marks of Global Mission.* Maryknoll, NY: Orbis, 2008.

Walumbwa, Fred Ochieng, and John J. Lawler. "Building Effective Organizations: Transformational Leadership, Collectivist Orientation, Work-Related Attitudes, and Withdrawal Behaviors in Three Emerging Economies." *The International Journal of Human Resource Management* 14, no. 7 (2003): 1083–1101.

Whiteman, Darrell L. "Anthropology and Mission: The Incarnational Connection, Part I." *International Journal of Frontier Missions* 20, no. 4 (2003): 35–44.

———. "Anthropology and Mission: The Incarnational Connection, Part II." *International Journal of Frontier Missions* 21, no. 2 (2004): 79–88.

Winston, Bruce E., and Barry Ryan. "Servant Leadership as a Humane Orientation: Using the GLOBE Study Construct of Humane Orientation to Show That Servant Leadership Is More Global than Western." *International Journal of Leadership Studies* 3, no. 2 (2008): 212–22.

Wofford, Jerry C. *Transforming Christian Leadership: 10 Exemplary Church Leaders.* Grand Rapids: Baker, 1999.

Zhu, Weichun, Alexander Newman, Qing Miao, and Agnus Hooke. "Revisiting the Mediating Role of Trust in Transformational Leadership Effects: Do Different Types of Trust Make a Difference?" *The Leadership Quarterly* 24 (2013): 94–105.

Zhu, Weichun, Bruce J. Avolio, Ronald E. Riggio, and John J. Sosik. "The Effect of Authentic Transformational Leadership on Follower and Group Ethics." *The Leadership Quarterly* 22 (2011): 801–17.

Zscheile, Dwight J. "The Trinity, Leadership, and Power." *Journal of Religious Leadership* 6, no. 2 (2007): 43–63.

198

Index

accountability, 97n33, 100, 102–3, 109, 149, 166–67

achievement, 5, 36, 38, 57n9, 63, 90, 133, 141, 146–49

Adair, John, 83, 84, 160

allocentric, 138–39

altruism, 6, 40–41, 52, 62, 72, 86, 109, 111, 113, 164–65, 184

aspiration, drive, 6, 22, 26, 28, 32–33, 39, 45, 60, 67, 70, 73–75, 82–83, 109, 132, 141, 162, 167–68, 181

authority, 4–5, 12–13, 26–28, 34, 42, 44, 46–47, 55, 53, 66n2, 67–69, 91, 93–103, 104–5, 107–9, 111, 113, 137, 148, 156, 159, 160–64, 166–68, 175–76, 179, 181–83, 186
source of, 95–99. *See* power

Bass, Bernard, 43–43
Contingent Reward, 35–36, 59–60, 61n25
Full Range of Leadership, 6, 25, 36–43, 46, 60, 162
Laissez Faire, 6, 36–37, 162
Management—by—Exception, 36
See Four Factors

be—know—do, 178

behavior. *See* ethic

Burns, James MacGregor, 6, 25, 42–43, 45–46, 100
on power and authority, 26–28
on transactional leadership, 28–30
on transformational leadership, 31–34

calling, 17, 79–82, 181

capacity, 17, 26–27, 44, 67, 88, 91–95, 100, 103, 156, 175, 182, 186
corporate, 9, 42

character, 12, 29, 52–54, 59, 60, 65, 67, 69–70, 79–80, 83–86, 90, 95, 97–99, 103, 109–111, 113, 156, 162–63, 165–66, 175, 178, 181, 186
courage, 83–86, 110–11, 113, 167, 181
humility, 53, 84–86, 98n35, 102n52, 166, 181, 184
integrity, 2, 32, 50, 52, 58, 64, 79, 83–86, 89, 98n35, 121, 181

charisma, charismatic, 6, 35, 37–38, 45, 51, 54, 58, 60, 63, 83, 95, 103, 111, 119, 121, 142, 145, 163–4

Chinese Value Survey (CVS), 117, 126, 133, 151
coercion. *See* power
communication, 11n45, 41, 45, 50, 56, 58, 64, 90, 126, 138, 153
competency, 17, 50, 52, 54, 65, 67, 79–80, 86–90, 148, 156, 165–66, 175
culture, intercultural, 1–3, 7–11, 10n45, 22–23, 62–64, 66, 92, 115–19, 159, 161, 167–72, 175
   corporate, 46, 49, 51–54, 56, 60
   as mediating, 50, 56–59, 130, 137, 170–71, 175, 187
   as moderating, 49, 57, 63, 137–39, 143, 154, 170–71, 176, 187
   as modifying, 55, 137, 143, 149, 154, 170–71, 187
   and transformational leadership, 136–54

decision—making, 37–38, 45, 47,51, 85, 124, 137, 141, 144
desire(s), need(s), 31–34, 47, 73–74, 108, 113, 123–4, 135, 147, 156, 160–61, 164, 170
   and power in meeting needs, 26–30
   and transformational leadership 34–36
Dimensions of Culture, 115–18, 121–35, 143, 145, 168, 170–71, 176
   Individualism—Collectivism (IDV), 125–28, 137, 138–40, 150, 156, 168–69, 171, 176, 186
   Indulgence—Restraint (IVR), 135, 145, 148, 150, 152, 168–71, 187
   Long—Term and Short—Term orientation (LTO), 133–34, 137, 139, 141–43, 145, 147, 149, 152, 168, 176
   Masculinity—Femininity (MAS), 128–30, 133, 137, 140–41, 144–46, 150–51, 153, 168–70, 176, 187
   Power Distance (PDI), 122–28, 130, 137–38, 148, 150–53, 169–71, 186
   Uncertainty Avoidance (UAI), 130–33, 145–47, 149, 151, 153–54, 169–70, 187

disciple—making, discipleship, 9, 72, 76–78, 80, 179–80, 183
drive. *See* aspiration

ethic, behavior, 3, 11, 13–14, 22, 26, 29, 30, 35, 37–38, 67, 90
   biblical, 104–113
   conclusions of 162–64, 166–67, 175–78
   See Four Factors of Transformational Leadership *and* servant
excellence, 114, 62, 29, 178

faith, obedience of, 9–10, 179–80
fear, 28, 85, 145, 149
femininity. *See* Dimensions of Culture
Four Factors of Transformational Leadership, 6, 37–42, 143–54
   Idealized Influence (II), 35, 37–38, 53, 60, 75, 83, 95, 112, 143–45, 170
   Individualized Consideration (IC), 35, 40–42, 58, 60, 112, 144, 150–52, 170–71
   Inspirational Motivation (IM), 35, 38–39, 48, 60, 75, 83, 95, 112, 143, 145–48, 151, 162, 170–71
   Intellectual Stimulation (IS), 35, 39–40, 45, 50, 60, 95, 112–13, 144, 148–50, 151, 170–71
French and Raven, bases of power, 5, 12–13, 92
   coercive, 5, 12–13, 29, 32, 42, 46, 92–93, 100
   expert, 5, 12–13, 92–95, 103, 131–32, 166
   legitimate, 12–13, 28, 46, 92–95, 103, 137
   referent, 5, 12–13, 92–95, 103, 137, 166
   reward, 12–13, 29, 36, 46, 50, 92–93, 103, 125, 130, 153, 167
   in the New Testament, 93–95
Full Range of Leadership. *See* Bass

GLOBE study, 63, 115–16, 118–19, 136, 161

goals, objectives, 3, 5, 6, 17, 22, 29, 31, 33–34, 38–39, 42, 46, 49, 51, 54, 55–56, 57–58, 63, 65–67, 70–72, 76–78, 103, 108–9, 112, 127, 139, 144, 148, 151, 153, 156, 165, 169, 175, 180, 186

God,
glory of, 7, 10, 69, 72–75, 85, 89, 94, 101, 106, 109, 112–13, 155, 165, 177, 179–81
will of, 9, 69, 71, 85, 91, 94, 96–7, 99, 111, 168, 183
Word of, 72, 80–81, 86, 89, 92–95, 97–99, 103, 110–11, 113, 164, 166, 179, 181–2, 184

gospel, 6–10, 72, 73, 74–75, 76–78, 80, 96, 105, 111, 179–80

Hiebert, Paul, 102, 160
Hofstede, Geert. *See* Dimensions of Culture

idiocentrics, 138–39
individualism. *See* Dimensions of Culture
indulgence. *See* Dimensions of Culture
influence, 3–5, 8, 13, 22–23, 33, 44, 47–48, 56, 58, 66, 69, 72, 92–93, 102, 108, 110n31, 160–61, 178, 186
by affect, feelings, 51–52
by behaviors, 49–50
by reason, 50–51
by the leaders' traits, 48–49
of context, situation, 61–62

leadership,
authentic, 2, 44, 51
behavior. *See* ethic
definition of, 4–5
exemplary, 30, 37–38, 44, 51, 71–72, 78, 85–86, 90, 94–95, 105–7, 111–13, 140, 163, 178, 182
locus of, 22, 46–47, 156, 159, 160–62
misunderstood, 174
outcomes of, 22–23, 50, 52, 55–64, 66–67, 69, 78, 93, 118, 127–31, 139, 143–44, 147, 153–54, 156, 159, 163, 170–71, 182, 186

servant, 31, 71, 84, 91, 95–97, 100–102, 164, 169, 182–84. *See* servant of God
transactional, 35–36, 45–46, 53, 55, 58–59, 61, 90, 100, 149, 160, 162. *See* Burns
transformational, defined 5–6
virtual, 57

Leadership Assessment Matrix (LAM), 4, 23, 66–67, 155–57, 159, 162, 168, 173–78
long-term orientation. *See* Dimensions of Culture

masculinity. *See* Dimensions of Culture
Maslow's Hierarchy, 26, 75, 133, 147, 164
mentor. *See* leadership, exemplary
missiology, 10–11, 70
mission drift, 70, 162
mission, missions, 1–3, 6–10, 65–68, 70–72, 76, 78, 80–82, 91, 102, 104–6, 155, 176–77
model. *See* leadership, exemplary
motivation, 26, 29, 31–33, 41–42, 49, 54, 60, 70, 73–76, 78, 82, 90, 100, 107–8, 112, 132, 138, 146–48, 153, 156, 160, 162, 164, 165, 170, 175, 180
Multifactor Leadership Questionnaire (MLQ), 35, 43, 58

objectives. *See* goals
ontology, 11–12, 67, 79–80, 105, 113, 164–66, 175
organizational models, 151–52

peer. *See primus enter pares*
performance, *See* leadership, outcome
Pleuddemann, James E., 9, 66, 71
policy and procedure, 36, 45, 95, 132, 137, 153, 160, 162
power distance. *See* Dimensions of Culture
power, 9, 42, 74–75, 105, 107, 111. *See* authority *and* French and Raven
primus enter pares, 106
productivity. *See* performance

purpose, 1, 8–9, 21–23, 28–29, 33, 39–40, 42–43, 44–46, 50, 54, 67, 77, 78, 102, 108, 152, 160, 162, 164–65, 179, 186. *See* teleology

responsibility, 31, 38, 41, 53, 67, 87, 91, 100–103, 111–12, 156, 160, 175, 182, 183
results. *See* performance
role model. *See* leadership, exemplary

servant,
    leadership. *See* leadership
    of God,104–9, 156
    of others, 109–111, 156
    in 2 Timothy, 109–111
short-term orientation. *See* Dimensions of Culture
spiritual gifts, 87–88
structural distance, 137–38

teach, teaching, teachers, 7, 9–10, 43, 72, 78, 89, 93–97, 99–101, 109–12, 140, 150, 166, 178, 181–84
teleology, 2, 4, 11–12, 67, 69–73, 156, 162, 164, 175–76, 179
Three–Circle model, 160–61
traits, 3–4, 22, 47–49, 67, 83–84, 86, 95, 103

transformational leadership, 44–64
    factors. *See* Four Factors of Transformational Leadership
    influence in, 47–52
    locus of, 46–47
    purpose of, 44–46
    stewardship in 52–53
    and culture, 136–54
trust, 13, 31, 37, 46, 52–54, 59, 84, 86, 92, 95, 98, 107, 112–13, 126, 139, 165–66, 181

uncertainty avoidance. *See* Dimensions of Culture
universal, universality, transferability, 23, 33, 55, 61–64, 88, 117–18, 121, 154, 156, 159, 161, 168–69

values, 1–2, 6, 12–14, 26–27, 32–33, 38, 40, 42, 45–47, 50, 53–54, 60–62, 70, 83, 92, 100, 103, 108–9, 112, 118, 123–28, 141–42, 144–45, 159–60, 163–64, 185
Values Survey Modules (VSMs), 117, 123, 133, 135
vocation. *See* calling

World Values Survey (WVS), 117, 133, 135

Printed in the USA
CPSIA information can be obtained
at www.ICGtesting.com
JSHW012333050324
58590JS00002B/7